"*God Has Chosen* is a brilliant contribution to a biblically grounded, historically sensitive, and theologically generous vision of election. May Lindsay's plea for a more expansive and comprehensive understanding of the doctrine find a wide readership and warm reception in the academy and in the church."

Christopher R. J. Holmes, associate professor of systematic theology at the University of Otago, New Zealand, author of *The Lord Is Good: Seeking the God of the Psalter*

"What a rich and stimulating book! Lindsay interprets election not solely in light of the various historical controversies regarding predestination, but also in light of the correlative understandings of the body politic and especially the Jewish people. In so doing he offers a theology of election or predestination that is also a subtly drawn political theology as well as an insistent engagement of ongoing Judaism within Christian theology proper. A rare work of systematic theology whose range actually lives up to its systematic ambitions."

Matthew Levering, James N. and Mary D. Perry Jr. Chair of Theology, Mundelein Seminary

"In this fine study, Mark Lindsay moves at pace and with sharp insight over the complex historical-theological terrain required for us to understand the doctrine of election in its long and contested development to the present day. The °lucid discussion that results illumines how this doctrine can be considered the very sum of the gospel by its proponents but impious speculation by its detractors, old and new. The closing exploration of the meaning of the doctrine for Christian-Jewish encounter in the shadow of the Holocaust confronts us with questions whose theological importance simply cannot be denied."

Philip G. Ziegler, professor of Christian dogmatics, University of Aberdeen

"The doctrine of election has elicited a number of fine studies in recent years, and Lindsay's volume deserves a high place among them. Eschewing the well-worn path of focusing primarily on issues of election and individual salvation, Lindsay highlights the ecclesial and sociopolitical contexts of key articulations of the doctrine. Of particular note are his reflections on how Christian accounts of election speak of the Jewish people, and on Jewish approaches to election post-Holocaust, with a concluding plea for us to recognize the consistent scriptural theme of the expansiveness of God's grace in election."

Suzanne McDonald, professor of systematic and historical theology, Western Theological Seminary, Holland, Michigan

"This volume offers a lucid and thoughtful exploration of one of the most vexing points of the Christian faith—the doctrine of election. Attending in turn to its scriptural foundation, historical development, and contemporary complexity, Lindsay does not shy away from any of the difficult aspects of the teaching, but seeks to further its understanding in a way that evidences his years of wrestling with its meaning and significance. In doing so, he provides readers less familiar with the doctrine with a sensitive, helpful guide that is sure to provoke deeper reflection and further reading."

Paul T Nimmo, King's Chair of Systematic Theology, University of Aberdeen

MARK R. LINDSAY

GOD HAS CHOSEN

THE DOCTRINE OF ELECTION
THROUGH CHRISTIAN HISTORY

IVP
Academic

An imprint of InterVarsity Press
Downers Grove, Illinois

InterVarsity Press
P.O. Box 1400, Downers Grove, IL 60515-1426
ivpress.com
email@ivpress.com

InterVarsity Press® is the book-publishing division of InterVarsity Christian Fellowship/USA®, a movement of students and faculty active on campus at hundreds of universities, colleges, and schools of nursing in the United States of America, and a member movement of the International Fellowship of Evangelical Students. For information about local and regional activities, visit intervarsity.org.

Scripture quotations, unless otherwise noted, are from the New Revised Standard Version of the Bible, copyright 1989 by the Division of Christian Education of the National Council of the Churches of Christ in the USA. Used by permission. All rights reserved.

Cover design and image composite: Bradley Joiner
Interior design: Daniel van Loon
Cover Image: © MirageC / Moment Collection / Getty Images

ISBN 978-0-8308-5322-9 (print)
ISBN 978-0-8308-5323-6 (digital)

Printed in the United States of America ∞

InterVarsity Press is committed to ecological stewardship and to the conservation of natural resources in all our operations. This book was printed using sustainably sourced paper.

Library of Congress Cataloging-in-Publication Data
A catalog record for this book is available from the Library of Congress.

P	23	22	21	20	19	18	17	16	15	14	13	12	11	10	9	8	7	6	5	4	3	2	1
Y	38	37	36	35	34	33	32	31	30	29	28	27	26	25	24	23	22	21	20

For Sonia and my boys,

who have tolerated more from me

than should ever have been asked of them

*Whatever may be said about the doctrine of
election, it is written in the Word of God as with
an iron pen, and there is no getting rid of it.*

CHARLES H. SPURGEON

*Die Erwählungslehre ist die Summe des Evangeliums,
weil dies das Beste ist, was je gesagt and gehört
werden kann: das Gott den Menschen wählt.*

KARL BARTH

CONTENTS

ACKNOWLEDGMENTS

WITH THE SAME INEVITABILITY as the dawn follows from the night, I have a multitude of friends and colleagues to thank, each of whom—in their own way, whether they know it or not—have been instrumental in the production of this book. First, I wish to record my thanks to David Congdon, easily one of the most creative and insightful theologians working today. As a one-time editor at IVP Academic, it was David who first encouraged me in this project and who steered the proposal through to its acceptance. Even though he has moved on to other work opportunities, I continue to learn from him. I am grateful also to friends at the University of Divinity, in particular Scott Kirkland, Geoff Thompson, and Chris Mostert, with whom I have enjoyed countless conversations about this book, and who have offered invaluable feedback. The end product is by far the better for their advice (and for me having taken it!). My thanks must also go to my colleagues at Trinity College Theological School, particularly to Dorothy Lee and Bob Derrenbacker—successive deans under whose leadership of the school this book has been written—and to Professor Ken Hinchcliff, warden of Trinity College, who has been unfailing in his support for the research ambitions of the theological school.

I am delighted to record my very sincere thanks to David McNutt, who took over the editorial reins for this project in early 2017 and has been wonderful to work with every step of the way. I am grateful to him for his sharp eye for detail and for the astute questions he posed of the text at various points.

Close friends are, of course, the often-unheralded supporters of projects such as this, and of their authors. Frequently unfamiliar with the material, their value is simply in *being there*: in enquiring about progress, in celebrating the reaching of project milestones, and—most importantly of all—in reminding us authors that there is a wider world out there, away from the books and the research. The company of dear friends, over meals and wine, is a gift of inestimable worth. And so I record here my thanks to Samuel and Jazz, Kath and Greg, Phil and Jane, Paul and Christina, and Luke and Alice. You have shepherded me and my family not only through the slow progress of this project but even more so through the various other ups and downs over the past few years. You know what I mean. Thank you.

Finally, to my family—I cannot repay the debt I owe you. You have been unfailingly good to me, and I cannot—no, *will* not—ever forget that. Let me say, and promise, simply this: each of you is infinitely more important to me than this or any book. Forgive me for those times when that has not been as evident as it should have been. Sonia, Jack, Tom, and Elijah—for what it is worth, this is for you, with my love.

ABBREVIATIONS

AT	Author's translation.
BAGD	Bauer, Walter. *A Greek-English Lexicon of the New Testament and Other Early Christian Literature*. Revised and augmented by W. F. Arndt, F. W. Gingrich, and F. W. Danker. Chicago: University of Chicago Press, 1979.
CD	Barth, Karl. *Church Dogmatics*. 4 vols., 13 parts. Edited by Geoffrey W. Bromiley and Thomas F. Torrance. Edinburgh: T&T Clark, 1936–1969.
CF	Schleiermacher, Friedrich D. E. *Christian Faith*. 2 vols. Edited by C. L. Kelsey and T. N. Tice. Translated by T. N. Tice, C. L. Kelsey, and E. Lawler. Louisville: Westminster John Knox Press, 2016.
Cl. *I Cor.*	First Letter of Clement, in *Ante-Nicene Fathers*. Vol. 1. Edited by A. Roberts and J. Donaldson. Grand Rapids: Eerdmans, 1979.
CO	*Ioannis Calvini opera quae supersunt omnia*. Edited by G. W. Baum, E. Cunitz, and E. Reuss. 59 vols. *Corpus Reformatorum*. Brunswick: CA Schwetschke & Son, 1863–1900.
C-Rom1	Calvin, John. *Commentaries on the Epistle of Paul the Apostle to the Romans*. Edited and translated by J. Owen. Edinburgh: Calvin Translation Society, 1849.
C-Rom2	Calvin, John. *Commentary on Romans*, Library of Christian Classics. Vol. 23. Edited and translated by J. Haroutunian. Philadelphia: Westminster Press, 1958.
DBWE	Bonhoeffer, Dietrich. *Dietrich Bonhoeffer Works in English*. 17 vols. Edited by Wayne Whitson Floyd Jr. Minneapolis: Fortress Press, 1995–2011.
Did.	*Didache*, in *Ante-Nicene Fathers*. Vol. 1. Edited by A. Roberts and J. Donaldson. Grand Rapids: Eerdmans, 1979.
Epistles	Cyprian of Carthage. *The Epistles of Cyprian*, in *Ante-Nicene Fathers*. Vol. 5. Edited by A. Roberts and J. Donaldson. Grand Rapids: Eerdmans, 1978.
ET	English translation.
GD	Barth, Karl. *The Göttingen Dogmatics: Instruction in the Christian Religion*. Vol. 1. Edited by H. Reiffen. Translated by G. W. Bromiley. Grand Rapids: Eerdmans, 1990.

Hom. On Eph.	Chrysostom, John. *Homilies on the Epistle of St. Paul the Apostle to the Ephesians*, in *Nicene and Post-Nicene Fathers*. First Series, vol. 13. Edited by P. Schaff. Grand Rapids: Eerdmans, 1979.
Ign. *Eph.*	Ignatius of Antioch. *Letter to the Ephesians*, in *Ante-Nicene Fathers*. Vol. 1. Edited by A. Roberts and J. Donaldson. Grand Rapids: Eerdmans, 1979.
Ign. *Mag.*	Ignatius of Antioch. *Letter to the Magnesians*, in *Ante-Nicene Fathers*. Vol. 1. Edited by A. Roberts and J. Donaldson. Grand Rapids: Eerdmans, 1979.
Ign. *Phil.*	Ignatius of Antioch. *Letter to the Philadelphians*, in *Ante-Nicene Fathers*. Vol. 1. Edited by A. Roberts and J. Donaldson. Grand Rapids: Eerdmans, 1979.
Ign. *Rom.*	Ignatius of Antioch. *Letter to the Romans*, in *Ante-Nicene Fathers*. Vol. 1. Edited by A. Roberts and J. Donaldson. Grand Rapids: Eerdmans, 1979.
Ign. *Smyr.*	Ignatius of Antioch. *Letter to the Smyrneans*, in *Ante-Nicene Fathers*. Vol. 1. Edited by A. Roberts and J. Donaldson. Grand Rapids: Eerdmans, 1979.
Ign. *Trall.*	Ignatius of Antioch. *Letter to the Trallians*, in *Ante-Nicene Fathers*. Vol. 1. Edited by A. Roberts and J. Donaldson. Grand Rapids: Eerdmans, 1979.
Inst	Calvin, John. *Institutes of the Christian Religion*. Translated by Henry Beveridge. Grand Rapids: Eerdmans, 1989.
1 Apol.	Justin Martyr. *First Apology*, in *Ante-Nicene Fathers*. Vol. 1. Edited by A. Roberts and J. Donaldson. Grand Rapids: Eerdmans, 1979.
KD	Barth, Karl. *Kirchliche Dogmatik*. Evangelischer Verlag Zürich, 1938–1965.
Or. *CC*	Origen. *Contra Celsus*, in *Ante-Nicene Fathers*. Vol. 4. Edited by A. Roberts and J. Donaldson. Grand Rapids: Eerdmans, 1979.
Summa	Aquinas, Thomas. *Summa Theologiae*. The Latin/English Edition of the Works of St. Thomas Aquinas. Translated by L. Shapcote, OP. Edited by J. Mortensen and E. Alarcón. Lander: Aquinas Institute for the Study of Sacred Doctrine, 2012.
Ter. *Apol.*	Tertullian. *Apology*, in *Ante-Nicene Fathers*. Vol. 3. Edited by A. Roberts and J. Donaldson. Grand Rapids: Eerdmans, 1978.
WA	Luther, Martin. *D. Martin Luthers Werke. Kritische Gesamtausgabe (Weimarer Ausgabe)*. Weimar: H. Böhlau Nachfolger, 1883–2009.

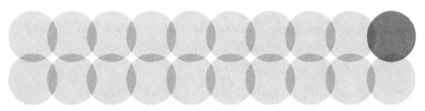

INTRODUCTION

IT HAS BEEN MY PRIVILEGE as a doctoral supervisor at Trinity College Theological School for the past six years and as director of research at the University of Divinity for eight years prior to that to have counseled dozens of graduate students through the various stages of their dissertations—from the most fragile of thought bubbles through to clear proposals, and from the frustrations and joys of research through to the nerve-wracking relief of final submission. As anyone who has had a similar role will know, one of the most common pieces of advice that almost all enthusiastic PhD students need to hear is that they cannot do everything in their dissertation that they would wish. When the final text is submitted for examination, there will inevitably be questions that have been left unanswered, threads of evidence and ideas that have remained unwoven, and intriguing lines of inquiry that have gone unexplored. Of course, those of us who have come out the other side know that this is as it must be, insofar as a doctoral project should only ever be the candidate's *first* word on their chosen subject, not their last. Indeed, nothing gladdens the heart of a PhD examiner more than to see, somewhere in the conclusion of the dissertation, a note from the candidate detailing all the avenues of further inquiry that they still would like to pursue.

In many ways, this book is similarly just one more byproduct of my own doctoral dissertation, which I completed twenty years ago. Even now I am still trying to weave together threads from that initial project.

I remember very clearly, as I embarked on my first major piece of research in 1994—in which I explored the theological foundations of Karl Barth's resistance to Nazi anti-Semitism[1]—it soon became evident that, no matter what the project's title may have suggested, the key themes were not going to be Barth's theology of Israel, his particular political ethic, or his principled hatred of National Socialist idolatry. Rather, I understood early on that my project would require me to focus on the manner in which, during those dark and difficult years, Barth tackled the doctrines of revelation and election. It was, therefore, Barth's utility of these two doctrines in particular—as key hermeneutical themes for both his resistance to Nazism and to his theology overall—that featured heavily in my PhD and in the three subsequent books that emerged from it.[2] Consequently, it is only now that I have been able to tackle the historical development of the church's formulation of divine election, considered more broadly than Barth's own version of it. That is to say, whereas Barth's distinctive contribution to this doctrine has been an ingredient in my earlier projects, I have always been conscious of the need to contextualize his contribution within the longer span of Christian history. This book is the result.

Let me hasten to add, however, that this book is not itself intended simply or even primarily as a project of Barthian contextualization. While it was Barth's creative reconfiguration of the doctrine of election that sparked my own interest, I have been more concerned here to provide something of an (admittedly and necessarily selective) overview of the doctrine's history. Barth's unique contribution thus appears, but only towards the end, and only as a later, albeit highly significant, aspect of a much larger picture.

Similarly, let me give two other caveats, in terms of what this book is *not*. It is not, as has been suggested to me, a genealogy of the doctrine

---

[1]M. Lindsay, *Covenanted Solidarity: The Theological Basis of Karl Barth's Opposition to Nazi Antisemitism and the Holocaust* (New York: Peter Lang, 2001).

[2]See my *Covenanted Solidarity*; and *Barth, Israel and Jesus: Karl Barth's Theology of Israel* (Aldershot, UK: Ashgate, 2007); and *Reading Auschwitz with Barth: The Holocaust as Problem and Promise for Barthian Theology* (Eugene, OR: Wipf & Stock, 2014).

of election. Genealogies, by definition, seek to demonstrate familial lineages, showing in the process where the lines of connection, as well as the points of separation, are between family members. Hopefully, readers of this book will indeed be able to see moments of connection, similarity, indebtedness, as well as disparity, between various forms of this doctrine that have been proposed down through the centuries. For example, we will see that Schleiermacher insists on the thoroughly Reformed orthodoxy of his own articulation of election, notwithstanding his otherwise quite evident departure from the views espoused by Calvin and Beza. Similarly, Aquinas is guided by Augustine's construal of election, even while also being influenced by Aristotelian metaphysics. Such lines of both connectivity and divergence should be evident to readers of the book, as they traverse their way through it.

But the fact that these lines are evident does not render them a genealogical structure. I would need to have been far more deliberate in tracing precisely how the various theologians I have looked at thought their own versions of the doctrine of election connected with, and departed from, their predecessors. That is, the familial pedigree—the articulation of one doctrinal model of election with the next—would have needed much more fleshing out than I have provided. I have not provided it, because that is not the intent of the project. Much more modestly, what I have sought to do here is suggest a set of snapshots-in-time, a sample of some of the ways in which various theologians have sought to respond to the mystery of God's electing will, in the light of Scripture, doctrinal tradition, and their own specific contexts. That there are familial similarities to be seen, as well as the occasional (and occasionally radical) departure from doctrinal expectations, should not be surprising. But that does not make this—and it has not been my intention for that to make this—an attempt at a genealogy of a doctrine. Thus, this book has been subtitled *The Doctrine of Election Through Christian History*, and not, as a genealogical study of the doctrine would have required, *A History of the Doctrine of Election*.

Second, this book is not an exploration of the many and various socio-political contexts in which theologies of election have been developed. Certainly, each chapter provides some brief historical background to the particular environments in which the theologians in question lived and worked. But to sketch these historical environs seems to me to be nothing more than good theological practice. That is to say, unless we believe in some sort of pure dogmatic immutability, it is incumbent upon theologians to recognize that their own work is inevitably shaped by the socio-political, and cultural, structures in which they operate, and equally incumbent upon historical theologians to draw attention to those influences.

I have been able, I believe, to show that many, if not all, of the individuals whose work I have considered in this book were at least tacitly affected by their particular contexts, in the ways in which they gave expression to God's mysterious decree. A largely uncontested medieval demonization of the *perfidis Judaeis* clearly provided an important contour for both Thomas and Scotus in their respective doctrines of election. Likewise at the end of the twentieth century, the range of Jewish articulations of what it now means to be "the People of God" were necessarily shaped by the horrors of the Holocaust.

To acknowledge the influence of historical context on the forming of discourse, both theological and non-theological, is thus no more than a minimum expectation. However, what I have not thereby tried to do in this project is explain, or even explore in any detail, precisely *how* historical context has shaped doctrinal content. I have not, that is, sought to demonstrate *how* Ignatius or Aquinas, Darby or Barth, exegeted their own historical locations as material norms for the construction of their doctrinal views, or even *that* they did so. Much more simply, I have tried to paint a picture, with a rather broad and coarse brush, of the respective milieu in which the people whom I have considered lived and thought, highlighting where possible and appropriate the ways in which their construals of God's electing will may have been informed by those contexts.

PREVIOUS APPROACHES TO THE DOCTRINE OF ELECTION

Of course, just as my doctoral dissertation was not *my* last word, neither is this book the last word on this topic, or even my own last word. It is offered here far more modestly as a contribution that, hopefully, will sit not too shabbily alongside the works of other scholars for whom the doctrine of God's gracious and unfathomable election has also been captivating. I mean, in particular, the expert voices of people such as, inter alia, Matthew Levering, Matthias Gockel, Bruce McCormack, and Suzanne McDonald. While my own project differs in form and intent from theirs, it has nevertheless benefited from interacting with them. And so it is my hope that, even in its difference, this book will not be unworthy of being in, or at least on the fringes of, their company.

In very general terms, much of the recent (and indeed not so recent) scholarship on the doctrine of election has followed one of two broad trends. The first and most obvious of these is what one might call the confessional argument. This line of scholarly inquiry can sometimes be, perhaps uncharitably, less inquiry and more assertion, insofar as it is often characterized by ecclesially specific pleas for particular versions of the doctrine. Arthur W. Pink's *The Doctrine of Election* represents an especially vigorous (which is not to say rigorous) endorsement of an uncompromisingly deterministic Calvinism, while Sam Storms's *Chosen for Life* offers a more nuanced—but nonetheless unapologetic—argument for the Reformed tradition against Arminianism.[3] Conversely, Franz Pieper's *Conversion and Election*, despite it now being well over a century old, remains one of the most forceful defenses of (what Pieper regards as) the normative Lutheran position.[4]

A second scholarly trend within the literature, which usually takes the heat out of such confessional exceptionalism, is the comparative

---

[3] A. W. Pink, *The Doctrine of Election* (Venice, FL: Chapel Library, n.d.); S. Storms, *Chosen for Life: The Case for Divine Election* (Wheaton, IL: Crossway, 2007).

[4] F. Pieper, *Conversion and Election: A Plea for a United Lutheranism in America* (St. Louis, MO: Concordia Publishing House, 1913). Pieper argues that the only truly scriptural understanding of election is the Lutheran balancing act between, on the one hand, *sola gratia* and, on the other hand, *universalis gratia*—a tension that finds its best expression, for him, in the Formula of Concord (article 11) of 1580.

study between two or three particular exponents of the doctrine. Richard Muller's *Christ and the Decree* is an outstanding recent example of this type of work. An invaluable contribution to Reformed understandings of election, this book treats in great detail the development of the doctrine from John Calvin to the next-generation English theologian William Perkins.[5]

In a similar vein to Muller's book is Suzanne McDonald's *Re-imaging Election*. Even though she also is writing from an intentionally Reformed perspective, her book does not fall into the first category of confessional scholarship, because she is uninterested in a simplistic restatement of "old Calvinism." On the contrary, she attempts a reconfiguration of that entire tradition through the loci of pneumatology and ecclesiology. Nonetheless, her work finds its particular focus through her engagement with "the two most prominent streams of thought . . . within the Reformed tradition, represented by John Owen . . . and Karl Barth."[6] Certainly, this book is much more than just an exercise in comparison between these two. But, insofar as McDonald's broader constructive agenda for Reformed theology as a whole relies on this comparative work, it can justifiably be put into this second scholarly category.

Other notable examples of this type of literature include Donna Bowman's ambitious *Divine Decision* and Matthias Gockel's quite brilliant comparison between Schleiermacher and Barth.[7] As far as Bowman's work is concerned, it is, in the words of one reviewer, an "elegant and constructive" piece of scholarship that represents the very best synthesis of Barthian and process theologies (most especially that of Alfred North Whitehead). Even more surprising than simply the synthesis,

---

[5]R. Muller, *Christ and the Decree: Christology and Predestination in Reformed Theology from Calvin to Perkins* (1986; repr., Grand Rapids: Baker Academic, 2008). There is no doubt that Muller's is a contribution to scholarship of a singular order. However, its historical and confessional boundaries are more tightly restricted than those within which I will be working.

[6]S. McDonald, *Re-imaging Election: Divine Election as Representing God to Others and Others to God* (Grand Rapids: Eerdmans, 2010), xiv.

[7]D. Bowman, *The Divine Decision: A Process Doctrine of Election* (Louisville: Westminster John Knox Press, 2002); M. Gockel, *Karl Barth and Schleiermacher on the Doctrine of Election: A Systematic-Theological Comparison* (Oxford: Oxford University Press, 2007).

however, is Bowman's conclusion. She suggests that, in the end, Barth's construal of election is not incompatible with process theology. That both affirm the priority of God's act *and* the necessity of creaturely response, and that both Barth and Whitehead speak of an ontology of "continual becoming," renders them productive, if unusual, conversationalists.[8] As for Gockel's work, it is arguably the essential text for understanding the modern evolution of the doctrine of election, at least in relation to the respective theologies of Barth and Schleiermacher. Undoubtedly one of the most significant comparative monographs on the doctrine of election in recent years, it nonetheless suffers from one small drawback; there is no contextualization of either theologian within a larger longitudinal study of the doctrine of election's change over time. This is precisely the gap that the present work seeks to fill.

Finally, a word needs to be said about Matthew Levering's seminal book, *Predestination*.[9] It is quite simply impossible to write on this topic these days without reference to Levering's work. This book probably comes closest to what I have hoped to achieve here, insofar as it takes a genetic-longitudinal approach, building a narrative around the evolution of the doctrine from Scripture through to the present day. However, there are some key differences between what Levering does and what I have sought to do. First, the title of Levering's book exposes a key differential; whereas he explores predestination as a doctrine that inevitably bifurcates into separable groups of people, the present book highlights the doctrine of election as something that has greater pertinence to our understanding of the being of *God* than the destinies of *people*. Second, in each chapter of Levering's book he engages with four representative thinkers. In what follows here, however, I limit my consideration to only two or three people or movements in each chapter and thus am able to explore each of them in greater depth. Third, Levering's book is quite naturally inhabited by a strong Catholic presence, with half

---

[8]T. J. Oord, review of *The Divine Decision*, by D. Bowman, *The Journal of Religion* 84, no. 4 (2004): 650-51.
[9]M. Levering, *Predestination: Biblical and Theological Paths* (Oxford: Oxford University Press, 2011).

of the theologians discussed in the central chapters being representative of different Roman traditions. As will become clear, my project has sought a more deliberately ecumenical and even interfaith engagement.

THE WAY FORWARD

Having set out how this book differs from others treating the same theme, I conclude with a short description of the way I have framed the following chapters. Starting from the assumption that the doctrine of election is indeed scripturally based, I begin the study with an admittedly selective exploration of key texts that have been used, and sometimes misused, to define both the meaning and the content of God's electing will. Most of the texts I consider are taken from the Pentateuch for the simple reason that the Christian articulation of this doctrine rests on an appreciation of God's earlier choosing of Israel. Regardless of whether one retains a supersessionist reading of Israel's relationship to the church, it is self-evident that, before the church emerged into history, there was already a community that understood itself to have been taken by God into a unique covenantal partnership, which pointed to its own scriptural tradition for the narration of that partnership. Insofar as the church has, for the most part, understood that it worships the same God as this other community of faith, it has thus predicated its own self-understanding as an elect community on these earlier scriptural texts while at the same time supplementing those texts with its own scriptural witness. For that reason, I begin with three Pentateuchal texts before looking at two key passages from two of the Pauline epistles.

In chapter two, I discuss how the early church developed a doctrine of election as part of understanding its own self-identity. Acknowledging that parameters of orthodoxy were only gradually formalized and that the major points of controversy in the first four centuries concerned Christology, on the one hand, and the triune being of God, on the other, I nonetheless seek to show that even as it sought to tighten up the boundaries of what ecclesial belonging meant, the church was inevitably drawn into a consideration of election. To ask questions of what it meant to be part of the church; to explore the tolerable limits of belief and practice when such limits were still under negotiation; and therefore to ask—implicitly, and at times also explicitly—who was "in" and who was "out" was to beg the question of the church's composition as determined in eternity by God. In this chapter, I particularly reference people such as Ignatius of Antioch, Origen, Cyprian, and Augustine precisely because their ecclesiologies—at a time when the very being of the church as such was under construction—speak profoundly to their belief in the eternally elect character of it.

Chapters three, four, and five explore the ways in which the church's teachings about election evolved within very different contextual realities. In chapter three, I consider the theme from the perspective of two quite different theologians—Thomas Aquinas and Duns Scotus—both of whom lived in an age in which the being of the church was almost invariably assumed to be contiguous with the boundaries of Christendom. To be one of the elect, therefore, was to have a particular relationship to the state. In this chapter, I explore not only how Aquinas and Scotus articulate this relationship but also what they have to say about the representatives of those who, as the non-elect, stood also in a particular—though much more precarious—relationship to the state.

In chapter four, the specific context in view is that of the Reformation. Naturally, it is impossible to avoid the looming figure of Martin Luther, and I do not do so. Nonetheless, the great debates about the doctrine of election during this period took place within the Reformed wing of Protestantism, and so my attention is drawn chiefly to the various ways in which Calvin, Beza, and then Arminius sought to understand and express God's election.

Chapter five moves us beyond the early modern period of Western Christianity and beyond even the Enlightenment, with which I do not specifically deal. Rather, as two very different representatives of post-Enlightenment religion, I compare and contrast Friedrich Schleiermacher and John Nelson Darby's contributions to the doctrine during the politically and theologically tumultuous nineteenth century. Their confessional distance from one another notwithstanding, Schleiermacher and Darby make intriguing case studies. They both found ways of giving expression to a fundamentally expansive concept of God's electing will in increasingly nationalistic contexts that were trying, conversely, to bind God's choice to politicized ethnic considerations.

In chapter six I depart from the pattern set by the rest of the book by exploring only one particular contribution, that of the Swiss Reformed theologian Karl Barth. Precisely because his mature doctrine of election has had such an extraordinary influence over so many later thinkers, and has generated such intensely polemical—indeed, at times, vitriolic—debate, I have thought it both appropriate and necessary to devote an entire chapter to Barth's version of this doctrine. Of course, Barth's own thinking about election changed considerably over the course of his career, with its (mostly) final form fixed by 1942. And so, lest anyone think that the way he presents the doctrine of election in *CD* II/2 is the *only* thing he had to say about it, I use this chapter to explore not only Barth's mature construal of the doctrine but also the way in which his theology evolved toward that final form. While I do not attempt any penetrating discussion of the more recent "Barth wars" that have emerged from contested readings of Barth's doctrine of election (I am referring here principally to the debates between Bruce McCormack, George Hunsinger, and Paul Molnar), I do offer a brief excursus on the topic and point interested readers to the voluminous body of literature that now exists in and around this debate.

Finally, in chapter seven, I consider God's electing will from yet another perspective—namely, the painful challenge to any beneficent notion of election that was occasioned by the Holocaust of the Jews. Having for so many centuries understood Israel to be God's "chosen people," Jews under and after Nazism were confronted by the awful reality that, whatever *election* might mean, it did not mean sanctuary from annihilation. On the contrary, if the Shoah proved anything, it was that, in the twisted logic of National Socialism, Jews were elected for death. In this chapter, therefore, I explore several ways in which Jewish theologians and philosophers have sought to reconstitute the concept of election in a post-Shoah world as well as two ways in which the church has responded in post-supersessionary confession.

The book concludes with something of a plea. Noting that, as humans, we have an unfortunate tendency to tribalize ourselves, and thus to find and fix the barriers where "we" are not "them," I offer two concluding reflections. First, and as much of this book will show, the history of the doctrine of election has served precisely that purpose of bifurcating tribalism, of seeking to define the "elect we" against the "reprobate them." Certainly, as I will demonstrate, the determinations of those definitions have variously relaxed and tightened, and those barriers between people have at times been more or less porous. Yet bifurcation between the elect and the reprobate has nonetheless been traditionally understood as contributing to the integrity of election. And it is here that I enter my closing plea for a more expansive view of God's electing will—a view that does not need to impose into God's own eternity a choice between groups of people but that instead takes quite seriously the radical inclusivity of God's call and offer. "Let *everyone* who is thirsty come. Let *anyone* who wishes take" (Rev 22:17).

1

SCRIPTURAL TRACES OF ELECTION

FOR FAR TOO MANY PEOPLE, Christians and non-Christians alike, the doctrine of election is regarded with suspicion, doubt, and often not a little trepidation. As Karl Barth put it, for much of its history the idea of election has existed in an interpretive and receptive "twilight" that has transformed what should by rights be a joyful summation of the gospel into an odious and inscrutable dogma.[1] Likewise, Barth's Swiss colleague, Emil Brunner, noted that, in considering this doctrine, we enter "the danger-zone, in which our faith might be injured and our theology distracted into heresy."[2] There are, perhaps, two overriding reasons why this has been the case. On the one hand, the doctrine often seems to presume at its head a God of arbitrary caprice. Indeed, the doctrine's general opprobrium is in large measure because it appears to be guided by neither rhyme nor reason but directed only by the mysterious will of a hidden God. For Theodore Beza, for example, the doctrine is founded not on the self-revelation of the triune God but on a God behind that revelation, "whose ways are past finding out."[3] On the other hand, it also suffers—or is thought to suffer—from that age-old doctrinal malady, "innovation." Christians by and large have tended to be a conservative

---

[1] *KD*, II/2, 12. AT.

[2] E. Brunner, *The Christian Doctrine of God: Dogmatics, Vol. I*, trans. O. Wyon (London: Lutterworth Press, 1962), 303.

[3] T. Beza, *Summa totius Christianismi* (1555), chap. 2. See G. Redding, *Prayer and the Priesthood of Christ in the Reformed Tradition* (London: T&T Clark, 2003), 141. It is for this reason that Brunner regards Beza's articulation of the doctrine as being derived from speculation rather than revelation. Brunner, *Christian Doctrine of God*, 345.

community, for which change and development is frequently associated with liberalizing heterodoxy. Stability and constancy act as proxy guarantors of dogmatic normativity, and any doctrine that seems to appear out of nowhere, as it were, is consequently in for a rough time.

Strangely, this is precisely the fate that has befallen the doctrine of election. While Augustine, Gottschalk, and Aquinas all spoke in differing ways about predestination between the fifth and thirteenth centuries, it was not until the sixteenth-century Reformation, particularly but not only through the influence of John Calvin, that the idea of election emerged with full force as an ingredient in Western theology. Nevertheless, while there is no doubt that Protestantism, most noticeably within the Reformed wing, has emphasized the doctrine of election to a degree not seen in either patristic or medieval writings, it is not thereby the case that this idea can or should be apprehended only lightly, as if it were a Protestant novelty.

On the contrary, the roots of this doctrine lie deep within the Hebrew and Christian Scriptures. If the exegesis of those Scriptures has obscured rather than clarified the intent of the idea, that should not detract from the doctrine's essential grounding in the Bible nor cause us to think of it only in the light of the last five hundred years. No genuine appreciation of the doctrine of election (and how indeed it is the sum of the gospel) is possible if we begin only, say, with Calvin and work forward. In this first chapter, then, we will explore just how ancient—and therefore un-innovative!—the idea of election is by considering a set of biblical texts (but by no means all) that foreground election as the most basic action by which God's relationship with his people is expressed.

A SCRIPTURAL DOCTRINE

All doctrines are, or should be, grounded in the church's Scriptures. That is an uncontestable axiom (at least rhetorically) across all Christian traditions.[4] But what this means in practice is a more complex matter that

---

[4]Of course, some traditions elevate the Bible more overtly and singularly than others. Consider, for example, the typical Baptist priority of Scripture alone, against the various Reformed churches

differs in its enactment from doctrine to doctrine. The nineteenth-century historical theologian George Fisher rightly insisted on the centrality of Scripture as "the objective rule of Christian faith."[5] Yet his successors were equally correct to remind us that the appeal to Scripture "has operated in different ways." Occasionally, the Bible is the "originating source" of a certain idea; more usually, it has been the provider of "confirmatory evidence for a conviction already reached." Of course, we are also now much more ready to accept that the Scriptures, as partially products of human endeavor, were written in contexts that themselves need careful cultural exegesis. Nonetheless, such interpretive complexities notwithstanding, doctrinal appeal to Scripture must still be made.[6]

However, an understanding of what it means for a doctrine to be "scriptural" still evades us. For example, the doctrine of the resurrection is scriptural in a way that the doctrine of the Trinity is not. That is, while there may be any number of ways of interpreting *what* the resurrection of Christ was and means, *that* the New Testament attests it is not in any doubt. The doctrine of God's triunity, however, is scripturally opaque. Although Dan Migliore contends that there is a "pervasive trinitarian pattern" to the witness of both Old and New Testaments, it remains the case that the doctrine of the Trinity itself must be extrapolated from the biblical witness rather than being found there in any self-evident sense.[7] What, indeed, were the earliest conciliar debates

---

that emphasize, alongside Scripture, the various confessional statements (e.g., the Heidelberg Catechism, the Belgic Confession, and the Canons of Dort). Both of these can be contrasted with the Roman Catholic tradition, in which the continuity of apostolic proclamation is perpetuated through the church, by the Holy Spirit, in a way that is "*distinct from* Sacred Scripture, though closely connected to it." See The Catechism of the Catholic Church, part I, sect. I, chap. 2, art. 3.78. My emphasis. None of these different traditions denies the primacy of Scripture, but each of them contextualizes that primacy in different ways.

[5] H. Cunliffe-Jones, introduction to *A History of Christian Doctrine*, ed. H. Cunliffe-Jones (Philadelphia: Fortress Press, 1984), 14.

[6] Cunliffe-Jones, *History of Christian Doctrine*, 14.

[7] D. Migliore, *Faith Seeking Understanding: An Introduction to Christian Theology*, 2nd ed. (Grand Rapids: Eerdmans, 2004), 68. Barth notes that the doctrine of the Trinity "as such does not stand in the texts of the Old and New Testament witness to God's revelation" (*CD* I/1, 375), and Bonhoeffer says, "The *deus uni-trinus* . . . can be grasped only by belief in revelation," and not through specific Bible texts (D. Bonhoeffer, "Faith and Revelation," *DBWE* 9:307). Millard Erickson affirms, "This doctrine [of the Trinity] is not overtly or explicitly stated in Scripture." M. Erickson, *Christian Theology* (Grand Rapids: Baker Academic, 1985), 321.

about—at Nicaea and then again at Chalcedon—if not heated controversies over the correct extrapolation of trinitarian theology from the
pages of Scripture? As Dietrich Ritschl has so eloquently put it, the
notion that "regulative statements [of doctrine] are present in the biblical writings" is true only approximately and with severe qualification.
Notwithstanding the obvious and necessary truth that Christian doctrine is grounded in, and based on, the testimony of Scripture, "scriptural doctrine" per se, if we mean by that a set of directly applicable
formulations of normative theology, is largely a fiction.[8]

So how are we to approach and understand this strange doctrine of
election and affirm its "scripturality"? It goes without saying that
election is in the Scriptures, much as the resurrection is and the Trinity
is not. God's decision "to choose" (בָּחַר—*bahar*) Jacob/Israel, the divine
"knowing" (יָדַע—*yada‘*) of his people that suggestively connotes so
much more than cognition, Jesus' "calling" of his disciples (καὶ εὐθὺς
ἐκάλεσεν αὐτούς—Mk 1:20)—each verbal metaphor depicts a God
who initiates and then activates a will to have a relationship with others
who are outside his own Godhead. Thus, and given that this whole
book is predicated on the affirmation of God's free decision to be with
us and for us, it seems right that we consider the relevant Scriptures not
so much as mere texts to investigate but rather as God's conversation
with us. Katherine Sonderegger articulates this beautifully when she
says that the "*dearness* of Scripture" is that we are drawn by it into the
presence of God, our eternal Teacher. No matter how strange and even
alien some parts of the Bible are to us—and this not least in connection
with the doctrine of election—to hear the words of Scripture is, says
Sonderegger, to enter into the "penumbra of a welcome Light," to
"touch and love a token of the One who irresistibly calls us."[9] In affirming the doctrine of election as scriptural, we mean here that in the
Bible's various expressions of this idea, we encounter over and again

---

[8]D. Ritschl, *The Logic of Theology*, trans. J. Bowden (London: SCM Press, 1986), 68-69.
[9]K. Sonderegger, *Systematic Theology: Volume 1, The Doctrine of God* (Minneapolis: Fortress Press,
  2015), 264-65.

this freedom of God's call. As we shall see, even in its shadow side, the confession that God chooses to call and beckon us into conversation and encounter—some first, then others; not all at the same time, but eventually some; always for the sake and on behalf of all—is the scriptural attestation of what it means to be elect. In other words, the Scriptures themselves are our conversation with God about his greater freedom to enter into conversation with us, which we rightly denote by the idea of election.

But we must also mean more than this. Conversations have a tendency to be heard discriminately, with us hearing only what we wish to hear. No matter how conversational our approach to the Scriptures is—and conversational it must indeed be if we know that in and through them we encounter not simply textual fragments and ideas but, on the contrary, God's attestation of his own self—the Scriptures must be for us not simply a dialogical sparring partner but the very foundation and testing ground of what we claim. Only if this doctrine of election, as we wish to propose it here, can legitimately be understood as a faithful representation "of what God has already said of himself, and continues to say," will it stand up to scrutiny.[10] Scripture thus becomes the starting point of all that we say and then the touchstone by which our and others' expressions of this doctrine are judged. With this in mind, we ought now to turn our attention to a selection of key passages in both Testaments.

GENESIS 12:1-9

> Now the LORD said to Abram, "Go from your country and your kindred
> and your father's house to the land that I will show you. I will make of you
> a great nation, and I will bless you, and make your name great, so that you
> will be a blessing. I will bless those who bless you, and the one who curses
> you I will curse; and in you all the families of the earth shall be blessed."
> So Abram went, as the LORD had told him; and Lot went with him. Abram
> was seventy-five years old when he departed from Haran. Abram took his
> wife Sarai and his brother's son Lot, and all the possessions that they had

---

[10]*KD* II/2, 36. AT.

gathered, and the persons whom they had acquired in Haran; and they set
forth to go to the land of Canaan. When they had come to the land of
Canaan, Abram passed through the land to the place at Shechem, to the
oak of Moreh. At that time the Canaanites were in the land. Then the
Lord appeared to Abram, and said, "To your offspring I will give this land."
So he built there an altar to the Lord, who had appeared to him. From
there he moved on to the hill country on the east of Bethel, and pitched
his tent, with Bethel on the west and Ai on the east; and there he built an
altar to the Lord and invoked the name of the Lord. And Abram jour-
neyed on by stages toward the Negeb. (Gen 12:1-9)

The story of Abram's call, while perhaps not the most fantastical story
in the Hebrew Bible, is nevertheless one of the most baffling. The creation of a universe ex nihilo may strike a somewhat more discordant
note in an age so devoted to science and technology as ours. In principle, however, it is not especially problematic if you have already accepted the premise of a sovereignly powerful God. Similarly unprob-
lematic are, on the acceptance of this premise, the sundry healing
miracles (e.g., of the widow's son in 1 Kings 17:17-24 and of Namaan in
2 Kings 5:1-19), the stopping of the sun (Josh 10:13), and the various
other manifestations of God's action in the natural world. This particular story, though, cannot be explained merely by reference to God's
presupposed almightiness, for the issue at hand is not power, but choice.
As James Kugel puts it, the ancient and indeed only reasonable response
to the call of Abram is "bewilderment"! What precisely had Abram
done to deserve God's promise that "he would become the ancestor of
a great and mighty nation . . . [and would be granted] so many good
things that his very name would turn into a blessing"? The only right
and possible answer is nothing.[11]

Walter Brueggemann presses this idea further in linking Abram's
undeservedness with that small but vital biographical detail at the end
of the preceding chapter: "Now Sarai was barren; she had no child"

[11]J. L. Kugel, *How to Read the Bible: A Guide to Scripture Then and Now* (New York: Free Press, 2008), 91.

(Gen 11:30). Such barrenness, says Brueggemann, "is the way of human history. It is an effective metaphor . . . [because] there is no human power to invent a future. But barrenness is not only the condition of hopeless humanity. The marvel of biblical faith is that barrenness is the arena of God's life-giving action."[12]

In other words, insofar as this passage is the first substantive introduction to Abram—the preceding verses in Genesis 11:26-31 being more about his father, Terah—its details provide no basis for extrapolating any merit on his part by which his divine call could have been justified. Indeed, it is exactly the deficit of merit, of which Sarai's infertility is a sign, that is the point. God's call is unexplained, precisely because it is unmerited, and rests only on God's free decision. True, a later passage in Joshua has been exegeted by Jewish, Christian, and Islamic scholars to prove Abram's monotheism, in an effort to cite that as the reason for his being singled out.[13] But Kugel reminds us that there is

> not a single verse in the book of Genesis [that] actually says that Abraham believed in the existence of only one God . . . There is nary a hint, even in the Bible's much later depiction of him, that Abraham's beliefs differed *in kind* from those of the people he encountered.[14]

What we see in this story, then, is a confounding example of God's freedom to choose one thing and not another—or in this case, one person and not another—not only for no good reason but seemingly for no reason at all.

Choice, however, is not the only ingredient to this story. Just as prominent are the promises of descendants and blessings, and the representative office to which Abram, and subsequently his "children," are

---

[12] W. Brueggemann, *Genesis* (Atlanta: John Knox Press, 1982), 116. See also V. P. Hamilton, *The Book of Genesis: Chapters 1-17* (Grand Rapids: Eerdmans, 1990), 372.

[13] "Joshua said to all the people, 'Thus says the LORD, the God of Israel: Long ago your ancestors—Terah and his sons Abraham and Nahor—lived beyond the Euphrates and served other gods. Then I took your father Abraham from beyond the River and led him through all the land of Canaan and made his offspring many'" (Josh 24:2-3). Some interpreters have claimed that Abraham was distinguished by God from Terah and Nahor because in fact he did not "worship other gods." This, then, becomes his "merit." See Kugel, *How to Read the Bible*, 91.

[14] Kugel, *How to Read the Bible*, 103.

called. Claus Westermann argues here for a historically contingent manifestation of blessing. Presuming the existence of the J source, Westermann contends that the blessing and promise of greatness refer solely to the period of Israel's history when it was "at the height of its prosperity . . . [which] is best thought of [as] the era of David-Solomon, that is, at the time of the Yahwist."[15] Yet such a reading misses the vicarious mission implicit in the blessing. Not only for himself or his family is Abram promised the gift of children; on the contrary, there is a *catholicity* to God's gift.[16] "Israel," says Brueggemann, "is never permitted to love in a vacuum. It must always live with, for, and among the others."[17] And thus, what Abram's/Israel's experience has been—undeserving recipients of God's gifts—becomes paradigmatic for the whole world: "God freely gives, and none must 'qualify.'"[18] As Sibley Towner puts it, this "extraordinary promise of God to Abram [and through him to all nations] is an open-ended, abiding announcement of potentiality."[19] Without merit or deserved favor, the free gift of God to Abram flows out subsequently to "all the families of the earth" (Gen 12:3). Articulating "a divine plan for universal salvation," verse 3 proclaims "Yahweh's programmatic statement. [Even] sinister nations and people of the earth . . . are to be blessed through Abram."[20]

---

[15]C. Westermann, *Genesis 12–36: A Commentary*, trans. J. J. Scullion (Minneapolis: Augsburg, 1985), 149-50. "J" and "the Yahwist" refer to the Graf-Wellhausen source theory (otherwise known as the JEDP theory), according to which the Pentateuch was composed not by Moses or any other single author but by four independent sources that date from different times in Israel's history and which were later (ca. 400 BCE) redacted and compiled into a single book. The theory was extensively critiqued during the last third of the twentieth century, notably by Rolf Rendtorff in *Das überlieferungsgeschichtliche Problem des Pentateuch* (Berlin: De Gruyter, 1977). More recent scholarship has tended to moderate Rendtorff's criticism, but the independent existence of a J source has remained highly contentious.

[16]See, for example, T. F. Torrance, "The Divine Vocation and Destiny of Israel in World History," in *The Witness of the Jews to God*, ed. D. W. Torrance (Edinburgh: Handsel Press, 1982), 85-104.

[17]Brueggemann, *Genesis*, 120. Hamilton notes that the Hebrew word choice reinforces this vicarious solidarity, insofar as Abram's descendants will become, according to this passage, not so much a great *people* (*am*, עַם) but a great *nation* (*gôy*, גּוֹי) among all the other nations (*gôyim*, גּוֹיִם). Israel's representative mission, by which it is singled out but not differentiated, is thus signaled lexically.

[18]Brueggemann, *Genesis*, 120.

[19]W. S. Towner, *Genesis* (Louisville: Westminster John Knox Press, 2001), 136.

[20]Hamilton, *Book of Genesis*, 374.

Even here, though, the motif of undeservedness shines through, most notably in the repetition of the "I will" phrases (וְאֶעֶשְׂךָ; "I will make you . . ."; וַאֲבָרֶכְךָ; "I will bless . . ."). Again, in Brueggemann's words, the future hope that is promised to Israel "is no accomplishment or achievement by Israel. It is a gift by the one who is able to give good gifts."[21] Just as important as the verbs of making and blessing, therefore, is the subject of those verbs—the divine I, whose initiative is both sovereign and free. In sum, this call of Abram, which is in fact a call through him to all peoples, demonstrates archetypally what election in Scripture looks like: divinely and freely initiated, extravagantly global in its embrace, and without the need for any human merit. As we shall see, this pattern recurs in each of the other texts to which we shall turn.

GENESIS 32:22-32

> The same night he got up and took his two wives, his two maids, and his eleven children, and crossed the ford of the Jabbok. He took them and sent them across the stream, and likewise everything that he had. Jacob was left alone; and a man wrestled with him until daybreak. When the man saw that he did not prevail against Jacob, he struck him on the hip socket; and Jacob's hip was put out of joint as he wrestled with him. Then he said, "Let me go, for the day is breaking." But Jacob said, "I will not let you go, unless you bless me." So he said to him, "What is your name?" And he said, "Jacob." Then the man said, "You shall no longer be called Jacob, but Israel, for you have striven with God and with humans, and have prevailed." Then Jacob asked him, "Please tell me your name." But he said, "Why is it that you ask my name?" And there he blessed him. So Jacob called the place Peniel, saying, "For I have seen God face to face, and yet my life is preserved." The sun rose upon him as he passed Penuel, limping because of his hip. Therefore to this day the Israelites do not eat the thigh muscle that is on the hip socket, because he struck Jacob on the hip socket at the thigh muscle. (Gen 32:22-32)

Whereas Israel had been prefigured in the previous narratives of call and blessing, it is only in this passage that the name, and thus the

---

[21]Brueggemann, *Genesis*, 118.

people, come into being. Two generations removed from Abram/ Abraham, Jacob the deceiver becomes Israel, the one who contends with God and is blessed but not defeated.[22]

This particular story sits within the broader context of Jacob's hesitant and fearful return from the land of his father-in-law, Laban, to the land of his birth—and, of course, thereby also to the land in which his estranged brother, Esau, still lives. Brueggemann highlights that this larger context is not incidental but is indeed a vital connection with the call of Abram (12:1-9) at which we have just looked. In God's command to Jacob that he is to *go back to* "the land of [his] ancestors and to [his] kindred" (31:3), we see an inverse parallel of 12:1, in which God tells Abram to "*go from* [his] country and [his] kindred." Thus, says Brueggemann, Jacob's return

> is not only his own homecoming . . . [but] also the homecoming of Abraham, who had left long ago. Jacob is presented as completing the sojourn which has been underway for three generations. Something more is at stake here than simply reconciliation with Esau. The family of Abraham now finally comes to its own country and that concerns Yahweh as much as Jacob.[23]

Because this homecoming concerns God as well, perhaps we ought not shy away from identifying the anonymous assailant of verses 24-29 with God. While some commentators have argued that in the earliest versions of the narrative "the man" is a demon of Canaanite animism,[24] the hermeneutical tradition has favored an identity of this attacker with God. Thus Calvin: "Moreover, it is not said that Satan, or any mortal man, wrestled with Jacob, but God himself."[25] And also Ephrem the

---

[22] The name *Yaʿaqov* (יַעֲקֹב) means either "heel" or "supplanter." The narratives of Jacob's birth, and subsequent rivalry with his brother, Esau, permit either interpretation, or more probably both. The meaning of the name *Yisraʾel* (יִשְׂרָאֵל), however, is more contested and may mean "God strives," "God protects," or even, "The one who strives with God." See Brueggemann, *Genesis*, 268; and J. Skinner, *Genesis* (Edinburgh: T&T Clark, 1910), 409-10.

[23] Brueggemann, *Genesis*, 263-64.

[24] See, for example, Westermann, *Genesis 12–36*, 516-18.

[25] "*Porro non dicitur vel Satan vel mor- talis quispiam homo cum Iacob luctatus esse, sed ipse Deus.*" CO 23:442.

Syrian: "The angel himself was God and the man was God. While the
fighting was of the man and the deed was of the angel, yet the perpe-
trator was God."[26] Indeed, this makes the best sense in that the chief
outcome of the encounter is not so much the fight itself, or even the
"draw" that both protagonists play out and that as such prefigures the
New Testament depiction of God,[27] but rather the creative act by which
the encounter is punctuated. In the Bible, it is only ever God who
brings something into being that was not there before (e.g., Gen 1:1-3;
Ps 104:30; Rom 4:17); insofar as that is what happens here, the assailant
must be God.

But what is made? Simply—but, in fact, momentously—in response
to Jacob's demand for a blessing, God gives him a new name instead.
However, in doing so, God is not being disingenuous—the name is not
in place of the blessing; it *is* the blessing. In an age when names were
identity-forming, Jacob shifts from being a somewhat unsympathetic
trickster to a person named (and thus called) by God himself. That is
to say, in bestowing on Jacob a different name, the unknown assailant
initiates an irreversible transaction: a "new being has been called forth
. . . Israel is something new in the world."[28]

In the first instance, the new entity that is Israel is a man no longer
frightened to meet his brother. Even though from this point on he is
physically restricted, his limp serves as a reminder not of weakness so
much as of his having prevailed in the riverside fight. Thus, Jacob/Israel
now knows himself as one who needs to be respectful but who no
longer needs to be fearful. His encounter with God has left him forever
wounded but also strengthened in resolve.[29]

---

[26]E. G. Mathews Jr., *The Armenian Commentary on Genesis Attributed to Ephrem the Syrian* (Louvain: Peeters, 1998), 127.

[27]That is, the God who wrestles with Jacob allows himself to be vulnerable, to the point of (almost) being beaten. The resonances with Christ's *kenosis* and crucifixion—his vulnerability and death—are impossible to miss.

[28]Brueggemann, *Genesis*, 268. Note that throughout the rest of the Genesis narrative, the names Jacob and Israel are both used for the one person. There are allegorical, geographical, and source critical explanations for this. See Kugel, *How to Read the Bible*, 160.

[29]Brueggemann, *Genesis*, 269; Westermann, *Genesis 12–36*, 521.

In the second instance, Israel is an identity—both a person and a people—formed from divine freedom. In much the same way that St. John says Christ was born "not of blood or of the will of the flesh or of the will of man, but of God" (Jn 1:13), so too Jacob's new identity as Israel is formed "not by success or shrewdness or land"[30] but by God's own determination.

In this passage, then, we have the miraculous creation—*ex Iacobus*—of a new character in God's economy of salvation. Israel is called forth out of struggle and perseverance, out of woundedness and undeservedness, out of God's freedom rather than Israel's merit. But equally, Israel is called forth *for a particular purpose*. As we have already noted, Israel never lives on its own or for its own, but always in and among, and for, others. That the first of Jacob/Israel's actions after Jabbok is to pursue reconciliation with his brother exemplifies the service of Israel to the world: to be that community through which God's love is made known to all people, to be that "light to the nations [*gôyim*, גּוֹיִם], that [God's] salvation may reach to the end of the earth" (Is 49:6). Creation and vocation thus come together in the emergence of Israel, as person and people, from the banks of the Jabbok.

DEUTERONOMY 7:6-11

> For you are a people holy to the LORD your God; the LORD your God has chosen you out of all the peoples on earth to be his people, his treasured possession. It was not because you were more numerous than any other people that the LORD set his heart on you and chose you—for you were the fewest of all peoples. It was because the LORD loved you and kept the oath that he swore to your ancestors, that the LORD has brought you out with a mighty hand, and redeemed you from the house of slavery, from the hand of Pharaoh king of Egypt. Know therefore that the LORD your God is God, the faithful God who maintains covenant loyalty with those who love him and keep his commandments, to a thousand generations, and who repays in their own person those who reject him. He does not

---

[30]Brueggemann, *Genesis*, 269.

delay but repays in their own person those who reject him. Therefore, observe diligently the commandment—the statutes and the ordinances—that I am commanding you today. (Deut 7:6-11)

With his insistence on the primacy of God's grace, and on our faith in that grace, Martin Luther might be presumed to have had little love or time for the "book of the law" that is Deuteronomy. Yet such was not the case. In 1525 Luther presented to Georg von Polenz, bishop of Samland, the published version of his lectures on Deuteronomy, which he had started in Wittenberg in 1523. In his opening remarks, Luther declared that "there is nothing in the whole range of life that is not arranged here most wisely and properly."[31] There remains, however, an apparent dissonance between the German reformer's insistence on religious freedom, on the one hand, and this text of command and curse, on the other. How could Luther, of all people, have understood these divine dictates as being in any way "wise and proper"?

The answer is simply that this passage, and indeed the entire book of which it is a part, is less about command and more about covenant.[32] In Von Rad's words, "the basic theological fact about Israel," is that it has been chosen as God's undeserving (and at times, reluctant) beloved; Deuteronomy returns to this theme time and again.[33] This passage in particular lays stress on that identity-forming reality. Following hard on the heels of the Decalogue (Deut 5:6-21) and the Shema (6:4), the text before us here provides the foundational reason for all the preceding commandments and thus all the future behaviors that will be expected of Israel. For, notwithstanding all that has already been said about Israel's representative character, it is nonetheless *unlike* all other nations and peoples. Alone among all others, Israel has been *chosen* (בָּחַר) by God, intentionally set apart to be so exclusively bound to YHWH that, collectively and personally, it must

---

[31]"*ut nihil sit in universo genere vitae, quod hie non sit sapientissime et aequissime dispositum.*" M. Luther, *WA*, 14:545.

[32]See, for example, R. E. Clements, *God's Chosen People: A Theological Interpretation of the Book of Deuteronomy* (London: SCM Press, 1968), 28.

[33]G. von Rad, *Deuteronomy: A Commentary* (London: SCM Press, 1966), 68.

"abstain from everything which might prejudice" its commitment to God's supremacy.[34]

Despite the wider context of commands and prohibitions, blessings and curses, it would be a mistake, however, to associate Israel's chosenness—its election—as a reward for unwavering obedience and unequivocal allegiance, no matter how sternly God requires those things. Their requirement is not thereby a merit. As Weinfeld puts it, God's choice of Israel must not be employed as a basis for a national "superiority complex."[35] On the contrary, the Deuteronomist hurries on to insist that Israel has not been chosen by God because of its size and power, or its meritorious virtue in obeying his precepts. Israel's election does not find its ground in the idea "that Yahweh . . . allowed himself to be impressed by Israel in any respect, but simply from an impulse in love," which had first been expressed in God's promises to the patriarchs.[36] Perhaps this is why Luther had such regard for this "book of the law," because, in fact, it is at its core a book of the gospel.[37] In spite of what has often been preached from Christian pulpits, Deuteronomy is not merely (or even essentially) a codification of Israelite cultus from which, under Christ, we have been freed.[38] Rather, it is the application, in the several and corporate lives of his people, of his freely given love.

Weinfeld's close exegesis of this passage underscores just how robust this divine love for Israel is. For example, that God has taken Israel to be his "treasured possession" (לְעַם סְגֻלָּה, l'am segullah) (Deut 7:6) suggests Israel is valued by God in the manner that a king treasures his

---

[34]Von Rad, *Deuteronomy*, 68. See also Clements, *God's Chosen People*, 34. Note that the word *chosen* (בָּחַר) is used for the first time here in Deuteronomy with an expressly theological meaning denoting election. M. Weinfeld, *Deuteronomy 1–11*, Anchor Bible 5 (New York: Doubleday, 1991), 368.

[35]Weinfeld, *Deuteronomy 1–11*, 368.

[36]Von Rad, *Deuteronomy*, 68.

[37]It is worth remembering that Luther's distinction between law and gospel did not, as is commonly supposed, correspond to the division between the Old Testament and the New. The distinction applies to the collected entirety of Scripture, with the Old Testament being "saturated with gospel." See B. Schramm and K. Stjerna, eds., *Martin Luther, the Bible, and the Jewish People: A Reader* (Minneapolis: Fortress Press, 2012), 87.

[38]This is not to deny the cultic element of Deuteronomy, but it is to argue that a more fundamental evangel is at work.

private wealth.[39] Even more starkly, God having *desired*, or "set his heart on," Israel (7:7) (חָשַׁק) is, as Weinfeld says, best understood as a passionate yearning that might, in fact, be accurately thought of as an almost lustful longing.[40] Far from being a litany of commands and precepts, Deuteronomy is thus grounded in the insistence on God's zestful and zealous desire for his people. Israel's sociality as a nation, therefore, is founded not on a shared culture or cultus but on its divine election, *out of which* its culture and cultus emerged as an obedient response.

ROMANS 9–11

I am speaking the truth in Christ—I am not lying; my conscience confirms it by the Holy Spirit—I have great sorrow and unceasing anguish in my heart. For I could wish that I myself were accursed and cut off from Christ for the sake of my own people, my kindred according to the flesh. They are Israelites, and to them belong the adoption, the glory, the covenants, the giving of the law, the worship, and the promises; to them belong the patriarchs, and from them, according to the flesh, comes the Messiah, who is over all, God blessed forever. Amen. . . . What if God, desiring to show his wrath and to make known his power, has endured with much patience the objects of wrath that are made for destruction; and what if he has done so in order to make known the riches of his glory for the objects of mercy, which he has prepared beforehand for glory—including us whom he has called, not from the Jews only but also from the Gentiles? As indeed he says in Hosea, "Those who were not my people I will call 'my people,' and her who was not beloved I will call 'beloved.'" "And in the very place where it was said to them, 'You are not my people,' there they shall be called children of the living God." . . . I ask, then, has God rejected his people? By no means! I myself am an Israelite, a descendant of Abraham, a member of the tribe of Benjamin. God has not rejected his people whom he foreknew. . . . So I ask, have they stumbled so as to fall? By no means! But through their stumbling salvation has come to the Gentiles, so as to

---

[39]Weinfeld, *Deuteronomy 1–11*, 368. Weinfeld also notes that the LXX translates *segullah* as "superior" rather than "treasured," whereas the Vulgate rendering of *peculium* denotes more correctly the idea of having been set apart because of its value.
[40]Weinfeld, *Deuteronomy 1–11*, 360.

make Israel jealous. Now if their stumbling means riches for the world, and if their defeat means riches for Gentiles, how much more will their full inclusion mean! (Rom 9:1-5, 22-26; 11:1-2, 11-12)

Before concluding this chapter on the scripturality of election, we cannot avoid looking at two of the key New Testament texts on the matter, which we find in St. Paul's letters to the churches in Rome and Ephesus. We will first consider an extended three-chapter portion of Romans and then look briefly at the opening verses of Ephesians.

In discussing Paul's hermeneutic of the relationship between Israel and the church, as expressed in the middle three chapters of his letter to Rome, we encounter what Karl Barth described as "the crooked path of the chief New Testament passage" on election.[41] We may not wish to go as far as Christiaan Beker, who has contended that these chapters ought to be regarded as the letter's material climax because, in his view, the letter itself is nothing less than an extended "dialogue with Jews."[42] Nor can we agree with David Martyn Lloyd-Jones's alternative suggestion that these three chapters are merely "a kind of postscript."[43] They are indeed far more than that. As Leon Morris has observed, the entirety of Romans 1–11 is a unity, designed to show forth God's plan to save humankind. The purpose of chapters 9–11, therefore, is to bring into particular focus the question of how, *post Christum*, that plan continues to include Israel.[44] Quite logically, then, when Karl Barth penned his remarkable *Römerbrief* in 1922, he noted that the theme of the letter is the universal suffrage of every person for the gift of God's grace: "Both Jew and Greek are enfranchised for the Gospel."[45]

---

[41]*CD* II/2, 15.

[42]J. C. Beker, *Paul the Apostle* (Edinburgh: T&T Clark, 1980), 77, 86.

[43]D. M. Lloyd-Jones, *Romans: An Exposition of 8:17-39; The Final Perseverance of the Saints* (London: Banner of Truth, 1975), 367.

[44]L. Morris, *The Epistle to the Romans* (1988; repr., Grand Rapids: Eerdmans, 1992), 344.

[45]K. Barth, *Der Römerbrief 1922* (1940; repr., Zurich: Theologischer Verlag, 2015), 16. AT. Note that Hoskyns's famous translation of 1933 renders this sentence in the negative: "Neither the Jew nor the Greek are disenfranchised from the Gospel." K. Barth, *The Epistle to the Romans*, 6th ed., trans. E. C. Hoskyns (Oxford: Oxford University Press, 1933), 40. This negative is perhaps more faithful to the first edition of the commentary, in which Barth says, of the same two verses (1:16-17), that "The world to come does not know these barriers [of Jew and Gentile]." K. Barth, *Der*

If this is so, then one might well ask why Paul seems to lay such stress in chapter 9 on the *disobedience* of Israel and their apparent *exclusion* from God's grace. Morris argues that, despite his own wishes, Paul must have thought that his "brothers according to the flesh"—that is, the whole community of the Jews of his day—were indeed destined for annihilation (ἀνάθεμα),[46] insofar as he expresses his desire to "take their place, to be lost so that they may be saved."[47] Morris argues this, despite the fact that the text does not unequivocally permit a substitutionary reading.[48] Gifford is even blunter in his assessment. The "vessels of destruction" (9:22), he argues, is the "eminently applicable" term "for the mass of the Jewish nation in St. Paul's day."[49]

Yet the point of these chapters is not that ultimate culpability and thus divine punishment fall on the collectivity of ethnic Jews as such and primarily, nor even that their historic sufferings are proleptic of an eternal fate that awaits at least some of them.[50] On the contrary, Paul's contention is nothing other than a repetition of the gospel we have already discerned in the earlier Old Testament passages: that God's mercy and grace are the free gifts of his own sovereignty, which he distributes according only to his own will, without reference to merit, heritage, or the privilege of birth.

David Congdon very helpfully reminds us of two dangers in positing God's free sovereignty (one of which he argues is real, the other perceived).

Römerbrief, Erste Fassung. GA II.16, 21. That is, while Hoskyns is not wrong, it is instructive to note that Barth himself saw fit to speak of the universality of the gospel more positively in the second edition than he did in the first.

[46]That is, something "laid up" on an altar to be utterly consumed and thus forever lost. BAGD, 54.

[47]Morris, *Epistle to the Romans*, 347.

[48]David Wallace, Douglas Moo, and Leon Morris all interpret ὑπὲρ to imply that Paul knows his fellow Jews to have been damned by God and is thus pleading for the impossible—that is, that he may, Christ-like, take their place. See Morris, *Epistle to the Romans*, 347; D. Moo, *The Epistle to the Romans* (Grand Rapids: Eerdmans, 1996), 559; D. Wallace, *The Election of the Lesser Son: Paul's Lament-Midrash in Romans 9–11* (Minneapolis: Augsburg Fortress, 2014), 38. For a contrary position, see L. Windsor, *Paul and the Vocation of Israel: How Paul's Jewish Identity Informs His Apostolic Ministry, with Special Reference to Romans* (Berlin: De Gruyter, 2014), 202-6.

[49]E. H. Gifford, *The Epistle of St. Paul to the Romans* (London: John Murray, 1886), 174.

[50]Note that the (unofficial but nonetheless pervasive) doctrine of Jewish "collective guilt" for the death of Jesus was not finally rescinded by the Roman Catholic Church until the promulgation of *Nostra Aetate* in October 1965.

On the one hand, the assumption of much of what Congdon calls the "Augustinian-Reformed tradition," based exactly on these three chapters of St. Paul's letter, in particular Romans 9:18-21, is that "God's freedom is a *freedom to condemn*."[51] Rather than understanding God's essential character to be one of love, this construal of God's being instead prioritizes his wrath. The hermeneutical presumption is that, in the employment of his freedom, God tends always toward the willing, or at least the permitting, of the eternal damnation of most of us. Grace and salvation are the mitigations of God's more proper aspect of righteous justice (Rom 3:23). Grace is thus pitted against God's default will, as something akin to a reluctant concession that is inherently at odds with God's better judgment.

But there is an equally problematic presumption on the other side, where God's radically generous grace is (or is perceived to be) constricted by an abstracted rule from which God cannot escape. That is, an explicit doctrine of universalism—according to which God's forgiving and salvific love is not only extended to but is effective for all of humanity—is said to destroy the freedom of God's grace by binding him to the principle that his grace obliges him to save everyone. As Barth put it during his visit to Princeton in 1962, while "we cannot avoid to, if we understand Jesus Christ and his work, than to look for, yes, look for universal salvation," we are not thereby permitted to proclaim it as a fait accompli about which we can be certain. "Because salvation is an act and a decision of God's free grace . . . if we proclaim [it] . . . , then we take away God's freedom to do it."[52]

Of course, as Congdon has argued, the dogmatic unsustainability of this position is valid only if we have already committed ourselves to the view inherent in the first of these two dangers—namely, that God's default will is to condemn and that this will is ameliorated, reluctantly, by the decision to allow some to live and not be damned.[53] Only if that

---

[51]D. W. Congdon, *The God Who Saves: A Dogmatic Sketch* (Eugene, OR: Cascade Books, 2016), 13.
[52]K. Barth, *Gespräche, 1959–1962*. In *Gesamtausgabe IV.25*, ed. E. Busch (Zurich: TVZ, 1995), 503-504.
[53]Congdon, *God Who Saves*, 14.

is our premise is the suggestion that God might save all a contradiction of his freedom. To put it the other way around, there is no obligation on God, and thus no damage to the free exercise of his will, if his eternal (and free) commitment is to the salvation of all instead of only some.

My argument here, though, in the context of Romans 9–11, is not that Paul teaches, or even implies, a proto-doctrine of universalism (*apokatastasis*). Nor does he teach—though he has frequently been understood as *at the very least* implying—an unyielding righteousness that prefers perdition over salvation. Rather, he proclaims an irrevocability of Israel's election that is neither confined to a single ethnicity nor oblivious to the failings and faults of the chosen. No one could accuse Paul of letting his fellow Jews "off the hook." They have been, he insists, "ignorant [ἀγνοοῦντες] of the righteousness that comes from God" (10:3)—desperate to obtain it but, in seeking for it in all the wrong places, failing to find it (9:30-31). Moreover, Israel's failures have opened up the possibility of salvation for the Gentiles. Using that potent symbol, Paul notes that in cutting off the natural branches of the olive tree, room is made for the ingrafting of unnatural branches—yet with a crystal-clear caveat that precisely in their unnaturalness, the ingrafted branches ought not think themselves as superior to those whose place they have taken. More to the point, though, Paul's argument in Romans 11 is not so much that everyone—Jews and Gentiles, natural branches and unnatural ones—is vulnerable and at ever-present risk of being "cut off." Rather, the emphasis falls on the universality of God's grace, from which no one—neither natural branches nor unnatural branches; neither the Gentiles who did not receive the promises, the law, the patriarchs, or the divine glory (9:4-5); nor the Jews who have stumbled—is in principle excluded.

EPHESIANS 1:3-14

> Blessed be the God and Father of our Lord Jesus Christ, who has blessed us in Christ with every spiritual blessing in the heavenly places, just as he chose us in Christ before the foundation of the world to be holy and

blameless before him in love. He destined us for adoption as his children through Jesus Christ, according to the good pleasure of his will, to the praise of his glorious grace that he freely bestowed on us in the Beloved. In him we have redemption through his blood, the forgiveness of our trespasses, according to the riches of his grace that he lavished on us. With all wisdom and insight he has made known to us the mystery of his will, according to his good pleasure that he set forth in Christ, as a plan for the fullness of time, to gather up all things in him, things in heaven and things on earth. In Christ we have also obtained an inheritance, having been destined according to the purpose of him who accomplishes all things according to his counsel and will, so that we, who were the first to set our hope on Christ, might live for the praise of his glory. In him you also, when you had heard the word of truth, the gospel of your salvation, and had believed in him, were marked with the seal of the promised Holy Spirit; this is the pledge of our inheritance toward redemption as God's own people, to the praise of his glory. (Eph 1:3-14)

The celebrated classical philologist Eduard Norden once said that this opening section of St. Paul's letter to the Ephesian church is "the most monstrous sentence conglomeration . . . I have ever met in the Greek language."[54] Be that as it may, the "heavy clumsiness" of this opening passage, to use Markus Barth's words, cannot mask the sheer extravagance of God's electing grace described here.[55] Barth reminds us that—whomever it may be who is making these statements, Paul or an otherwise unknown author—the statements themselves about God's decision to choose people for himself are "adoring rather than calculating or speculative." What is in view here is neither "a fate or system above God," nor does this passage describe merely one particular feature of "an impersonal omnipotent rule."[56] On the contrary, the election of which Paul speaks is deeply personal, referring not, in the first instance,

---

[54]E. Norden, *Agnostos Theos: Untersuchungen zur Formengeschichte Religiöser Rede* (Berlin: Verlag B. G. Teubner, 1913), 253n1. Cited in M. Barth, *Ephesians 1–3*, Anchor Bible 34 (New York: Doubleday, 1974), 77. Note that while, for the purposes of this section, I will speak of St. Paul as the author of Ephesians, I am nonetheless aware of the continuing debates as to Pauline authenticity. However, I neither wish nor need to engage with those debates in this context.

[55]Barth, *Ephesians 1–3*, 77.

[56]Barth, *Ephesians 1–3*, 105.

to individuals about whom a certain destiny has been decreed but rather to the God who has taken people to himself as his children.

Andrew Lincoln has made much the same point. The writer of the letter, he argues, seems not at all interested in speculating about the whys and wherefores of election, nor indeed about its shadow side of reprobation. Rather, having been "overwhelmed by the blessing of being chosen," he can do nothing other than "praise the God who is the source of such blessing."[57]

Of course, the frequently used language of election "in Christ"[58] renders this passage particularly susceptible to an exclusivist reading, in which God's blessings of "sonship"—υἱοθεσία ("adoption as his children," v. 5)—might be assumed to accrue only to members of the Christian community. St. John Chrysostom, for one, represents precisely this view. In the first of his homilies on this letter, he exegetes verse 3 ("who has blessed us in Christ with every spiritual blessing in the heavenly places") as an explicit denunciation of the allegedly carnal blessings enjoyed by Israel. "The Jews," he says, "had blessing also, but it was not spiritual blessing." Thus, as the possessors of carnal things only, Jews are now "unable to hear of spiritual things," including, most importantly, those bessings that have now been bestowed from the heavenly places in Christ Jesus. With searing logic, yet with no textual justification whatsoever, Chrysostom concludes that "we"—that is, those who have been chosen "in Christ"—"surpass [the Jews] not only in the quality of the blessings, but in the Mediator also."[59]

Fifteen centuries later the Reformed theologian Charles Hodge, in his own exegesis of this letter, drew similarly narrow limits around God's electing will, albeit without the anti-Jewish overtone. The blessings of election, he contends, are bestowed "not on any external community or

---

[57]A. T. Lincoln, *Ephesians*, Word Biblical Commentary 42, ed. D. A. Hubbard and G. W. Barker (Dallas: Word Books, 1990), 24.

[58]Such language of incorporation—"in Christ," "in him," "in the beloved," or its cognates—is used no fewer than six times in just eleven verses.

[59]*Hom. on Eph.* 50-51.

society as such" but to "believers, scattered here and there."[60] Moreover, while "the purpose of [God's] election is comprehensive," only those who supplement God's prior federal union with their own voluntary union of faith are actually the recipients of its benefits.[61]

Markus Barth, however, reads this passage in an entirely different way. The "in Christ" language does not, he suggests, imply a constriction of God's grace but, on the contrary—when taken in concert with what many have described as the "cosmic Christ" of verse 10—a "universalist" application of it.[62] Certainly, this Christological election must mean that it is only "as members of [the] community" of God's people that individuals "share in the benefits of God's gracious choice." Yet, insists Barth, this ought not be parsed as "the creation of a scheme which divides mankind [sic] into two opposite groups."[63] The reason for this is surprisingly simple. Insofar as the acting subject, and first object, of God's electing will is Jesus Christ himself "before the foundation of the world" (v. 4), and that the goal of God's purposes is the eschatological summing up of all things in that same Christ (v. 10), then it follows that "God's comprehensive purpose goes beyond simply humanity to embrace the whole created order."[64] John Muddiman has argued that this "'christologization' of the doctrine of election," in terms of the preexistent Christ, means that "it is not so much that Christians claim to be an elect race apart from ordinary humanity, but that they are those who believe in the one who is the unique object of God's elective love."[65] That is true, but it does not go far enough. Rather, the blessing that accrues to the believing community is not that they *alone* are the ones who exist in elected solidarity with Christ but simply that they are the ones who are *aware* of that solidarity.[66] The election, in fact,

---

[60]C. Hodge, *Commentary on the Epistle to the Ephesians* (New York: Robert Carter & Brothers, 1866), 29-30.

[61]Hodge, *Ephesians*, 30-31.

[62]Barth, *Ephesians 1–3*, 106.

[63]Barth, *Ephesians 1–3*, 108.

[64]Lincoln, *Ephesians*, 34; Barth, *Ephesians 1–3*, 109-10.

[65]J. Muddiman, *The Epistle to the Ephesians* (Peabody, MA: Hendrickson, 2004), 67.

[66]Cf. Lincoln, *Ephesians*, 23.

is representatively true of all people, for all are included in the pre-foundation election of Christ. The divided humankind, implies Barth—divided erroneously between the false categories of "the elect" and the "reprobate"—is reunited, through the work of Christ, into "a new man," *ut omnes unum sint* (that they all may be one).[67]

CONCLUSION

Very much more could be said on the ways in which the theme of election is discussed within the Hebrew and Christian Scriptures. In this chapter, I have not sought to give an exhaustive summary of this motif or its myriad lexical variants. I have, however, tried to present a suggestive sample of texts, from the tradition of Abraham's patriarchy, through Jacobean and Mosaic stories, before returning again to Abraham, but this time through a Pauline lens. In each case, I have brought to the foreground the manner in which these texts affirm *both* the unfettered freedom of God in his decisions *and* the munificence of his will.[68] Moreover, it has been my contention here that these texts demonstrate a pattern of God's free willing that is characterized more prominently by an expansive inclusivity that extends even to the most unlikely and alien than by either arbitrary or punitive exclusion.

In other words, in claiming as I did at the start of the chapter that the idea of election is indeed scriptural, my subsequent claim now is

---

[67]Barth, *Ephesians 1–3*, 110.

[68]Much of the recent "Barth Wars" that have bombarded the "playground of (modern) theologians" have been shaped by an assumption, at least on one side of the debate, that there is a necessary distinction between freedom and will, such that God's *will* to be graciously for us can be and is qualified by his *freedom not* to be for us. So, Paul Molnar insists that God's being is eternally triune *antecedentally* to his decision to be and act for us in the person of Jesus Christ, whereas Bruce McCormack argues that such a view (a) "temporalizes" the process of divine decision-making into an illegitimate (and indeed nonsensical) "before-and-after" and (b) thus inserts a change in God in which God *becomes* for us in a way that he had not been previously. On the contrary, argues McCormack, "There [must] be no metaphysical gap between God's being and his acting. . . . [Therefore] in that God chooses to be for us in Christ, he is giving himself the being he will have for all eternity. . . . [In other words] God's freedom is the freedom of love that God is to set itself in concrete relationship to that which is other than itself." See B. L. McCormack, "Trinity and Election: Theses in Response to George Hunsinger," in *Trinity and Election in Contemporary Theology*, ed. M. T. Dempsey (Grand Rapids: Eerdmans, 2011), 135; and P. Molnar, *Divine Freedom and the Doctrine of the Immanent Trinity*, 2nd ed. (London: Bloomsbury T&T Clark, 2017), 131-205.

that its scripturality is not simply that election is vaguely present as some sort of undefinable trope, but that it has rather a very specific shape that is both unqualifiedly free and unendingly loving. It is this patterning from Scripture that will be the doctrinal assumption on which the rest of the book will be grounded and the criterion by which the various theologies of election I interrogate will be assessed.

2

THE DOCTRINE OF ELECTION IN
THE WRITINGS OF THE FATHERS

KARL BARTH WAS QUITE RIGHT when, in his magisterial study of election in *Church Dogmatics* II/2, he gave priority to the election of the community over the election of the individual.[1] This was not, he hastened to add, because the community (*Gemeinde*) can ever itself be the object of election in and for itself. No, there can be no legitimate elevation of Israel, or the church, or indeed any other group that considers itself to be divinely chosen, over and above the one Jesus Christ in whom election finds its truest ground and embodiment. There can be, and is, no community that is elected independently (*selbständige*) or, worse, in its own right.[2] Nonetheless, the community of the elect forms the necessary "mediating" environment through which the election of Jesus Christ is attested and into which the election of individuals takes its proper, if only provisional, shape.[3] A responsible appreciation of what it means for any particular person to be elect therefore makes sense only in the far broader context of what we might call "elected sociality"—the communal relationship with others, without whom one is not in fact elected at all.

---

[1]Of course, the election of the community is, in Barth's work, itself preceded by and subsidiary to the election of the one individual, Jesus Christ (§33).
[2]*KD* II/2, 216. This was precisely the danger that Barth saw in a Nazified *Volkskirche* (people's church) in which the sole lordship of Jesus was replaced by the new revelatory medium of "Germanness." See also D. Ritschl, *The Logic of Theology*, trans. J. Bowden (London: SCM Press, 1986), 115.
[3]*CD* II/2, 196-97.

The doctrine of election thus inevitably invites questions about the nature of the community into which one is either elected or from which one is (if this is, ultimately, even possible!) kept apart. As Markus Barth has provocatively asked, "Who are the people of God? Jews, Christians, both together, or neither of them?"[4] Again, Dietrich Ritschl has expressed the issue with generous clarity. Israel and the church are together, he says, "part of the ecumene," but that ecumene itself must be understood as broadening out considerably beyond the scope of those two. Indeed, asks Ritschl, "Is it at all theologically legitimate to distinguish the people of God from others as though the whole of humanity were not affected by the coming, death and resurrection of Jesus in a way that 'extended' the history and election of Israel to all people?"[5] We shall be compelled to return to this idea in later chapters.

At this time, however, it is important simply to recognize the more basic point that the boundaries of the elect community—assuming, in fact, that we can indeed speak in the singular—are uncertain, blurred, and porous. Mindful of this recognition, we turn in this chapter to a consideration of the ways in which certain of the Fathers mapped election onto the being of the church, at a time when the very nature of "church" itself was still a matter of controversy. What we have said already suggests, of course, that we must reckon with the possibility that the elect community is far broader than the church, a possibility to which Origen implicitly points. But, as we shall see with Augustine and a number of the other Fathers, it is also in a certain sense far narrower. Consequently, there must be an overlap, even if only a partial one, between these narrow and broad conceptions of this community.

The extent, nature, and reasons for this overlap were precisely what the church's first leaders and thinkers had to wrestle with as they sought in their own ways and contexts to determine what it meant to be "the elected community of God." It is evident from some of the later New Testament letters that the idea of the church as a multiethnic chosen

---

[4]M. Barth, *The People of God*, JSNT Supplement Series 5 (Sheffield, UK: JSOT Press, 1983), 9.
[5]Ritschl, *Logic of Theology*, 45.

people in the manner of a new Israel—the church is, says the author of the Petrine letters, a "holy nation, God's own people" (1 Pet 2:9)—took root within the first few decades of the church's existence.[6] Insofar as Israel was already understood to be, or perhaps to have been, the elect people of God, the assumption of that title by the church to itself is suggestive of a deliberate and developed concept of ecclesial election. But in fact, despite the Petrine language, this was not the case. The church's early theologians only unevenly employed this particular imagery. Some did not use Israel symbolism at all, preferring to find other ways of depicting and defining the church's constituency.[7] In contrast, therefore, to those like Matthew Levering who explore patristic doctrines of predestination independently of the ecclesial context, in this chapter we will explore the opinions of the Fathers on the nature of election and predestination in the very particular context of their evolving understanding of the nature of the church as the visible iteration of the elect community. *Mt 25 X hr* ✓

THE ECCLESIOLOGICAL CONTEXT

When we ask how the early church tried to conceptualize itself, it soon becomes abundantly clear that, even as various and competing ecclesiologies were being worked out, there was a determination to find the limits of the church. As Howard Clark Kee has observed, any serious attempt to inquire into the self-understanding of the early Christian communities needs to address what he calls "boundary questions": What were the markers of group identity, how and by what authority

---

[6] One could also cite here Paul's reference to the "Israel of God" (Gal 6:16). While the precise meaning of this phrase is contested, John Chrysostom, Martin Luther, and John Calvin each understood it to refer exclusively to the (non-Jewish) church, with this becoming the dominant exegetical view. For the alternative opinion, that "Israel of God" refers to ethnic and/or Christian Jews, see P. Richardson, *Israel in the Apostolic Church* (Cambridge: Cambridge University Press, 1969); F. F. Bruce, *Galatians*, New International Greek Testament Commentary (Grand Rapids, Eerdmans, 1982); S. Lewis Johnston, "Paul and 'Israel of God': An Exegetical and Eschatological Case-Study," in *Essays in Honor of J. Dwight Pentecost*, ed. S. D. Toussaint and C. H. Dyer (Chicago: Moody, 1986).

[7] For example, images of mother, ark, and virgin bride were all used to describe the church with varying degrees of regularity. B. Ramsey, *Beginning to Read the Fathers*, rev. ed (Mahwah, NJ: Paulist Press, 2012), 99.

were the boundaries determined and defended, and through what processes could those boundaries be crossed?[8] Baptismal belonging gave
expression to membership around the eucharistic table, but, as Papandrea rightly says, this does not really answer the question. "On the
one hand, some who were not yet baptized could consider themselves
Christians . . . On the other hand, some who were baptized might not
be considered within the true Church."[9]

Taking seriously Jesus' commands to go to the ends of the earth (Mt
28:19; Acts 1:8), but in equal seriousness the *Christ*ian specificity of
the gospel, the Fathers realized their need for an ecclesiological
grammar that could hold together the church's universality as well as
its particularity—a particularity that took not only doctrinal but also
(and in the first instance, primarily) ethical shape. For this, a determination to define the marks of membership was needed.[10]

In other words, when one considers the multitude of controversies
and schisms with which the early Christian communities were riven
between the middle of the first century and the middle of the fifth,[11]
one major factor stands apart from all others. The apologies for the
faith—one thinks, for example, of the apologetic works of Justin Martyr
and Tertullian—as well as the refutations of heresies and heretics, were
done with the singular aim of ensuring the faithfulness and purity of
God's community on earth. No matter whether one considers the repudiation of Arian Christology or the insistence on a proper ordering
of baptismal catechesis, the determinative agenda was to retain the
holiness of the Christian ecclesia. Even if Rowan Williams is correct

---

[8]H. C. Kee, *Who Are the People of God? Early Christian Models of Community* (New Haven, CT:
Yale University Press, 1995), 13-14. Kee also notes the importance of "authority questions" and
"ritual questions"; that is, what were/are the governance structures, and how were/are formative
experiences of change and transition liturgized? We will touch on both of these matters throughout this chapter.

[9]J. L. Papandrea, *Reading the Early Church Fathers: From the Didache to Nicaea* (Mahwah, NJ:
Paulist Press, 2012), 173.

[10]C. Gunton, *The Christian Faith: An Introduction to Christian Doctrine* (Oxford: Blackwell, 2002),
128-29.

[11]For the purposes of this chapter, the "early church" is taken to extend only until the Council of
Chalcedon in 451 CE.

(and I believe that he is) that the Arian debates and their ilk were primarily exegetical,[12] they were nonetheless contests in which certain exegetical principles (as well as their logical doctrinal consequences) came to be deemed beyond the ecclesial pale.

Acknowledging this, however, poses two difficulties. First, much of the initial determination around ecclesial limits was decided on doctrinal grounds that were themselves ambiguous. Definitions of orthodoxy—and therefore what was *extra ecclesiam*—were not readily apparent until the church decided them. Thus, the basis on which any given group or individual might be excluded from the church's fellowship, and by implication from the community of the elect—other than by recourse to allegations of visible moral imperfection[13]—was not always altogether self-evident.

Denials of Jesus' resurrection were easy enough to handle. For example, Ignatius warns the Christians in Smyrna to distance themselves from those who "make a jest of the resurrection" and in so doing deny the Eucharist.[14] Similarly, Irenaeus castigates those who "do not take into consideration the power of God who raises it [flesh] from the dead."[15] Such refutations were clearly directed against various Docetic tendencies within or hovering at the fringes of Christian communities. More complex doctrinal matters, on the other hand, took considerable time to configure and were not so easily adjudged. There was simply no formula for describing the proper inter-relationship of the trinitarian persons until Constantine called the bishops to Nicaea in 325 CE. Similarly, there was no single authoritative statement of what constituted an orthodox account of the relationship of Jesus Christ's divine and human natures until Chalcedon in 451 CE.

---

[12]R. Williams, *Arius: Heresy and Tradition*, rev. ed. (Grand Rapids: Eerdmans, 2002), 108.

[13]Community discipline and exclusion—at least for a time—was part of early liturgical practice. See for example, Justin Martyr: "And this food is called among us Εὐχαριστία [the Eucharist], of which no one is allowed to partake but the man who believes that the things which we teach are true, and who has been washed with the washing that is for the remission of sins, and unto regeneration, and *who is so living as Christ has enjoined*." *1 Apol.*, 66. Emphasis added.

[14]Ign. *Smyr.*, 7 (longer version).

[15]*Against Heresies* 5.3.2.

This is not to suggest that the creedal statements and formulae that emerged from those councils were greeted with unanimous endorsement; there were, in both cases, smaller groups of Christians who for various reasons refused to accept the determinations. Nor is it to suggest that the final authoritative statements of faith were dreamed up in a conciliar vacuum, as though they had not been thoroughly explored and debated in the preceding years. It is, however, to say that until those landmark statements were approved in council there was, at most, only an intuitive sense of what best approximated orthodoxy, and a range of opinions were nearer to or further away from what those statements ended up defining. (As we have already noted in chapter one, appeal to Scripture did not always easily resolve the problem.) In Barth's memorable phrase, "All heretics are [only] relatively heretical"![16] Moreover, the fact that many of the "heretics" could cite otherwise orthodox theologians for support goes to show how fluid the nature of orthodoxy and heterodoxy was in the church's formative centuries.[17] As Hans Küng quite rightly asks, are we really to expect that "light and darkness are . . . equally distributed between Church and heresy? Or . . . that the power of evil is only effective outside the Church, and that faith only exists inside it?"[18] In other words, the opinions that were in the end rejected as heretical were rejected post facto only once the definitions and creedal affirmations had been finalized. Until that point, however, they were often nothing more than genuine, if ultimately unpersuasive, attempts to find conceptual paradigms for ideas that lie fundamentally beyond both discursive and cognitive capacity.[19] In many cases the holders of

---

[16]"Es gibt nur relative Ketzer." K. Barth, *Geschichte der protestantischen Theologie seit Schleiermacher* (Zurich: Hans Walt, 1943), 3, AT. The English translation appears as *Protestant Theology in the Nineteenth Century* (London: SCM Press, 2001), 3.

[17]For example, Arius was backed by Eusebius of Caesarea, Secondus of Ptolemais, and Theonas of Marmarica as well as by the renowned scholar Lucian of Antioch. Apollinaris cited Athanasius in support of his own Christology. Even Cyril of Alexandria was at times confused, apportioning a key phrase—"one incarnate nature of the Word of God"—to Athanasius, when in fact it had originated with Apollinaris.

[18]H. Küng, *The Church* (New York: Image Books, 1976), 321.

[19]We should therefore not be entirely surprised to note that some of the so-called heresies have been rehabilitated in more recent times, precisely because the construals of the first four centu-

such views eventually found themselves outside the limits of the church, but the holding of such views could not, in the first instance, be a self-evident proof that one did not belong.

Second, and much more significantly, there was no single understanding of what the "church" was or meant. While it may not be entirely incorrect to say that "church" was understood at least conceptually by its membership—that is, it was roundly understood to be the "body of Christ . . . the extension of the kingdom of God on earth, and [that] it existed wherever people gathered" in Christ's name[20]—such an affirmation nevertheless hides more than it reveals. Principally, it hides the fact that a more concrete sense of what being the "body of Christ" actually meant in any given region evolved only gradually and in different ways across different locations. Although now well over a hundred years old, the view put forward by James Bethune-Baker in 1903, that "of the doctrine of the Church . . . there was for some time no clear definition framed . . . [but only] a general sentiment about it," remains essentially as true now as when he first proposed it.[21] In his study of early worship practices, Andrew McGowan states, "Early Christianity was characterized by processes of community formation, involving both ritual and theory . . . through a variety of controversies and contests." What we now recognize to be in some sense normative, says McGowan, "was not always and everywhere the most or only obvious way to be Christian."[22] This is as true in ecclesiology as it was in the matter of liturgy and ritual development. Even though baptism provided a visible boundary to the church community,[23] it was not at all understood why only some ventured, through baptism, to cross the boundary into that community. Nor was it clear precisely what sort of community it was

---

ries are now recognized to be, at particular points, susceptible to critique (e.g., the renewed interest in divine passibility). Similarly, the Chalcedonian formula has never achieved complete ecclesial endorsement, with the continuation of non-Chalcedonian miaphysitism in the Egyptian and Ethiopian churches.

[20]Papandrea, *Reading the Early Church Fathers*, 7.

[21]J. F. Bethune-Baker, *Early History of Christian Doctrine* (1903; repr., London: Methuen, 1962), 356.

[22]A. B. McGowan, *Ancient Christian Worship* (Grand Rapids: Baker Academic, 2014), 14.

[23]See Papandrea, *Reading the Early Church Fathers*, 7.

that people were being included into by their baptism, or conversely from what they were being excluded if they were not baptized.

Perhaps the most concrete notion of church that assumed early and general endorsement was that of a eucharistic community, revolving around a bishop.[24] Irenaeus and Tertullian, for example, both insisted, as had Ignatius before them, on proper episcopal jurisdiction as part of the church's existence. In their view, episcopal continuity in any given see was the guarantor of doctrinal purity. As Irenaeus puts it,

> It is incumbent to obey the presbyters who are in the Church—those who, as I have shown, possess the succession from the apostles; those who, together with the succession of the episcopate, have received the certain gift of truth, according to the good pleasure of the Father.[25]

While this might have given visible and indeed ethical expression to church membership, it did not answer any questions about the nature of the larger eschatological community beyond the temporal sphere. This is the difficulty with Hans Küng's account of ecclesial being. For Küng, the first communities drew heavily on the imagery in the Pauline and Lukan texts in particular that spoke of the church as the ek-klesia of God (e.g., Acts 20:28; 1 Cor 12:28). Insofar as the members understood this to mean they were the "called-out" ones, gathering around a shared belief in the resurrection of Christ, they were justified, says Küng, in self-identifying as an eschatological community of faith, the new *kehal Yahweh* (community of God). For this very reason, he says, they were the ἐκλεκτοί (the elect).[26] Yet, as the doctrinal controversies were to prove, and Augustine's own "twin-city" typology would later confirm, mere membership within an ecclesial gathering, even on the part of

---

[24]The presence of a bishop at eucharistic celebrations seems to have been the norm in the early centuries until larger and more complex organizational structures of church life in the mid fifth century made it impractical for the bishop to be everywhere that services were held, resulting in greater roles for presbyters. Note, though, that Ignatius's need to stipulate episcopal authority in his letters from the second century perhaps suggests that even this minimal descriptor of "church" was not always operative. See McGowan, *Ancient Christian Worship*, 41, 174.
[25]*Against Heresies* 4.26.2.
[26]Küng, *Church*, 114-24.

those who affirmed faith in the resurrected Christ, did not prove that one was thereby a member of "the church" in any ultimate sense. Neither eucharistic participation, nor the confession of faith and baptism by which it was always preceded, said anything about the basis in God's predestinating will for any person's inclusion in or exclusion from this "ek-lektic" community of faith. Sociological belonging was not an altogether accurate proxy for what we have earlier called elected sociality.

Alister McGrath has suggested that a key factor in this lack of conceptual clarity was because "ecclesiology was not a major issue in the early church." Eastern theologians, he says, showed "no awareness" of the significance of ecclesiology, and the Greek fathers were content simply to use scriptural phrases "without choosing to probe [the issue] further."[27] Yet McGrath's claim itself needs further probing. Is it in fact true that the lack of precision regarding the nature, being, and extent of the church was because the Fathers were uninterested in the question? How did the community formational processes, of which McGowan has spoken, become concerned not only with the ordering of liturgy and governance but with the eternal divine willing of ecclesial membership? These are the questions to which we must now attend.

FROM THE APOSTOLIC FATHERS TO THE *SANCTORUM COMMUNIO*

At the turn of the second century, the so-called apostolic fathers[28] tended to lay heavy stress on more obviously institutional markers of the church's existence that spoke to communal order and ethical propriety. Given the precarious legality of Christian belief, this made great sense; there was little point in provoking the authorities by displays of overtly subversive actions. We should not, of course, overplay the danger faced by Christians during this time. Candida Moss has shown admirably that "while Christians were never a beloved group and that during the vast majority of [the first three centuries] they were actively disliked," there

---

[27]A. E. McGrath, *Christian Theology: An Introduction*, 2nd ed. (Oxford: Blackwell, 1997), 461.
[28]Typically understood to include Clement of Rome, Ignatius of Antioch, Polycarp of Smyrna, and the Didache, sometimes also including The Shepherd of Hermas and the Epistle of Barnabas.

is less evidence than is often assumed for wholesale, and specifically targeted, persecution.[29] Within a context in which judicial brutality was the norm rather than the exception, the deliberate pursuit of Christians as such was generally sporadic and localized.[30] Even so, it remains the case that church gatherings were unlikely to be peopled by members who did not genuinely wish to be there. Yet it was also important to be able to show that, contrary to rumor, such gatherings were not riotous events that caused civil disruption. They were not, as Suetonius and others would have had it, characterized by cannibalism or incestuous orgies.[31] It is no wonder, then, that early apologies emphasized the order and decorum of Christian worship. Thus, we see Justin confidently urging Emperor Antoninus Pius to judge the Christians' lives as well as their doctrines, and Tertullian outlining in considerable detail just how decorous Christian meetings and meals actually were.[32]

In Clement of Rome (d. 99) we see a similar theme. His first epistle, for example, focuses not only on the church's liturgy but also on its governance. We read him insisting that there be a proper ordering of services and offerings, that those services be offered at appointed times, and that there be a clear structuring of bishops, priests, and deacons. As he wrote to the Corinthian Christians,

> It behooves us to do all things in [their proper] order, which the Lord has commanded us to perform at stated times. He has enjoined offerings [to be presented] and service to be performed [to Him], and that not thoughtlessly or irregularly, but at the appointed times and hours. Where and by whom He desires these things to be done, He Himself has fixed by His own supreme will, in order that all things being piously done according to His good pleasure, may be acceptable unto Him . . . Our apostles also knew,

---

[29]C. Moss, *The Myth of Persecution: How Early Christians Invented a Story of Martyrdom* (New York: HarperCollins, 2013), 129.

[30]The Decian persecution of 249–251, for example, was empire-wide but not specifically targeted at Christians. Similarly, the persecutions that commenced under Diocletian in 303 and ended in 313, while undoubtedly brutal, were never consistently enforced across all the various imperial provinces.

[31]E.g., Suetonius, *Annals* 15.44; and *Life of Nero* 16. See the refutations of such charges in Athenagoras, *A Plea for the Christians* 3; and Theophilus, *To Autolycus* 3.4.

[32]*1 Apol.*, 1-4, 7, 10; Ter. *Apol.*, 39.

through our Lord Jesus Christ, and there would be strife on account of the office of the episcopate. For this reason, therefore, inasmuch as they had obtained a perfect fore-knowledge of this, they appointed those [ministers] already mentioned, and afterwards gave instructions, that when these should fall asleep, other approved men should succeed them in their ministry.[33]

The community of Clement's church was, in this view, a structured community of people who gathered for particular purposes at particular times. It was evidently also a community whose consent was needed for the appointment of its own leadership.

We see evidence of similarly prescriptive ordering in Justin Martyr's *First Apology* and in the Didache, in both of which set prayers are provided and improvisation within the *Eucharistia* is frowned on.[34] Andrew McGowan has said that these liturgical prescriptions suggest that the communities from which they emerged were more concerned with ensuring the proper functioning of worship than with explicating it theologically.[35] Allen Brent offers a suggestion as to why this might have been the case. In his view, such an emphasis on order is reflective of a situation in which order was conspicuously absent. In other words, Clement, Justin, and the Didachist lay stress on the need for things to be done "decently and in order" precisely because their communities were disordered and verging on fracture.[36]

Be that as it may, while there is a sense in all these writings of how proper ecclesial governance should be constituted and suitable worship should be conducted, what is noticeably lacking beyond these organizational rubrics is anything approximating conceptual clarity around the nature of the church's essentially willed being. This is an understandable and natural consequence of the particular issues the church grappled with in these early decades. Yet it is striking that one is unable to discern any articulation of the ultimate ground of the church's existence.

---

[33]Cl. *I Cor.* 40-42.
[34]See especially *1 Apol.*, 65-66; and Did., 8-10.
[35]McGowan, *Ancient Christian Worship*, 37.
[36]A. Brent, *Ignatius of Antioch* (London: T&T Clark, 2007), 26-29.

It is as though defining governance and liturgical propriety—thereby setting the parameters within which the Christian community could appropriately gather without provoking the ire of the imperial authorities—was by itself a sufficient determinant of ecclesial being. To put it otherwise, insofar as McGowan is right that the Clementine and Didachist communities were uninterested in expressing a deeply considered theology of worship, they seem to have been similarly uninterested in exploring and expressing what the church in fact eternally is and in which this worship was to be offered.

What one sees, therefore, in these first formative decades of the church's life into the second century is an increasingly sophisticated variety of organizational models, the need for which was made all the more urgent by the church's rapid growth in numbers and sociological complexity. Duties of bishops and presbyters, and the manner in which community meals and other services[37] were to be hosted, were set down in considerable detail. Certainly there was variety; liturgical orders and exhortatory epistles described, and prescribed, practiced in specific localities, without those being necessarily copied into other regions. But answering the question of how the church properly does what it does did little, by itself, to solve the question, What is the church?

Significantly, creedal formulations did not do much to clarify the issue. One of the earliest liturgical references to the church community is to be found in the Old Roman Creed (ca. 140).[38] Employing very simple terms, the creed speaks of belief in "the Holy Spirit; the holy church."[39]

Tertullian, in the late second century, affirmed the simplicity of this creedal structure by being even more minimalist. In the various places in which he summarizes the "rule of faith that has come down to us

---

[37]Note, for example, that whereas Ignatius seems to have assumed that the Eucharist would be celebrated within the context of a broader "love feast" meal (Ign. *Smyr.* 5), Justin sets it aside as a specific service on a given day of the week. *1 Apol.*, 67.

[38]It was this creed that gradually developed into what we now know as the Apostles' Creed, the first references to which are from the southwest of France in the sixth century.

[39]See Rufinus (ca. 400), cited in A. E. Burn, *An Introduction to the Creeds and to the Te Deum* (London: Methuen & Co., 1899), 46-48.

from the beginning of the gospel," he does not even mention the church other than as the implicit community in which the faith is professed. His emphasis—at least in his overviews of the creed—is squarely on the triune God in whom the believer believes, not at all on the ecclesial community within which that belief is enacted.[40] This perhaps reflects both the baptismal usage of the creed (in that what is at stake at baptism is the object of profession; the professing subjects are somewhat more self-evident) and the particular nature of the trinitarian heresies against which Tertullian was writing. In any event, the church as such lies in the background of early creedal formulae and is not highlighted as a particular element of critical belief.

By the fourth century, this minimalist statement had been expanded to include the explanatory clause "the communion of saints." As we shall see, however, it did not in fact explain very much at all. There are contested readings as to the origin and meaning of this addition. The so-called Creed of Jerome (ca. 374–379) reads, in its third article, "I believe in the remission of sins in the holy catholic church, the communion of saints."[41] There is also an instance in the writings of the missionary-theologian Nicetas of Remesiana (ca. 400), who had in turn been heavily influenced by the catechetical lectures of Cyril of Jerusalem.[42] Nicetas asks rhetorically, "What is the church but the community of all the saints?"[43] By the end of the fourth century, the creed thus read, "We believe in the Holy Spirit, the holy catholic Church, the communion of saints."

In the first instance, it is important to note that the clause *sanctorum communionem* is in restrictive apposition to the preceding. The saintly communion is the church, and vice versa. One of the more striking

---

[40]See, for example, *Against Praxeas*, 2; and *On the Prescription Against Heretics*, 13, 36.

[41]"*Credo remissionem peccatorum in sancta ecclesia catholica, sanctorum communionem.*"

[42]Note that an imperial edict from 388 CE banned Apollinarians from the *communio sanctorum*. It also appears in a canon from the Synod of Nimes in 394 CE, in the context of participation in the Eucharist.

[43]"*Ecclesia quid aliud, quam sanctorum omnio congregatio?*" See editor's note, D. Bonhoeffer, *DBWE* 1:123.

things about this clause is that it not only "embodies" the ecclesial institution but intentionally references the Eastern idea of κοινωνία των
ἀγιων (the fellowship of the holy), by which the Eastern fathers meant
the shared participation in the eucharistic elements of bread and wine.
Notwithstanding the reference to the sacramental elements, this represents a clear development of the idea of church: not simply the place
where the Eucharist is offered according to certain rubrics but a community of a particular type of people. In other words, the use of the
term *sanctorum communio* as a descriptor of the church did a number
of things at once. It carried the sense of a spiritual community, by which
the living were conjoined in fellowship with the faithful departed (e.g.,
Heb 12:1). Even in Cyprian's day, for example, the African church tied
eucharistic celebration to a commemoration of martyrs.[44] It was also a
somewhat tightly defined term that connoted those people who, on
account of their baptism and right conduct, were entitled to be admitted to the table.[45] But we ought not overstate the theological profundity of this development, important as it was. What the inclusion of
the term *sanctorum communio* did not do was provide a descriptive
commentary on the identification of the elect or suggest in any way that
the elect might necessarily include, but also be demographically distinct from, this holy communion of saints.

Perhaps, then, McGrath is correct that ecclesiology did not, in its first
iterations within the patristic literature, seek to expound anything other
than the ritual and sociological patterns of function and constituency,
with more ultimate questions left essentially unexplored. To query whether
this is in fact the case, we now need to consider various Fathers in some

---

[44]McGowan, *Ancient Christian Worship*, 245.

[45]See E. A. Johnson, *Abounding in Kindness: Writings for the People of God* (Maryknoll, NY: Orbis,
2015); and E. Brunner, *The Christian Doctrine of the Church, Faith and the Consummation:
Dogmatics, Vol. 3*, trans. Thomas H. L. Parker and D. Cairns (Cambridge: James Clarke, 2002),
125. In this context, it is worth noting that various sectarian groups in the early church also
highlighted holiness of life—κοινωνία των ἀγιων (fellowship of the holy ones)—as the essential
mark of the true church. For example, the second-century Montanist movement embraced
celibacy, fasting, and a glorification of martyrdom, while Novationism in the third century refused to countenance second marriages and allowed no readmission to fellowship for lapsed
believers. Note that the Novationists called themselves καθαροι, meaning "Puritans."

detail, specifically to ask whether and how their understanding of the church incorporated any sense of what it meant to be the elect of God.

IGNATIUS OF ANTIOCH

Ignatius of Antioch (d. ca. 107[46]), traditionally thought to have been a disciple of St. John and then Antioch's third bishop after Saints Peter and Euodias, had his own uncompromising views about the proper constitution of the church. In his mind, the existence of the church in any given town was guaranteed by the authoritative presence of a single bishop, to whom all believers in that city were to be subject. To the Smyrnean church, Ignatius insists that "wherever the bishop shall appear, there let the multitude [of the people] also be; even as, wherever Jesus Christ is, there is the catholic Church [καθολικὴ ἐκκλησία]."[47] Similar sentiments are expressed in his other letters to the Trallians, Ephesians, Philadelphians, and Magnesians.[48] This should not cause us to think that the bishop was the only holder of responsible authority: there was also place for presbyters and deacons, whose roles were appointed by God to be *in locum apostolorum*. As Brent reminds us, Ignatius supposes a mutual cooperation between bishop, presbyters, and deacons, in which submission to authority is nuanced and shared; it is to the threefold order that lay submission is required, never to the bishop alone.[49] Nevertheless, the bishop in this model occupied a unique place in the church's order, as the "strings" to the "harp" of God's commandments.[50]

Hans Küng notes that this Ignatian ordering was the first example in the church's life of a three-tiered hierarchy, in which a single *episkopos* ruled in place of a college of equals. But, while this may seem to be

---

[46]Dating the martyrdom of Ignatius, and therefore the composition of his letters, is notoriously difficult. The general consensus puts it somewhere between 105 and 115 CE. In any case, if both tradition and literary evidence is correct, that Ignatius died during Trajan's rule, then it must have been before 117 CE, the year of Trajan's own death.

[47]Ign. *Smyr.* 8. This is the first time that the word *catholic* was used to describe the church.

[48]See, for example, Ign. *Eph.* 6; Ign. *Mag.* 3-4; Ign. *Trall.* 2-3; and Ign. *Phil.* 1-2, 4. Note that these constitute those letters generally considered to be authentic.

[49]Brent, *Ignatius of Antioch*, 32-33.

[50]Ign. *Phil.* 1.

nothing more than a particularly formalized model of governance, Küng argues that it denotes, in fact, an image of church that is both mystical and pneumic.[51] It is so precisely because of the way in which the three orders of clergy represent, in their offices, God himself and Christ's apostles. Throughout his letters, Ignatius commends union with the bishop as being analogous to union with Christ, with the bishop indeed standing "in the place of" (εἰς τόπον θεοῦ) God himself and the presbyters delegating in the place of the apostles.[52]

This is not, however, merely a governmental issue. On the contrary, it is a matter that goes to the very heart of what it means to be in, and to be, the church. We know from the Ignatian letters themselves as well as from inferences within the Didache and the Gospel of St. Matthew—both of which likely also originated from Syria, and within a few decades of each other—that the Syrian churches were riven by factionalism in and around the turn of the second century. The First Evangelist, for example, has in view those who read the messianic promise in a universal sense; thus, he writes of eastern sages who recognize the baby Jesus to be the Christ (Mt 2:2, 10), then concludes the Gospel with the dominical injunction to "go . . . and make disciples of all nations" (Mt 28:19). At the same time, however, Matthew is also conscious of a more sectarian view among some who read the messianic promise in exclusively Jewish terms; for such as these, Jesus is sent "only to the lost sheep of the house of Israel" (Mt 15:24). Similarly, the Didachist speaks into a church context in which it has become hard to distinguish true prophets from the false, with the members of the community being urged to beware those who would turn them against each other.[53] Conflict and division are evidently at play in both Syrian communities from which these writings emerge.

The letters of Ignatius, the preeminent Syrian bishop of the time, demonstrate the same set of problems. He repeatedly insists that division

---

[51]Küng, *Church*, 524-25.
[52]Ign. *Eph.* 5; Ign. *Mag.* 6.
[53]Did., 11, 15.

within the church is the worst of all errors,[54] and so much of the content of his letters is given over to proposing what, in his mind, is the only workable solution. Disharmony, he insists, is to be avoided most effectively by maintaining happy communion with the bishop. And so, "nothing should be done" without or apart from the bishop, to whom the church is to be subject "as to Jesus Christ."[55]

Strangely, perhaps, it is in this very context that we at last encounter references to election:

> Ignatius, who is called Theophorus, to the Church which is at Ephesus . . . being blessed in the greatness and fullness of God the Father, and predestined [προωρισμενη] before the ages, that it should always be for an enduring and unchangeable glory, [the ones having been] united and elected [εκλελεγμενην] through the true passion by the will of the Father.[56]

Ignatius writes also to the Trallian church, which is, he says, "beloved of God, the Father of Jesus Christ, elect [εκλεκτη] and worthy."[57]

These epistolary prefaces provide some important clues about how Ignatius understood election. First, election is only ever construed communally. For Ignatius, there is no other object of election than the church. Contrary to so much of this doctrine's history, individualized election is never mentioned within his letters. Second, the predestining decision of God, of which Ignatius speaks in reference to the Ephesian church, takes place "before the ages" (πρὸ τῶν αἰώνων). It is, in other words, a pretemporal act of the Father that has, as its purpose, the church bearing witness to an abiding (παραμονών) and immutable (ατρεπτον) glory. It is also important to see in this context that this eternality of the church is illustrated typologically by Ignatius's ordering of ministries. Ignatius draws explicit parallels between God the Father, Christ, and the apostles, on the one hand, and bishops, deacons,

---

[54]Because love is the greatest of all virtues, any sort of schism—understood as a breach of love—is thus the worst of all evils. See Ramsey, *Beginning to Read the Fathers*, 104.

[55]E.g., Ign. *Trall.* 2; Ign. *Smyr.* 8-9.

[56]Ign. *Eph.* Preface.

[57]Ign. *Trall.* Preface.

and presbyters, on the other.[58] But as John Behr reminds us, within this typology, the apostles "are always placed on the eternal, universal level of the Church."[59]

The third point to make is that the election of the church, of which Ignatius speaks, is accomplished "through [ἐν—that is, as a consequence of] the true passion." This could refer to the Ephesians' own suffering under persecution, by which they had been compelled to come together in self-defensive unity. This, though, would require evidence of far greater persecution from either Roman or Jewish opponents in the first decade or so of the second century than we in fact have.[60] Or, and I think this to be the more likely interpretation, "the true passion [or suffering]" could refer to the death and resurrection of Christ. If so, then Ignatius clearly has in mind that the election of the church is something willed in uncreated eternity, then brought into effective being through the cross. In any event, the concept of election that Ignatius proposes in this letter is marked by these discernible characteristics: that it is communal, eternally willed, and actualized Christologically at the cross.

We also learn in these letters that election is intrinsically tied to unity and worthiness. Those who belong to the church are "united and elected," "elect and worthy." Given his constant reiteration of the need for the church to be united against factionalism, it makes complete sense that the unity of which he speaks in the Ephesians preface is not so much a unity of the church with God (although it undoubtedly also includes that) but rather a unity of the church with itself. Only insofar as the church demonstrates this internal unity is it in fact also the elected community. Or, to put it the other way around, the church *is* only that community that is in harmony with itself. Moreover, the fact that Ignatius maintains in all his letters that the church exists where it

---

[58]See Ign. *Trall.* 3.1; and Ign. *Mag.* 6.1.

[59]J. Behr, *Formation of Christian Theology*, vol. 1, *The Way to Nicaea* (New York: St. Vladimir's Seminary Press, 2001), 82.

[60]See, for example, P. Trebilco, *The Early Christians in Ephesus: From Paul to Ignatius* (Grand Rapids: Eerdmans, 2007).

is united with the bishop as to Christ suggests that its worthiness is also tied to its obedient unity under episcopal rule. The church that is worthy, says Ignatius, "possess[es] peace [εἰρηνευούσῃ]," presumably as opposed to division.[61] In other words, while election occurs before all time, its characteristic markers in time, which demonstrate the community's worthiness to bear the mantle of election, are peaceable unity in obedient submission to the bishop and presbyters, in whom Christ's own presence and the guarantee of apostolic fidelity reside.

That is to say, Ignatius views the church as under constant threat of disunity and division. The church is not hermetically sealed from the danger of factionalism. Equally, however, the community that can withstand those threats and remain internally united under the leadership of a bishop who stands in the place of Christ himself demonstrates by such harmony that it is the church which has been elected from before the ages.

If we are not careful, the heavy emphasis on clerical governance in these Ignatian letters can blind us to what Küng calls the "spiritual-pneumic" aspect of the church, which Ignatius regards as the more important thing. Read in this light, the Ignatian letters describe in embryonic form the idea of ecclesial election that originates in the pretemporal will of God and manifests in the harmony of episcopally led peaceful obedience. Far from being merely a set of instructions about how to behave and whom to obey, Ignatius's letters to the churches start to indicate a very particular understanding of what elected sociality looked like.

ORIGEN OF ALEXANDRIA

From troubled Syria at the beginning of the second century, we turn now to northern Egypt at the start of the third, focusing our attention on that most ambiguous of figures, Origen (ca. 186–255). Remembered both for his exegetical genius and also for his advocacy of subordinationist Christology (among various other heterodox ideas), Origen

---

[61]Ign. *Trall.* Preface.

nonetheless has valuable things to say about the nature and being of the church in the eternal will of God. Levering may be overstating the case when he says that Origen's views on this topic "inform all later discussions."[62] Still, his is a vital voice to hear in this context. Moreover, the details of what he has to say take us significantly beyond Ignatius.

It is well known that Origen advocated an ultimately universalist view of salvation. Insofar as predestination generally, and election specifically, are typically concerned with ultimate destinies, this might be thought to exhaust Origen's views on the matter. In fact, it does not. Origen says that God does indeed predestine some to eternal life and not others. But the emphasis in this predestining lies heavily on the free choices made by God's creatures rather than on God's own arbitrariness. In particular, Origen understands the subjects of God's foreknowledge and predestination to be those who, by the freedom of their own created will, have chosen to love and obey him. Thus, it is those who "freely purify their souls from sin" whom God takes to be his chosen vessels.[63] Predestination is therefore the anticipatory consequence, and not the cause, of one's love for God. As Thomas Scheck puts it, Origen's doctrine of predestination and election is "essentially [God's] foreknowledge of [an individual's] merits."[64] Conversely, for those who do not freely purify themselves and as a result are not God's "chosen vessels," there remains the purifying fire of hell. Yet Origen insists that even this is not an eternal damnation. On the contrary, this punishment acts in a curative fashion as a "physician of the souls" in order that, in the end, God will achieve the restoration of all. Through restorative torment, all souls emerge gradually from bondage to freedom, with this "perfect restoration of the entire creation" being the final actualization of unity in Christ.[65]

---

[62]M. Levering, *Predestination: Biblical and Theological Paths* (Oxford: Oxford University Press, 2011), 38.

[63]Origen, *Commentary on the Epistle to the Romans*, 7.19.26. Cited in Levering, *Predestination*, 43.

[64]T. Scheck, *Origen and the History of Justification: The Legacy of Origen's Commentary on Romans* (Notre Dame, IN: University of Notre Dame Press, 2008), 70.

[65]Origen, *On First Principles*, ed. J. Behr (Oxford: Oxford University Press, 2017), 2.10.

In other words, Origen does not discount the type of bifurcation of individuals into righteous and unrighteous, elect and damned, that has come to be regarded as synonymous with the doctrine of election. Some are chosen, others are not. But for Origen, this bifurcation is not on the basis of God's arbitrary pretemporal choice, nor is it absolutized into eternity. Rather, it privileges, on the one hand, the freedom of individuals to choose for or against God and, on the other hand, the victorious power of God's unifying love that ultimately relativizes all human choice.

Nevertheless, this utterly eschatological vision of universal purification is not all that Origen has to say about the concept of election. Just as we miss much of significance in Ignatius if we focus only on structures of episcopal governance, so too we miss a vital element in Origen's view of election and predestination if we ignore how he sees the community of the elect taking shape in this life. And so, in keeping with this chapter's theme, we need to ask how Origen understood the being and limits of the church.

We have seen that Ignatius understood the church to be in some sense preexistent—or at least that the church was elected by God in pretemporal eternity πρὸ τῶν αἰώνων (before the ages) and then takes form in history as a united body in willing obedience to the local bishop. This sequential move from the elected ideal to the elected real is, as we shall see, a key point of difference between the ecclesiologies of Ignatius and Origen.

For Origen, the church of God is "the body of Christ, animated by the Son of God," in which the members are all who believe, having been vivified into that belief by the Word of God, without which they then do nothing.[66] In itself, this is a slightly different emphasis on church membership than what we see in Ignatius. The stress here is on individual belief rather than any particular order of liturgical praxis or episcopal governance. This focus on belief rather than structure accords

---

[66]Or. *CC*, 48.

well with Origen's broader claim that the church is the "autobasileia of Christ in the soul of each individual" and thus an earthly image of the heavenly kingdom.[67]

But these believers who constitute the church also exist beforehand in some way. As Origen puts it in his commentary on the Song of Songs 1:11-12,

> You must not think that it [the church] is called the bride of Christ only from the time of the coming of the Savior in the flesh, but from the beginning of the human race and from the very foundation of the world— indeed, if I may seek the origin of this deep mystery with Paul as my guide, even before the foundation of the world. For this is what he himself says, "As he chose us in Christ before the foundation of the world" [Eph 1:4].[68]

In the same commentary, Origen goes on to speak of the angelic ministration to the saints—those who belong to the church—during the time of the prophets and even as far back as Adam. He famously cites the prostitute Rahab and her house as an iteration of the church that is present before Christ.[69] Boniface Ramsey argues that Rahab functions in this homily merely as a sign and symbol.[70] I am not so sure that Origen's Rahab can be understood only semiotically. If he indeed holds that the church pre-dates the incarnation and has historic actuality back to Adam, then Rahab becomes not simply a symbol of the future church but indeed a very real member of the already existent but hidden church. That Origen even says in this homily that Rahab "knew that there was no salvation for anyone except in the blood of Christ" suggests that Rahab has more than just a proleptic symbolic function. Clearly, Origen holds that a church exists within history which yet remains hidden until the incarnation.

Insofar as he consciously recalls Paul's words in Ephesians, Origen also seems to be insisting that this preexistent church pre-dates not only

[67]Küng, *Church*, 127. Emphasis added.
[68]Origen, *Song of Songs* 2.8.
[69]Origen, *Homily on Joshua* 3.4-3.5.
[70]Ramsey, *Beginning to Read the Fathers*, 109.

the historic ecclesial community that exists from the time of Christ but also time itself, thus extending back into eternity. This is not dissimilar to the concept of a hidden, preexistent church that one finds in The Shepherd of Hermas from the mid-second century. In the Shepherd's second vision, he learns that the old woman, from whom he has received revelation, is the personified and idealized church—old because "she was created first of all," for whose sake the world itself was made.[71]

Both Origen and the Shepherd (of whom Origen was aware and whom he occasionally cites) thus develop Ignatian ecclesiology in one very particular and important way. The pretemporally elected church in Ignatius's letters becomes existent only in the historic actuality of harmonious fellowship around a bishop. Its elected preexistence is thus something of an abstract ideal until the coming of Christ. The Origenist church, however—also pretemporally elected (thus the reference to Ephesians)—is actualized in time prior to the incarnation, in the lives of the saints and prophets, and indeed even exists as such before the creation of the world. While Origen shares with Ignatius the idea of the church's election before time, he envisages the church as having a real (albeit hidden), and not simply ideal, existence right back to the beginning of time, and even before.

In other words, Origen's construal of predestination and election is somewhat more complex than just his universalist eschatological restoration of all things. True, he insists on that ultimate triumph of God's love that finally embraces and purifies even the unrighteous. But his doctrine of election is also tied to his concept of the church, according to which Origen extends the idea of elected sociality beyond the boundaries of any church membership that can be readily accessed through authorized rites of baptism or recognized by virtue of a community's bishop-facing unity. The church is indeed the body of the elect, constituted by those whose inward selves and beliefs have been vivified by the Word of God. But the possibility—and reality—that such vivification

---

[71]The Shepherd of Hermas, book 1, vision 2.4. See also W. Pratscher, ed., *The Apostolic Fathers: An Introduction* (Waco, TX: Baylor University Press, 2010), 222.

has encompassed countless people prior to the church's historic un-veiling radically enlarges the ecclesial limits and makes "the elect" a far more inclusive group than that depicted in the Ignatian epistles.

CYPRIAN OF CARTHAGE

Arguably the most influential ecclesiologist in the early church besides Augustine, St. Cyprian of Carthage (ca. 200–258) provides a valuable counterpoint to the vision of church as presented by Origen, with whom he was largely contemporaneous. Younger than Origen by perhaps twenty years, Cyprian's understanding of the church's being, as well as its polity, was forged during the Decian persecution. Decius's now-infamous edict of 250 CE had ordered that everyone in the empire, with the exception of Jews, be required to sacrifice and burn incense to the Roman gods and to the well-being of the emperor.[72] Moreover, they were to do so in the presence of a Roman magistrate, who would thereby act as witness and distribute a *libellus* (a form of receipt) to each subject as proof of their obedience. The edict was not specifically tar-geted at Christians. Rather, it was part of a broader propaganda cam-paign waged by Decius to shore up his own precarious emperorship, to which he had ascended in somewhat controversial circumstances.[73] It was nonetheless the first time that any imperial edict had forced all Christians throughout the entire empire to choose between their re-ligion and the religion of Rome.[74] As Candida Moss has said, Chris-tians were not simply at risk if they happened to be found out (as, for

---

[72]According to Clarke, the exemption of the Jews was on account of their antiquity and ethnic purity, both of which the Romans understood and respected. The Christians, however, enjoyed neither of these benefits, being religious newcomers and ethnically disparate. See G. W. Clarke, ed., *The Letters of St. Cyprian of Carthage* (Ramsey, NJ: Paulist Press, 1984), 1:24.

[73]Decius was emperor during a period of Roman imperial history that has come to be called "The Crisis of the Third Century," during which—over a fifty-year period—there were no fewer than twenty-six emperors.

[74]Moss notes that the edict was universal and was not directly aimed at Christians in particular. That Christians were caught up in it simply indicates they were members of the empire in which the edict was operative and that—as confessors of a religion at odds with the idea of imperial divinity—they were especially compromised by the edict's requirements. See Moss, *Myth of Persecution*, 150.

example, was the case under Pliny and Trajan). They were required to make a deliberate choice—to obey and apostatize or to resist and be punished.[75] At least on this occasion, the insistence on obedience, and therefore the experience of persecution by those who refused, was not mitigated by geographic variation in the edict's application.

The results of this persecution for the church as a whole were far-reaching—perhaps not so much because of the number of Christians who died or were imprisoned as because of the ensuing structural divisions within the church. While some chose martyrdom and others imprisonment, other Christians decided—discretion being the better part of valor—either to apostatize, flee into exile, or simply ignore the decree.[76] Self-imposed exile was itself a two-edged sword. At least since Tertullian's *On Flight in Times of Persecution* (written sometime around 208 CE), flight was considered self-evident proof of cowardice. Cyprian himself, however, argued that it was, in its own way, a form of martyrdom.[77] Indeed, he had fled from Carthage, taking refuge away from the city centers, from where he believed he could more usefully shepherd those in his care.[78]

Not surprisingly, such a range of responses to the Decian edict created tensions within church communities. Suspicion, animosity, feelings of superiority (on the part of the surviving resisters), and guilt (on the part of the apostates) rent the harmony of the church in Carthage and across the empire. These divisions became especially acute once the persecution was over and Christians sought to resume their previous lives. Most particularly in view was what should be done with those who had apostatized and who now wished to return to the

---

[75]Moss, *Myth of Persecution*, 146. See also the letters between Pliny the Younger and Trajan, ca. 112 CE, http://faculty.georgetown.edu/jod/texts/pliny.html.

[76]These latter were known as *stantes*: people who gambled on the fact that the authorities would not bother checking who had or had not sacrificed.

[77]See A. Brent, *Cyprian and Roman Carthage* (Cambridge: Cambridge University Press, 2010), 10.

[78]He did so by two means: first, by writing letters to Christians back in Carthage, but, second, and controversially, by ordering his presbyters and deacons to remain in the city on his behalf. See, for example, *Epistles*, 5. Moss argues that it is because of this command, as well as his decision to flee in the first place, that Cyprian's name was not finally redeemed until his own martyrdom under Valerian in 258 CE. Moss, *Myth of Persecution*, 147.

church's fold. Consideration of this issue led not so much to a greater articulation of ecclesial discipline but to a more developed theory of the church as such.

As bishop of Carthage, the now-returned Cyprian was compelled to respond to these post-persecution tensions within his see. Broadly speaking, Cyprian had to adjudicate three competing views. The hardline Novationists (named after the Carthaginian priest Novatus and the Roman theologian Novatian) argued that grave sinners—including in this case apostates who had obeyed the imperial decree—could not be reconciled to the church during their lifetime.[79] To readmit such people would be to contaminate both the church and its sacramental ministries. Such a view of the church permitted no breach of purity and (to the Novationists' detractors) ignored the fact that in the ark "there were shut up not only clean animals, but also unclean."[80] The so-called confessors—those who had themselves suffered persecution and survived, despite not giving in to the imperial dictates—insisted, on the contrary, that forgiveness and readmission to the church were possible for the lapsed but that the authority to grant absolution should be devolved to themselves alone who had been proven worthy. Indeed, even during Cyprian's absence, some of the lapsed had already sought absolution and readmission to eucharistic fellowship from the confessors, who were themselves generally laypeople with no authority from the bishop to grant any such thing.[81] The third option—and the one ultimately accepted by Cyprian himself—was that the authority to grant forgiveness and readmission to apostates should lie in the hands of bishops, who should judge each case on its merits and not on prior principle.

That Cyprian took the third view was no surprise; it was in harmony with his underlying ecclesiology that was, in turn, informed by his

---

[79]This was also largely the view that had previously been taken by Tertullian. See his *On Repentance*, 7.

[80]*Treatise Against the Heretic Novatian*, 2.

[81]This, in fact, was one of the issues: whether authority within the church was properly invested apostolically (to the bishops) or charismatically (to those whose lives, rather than their positions, commanded respect).

views on the ordering of ministries within the church. In Cyprian's view, and strongly reminiscent of the Ignatian tradition, the bishop was key to the church's unity. The continuity of bishops in their sees, in succession to the apostolic founders of those sees, was the guarantee that the churches over which those bishops presided were parts of the authentic church of Christ. This was not, he stressed, due to any personal holiness of the bishops themselves but rather because the word of Christ that established the church at the same time established the office of bishop within the church, as a *vicaria ordinatio* to act with the fully delegated authority of Christ. As William Weinrich puts it, the bishop "as the one placed into [that] office . . . by Christ's ordinance for and on behalf of the people of the church is the one who alone can lawfully and in power administer the things of Christ."[82] Cyprian himself says in a letter to some of the lapsed Christians, "Through the changes of times and successions, the ordering of bishops and the plan of the Church flow onwards; so that the Church is founded upon the bishops, and every act of the Church is controlled by these same rulers."[83] In consequence, membership in the church was defined by Cyprian as being in communion with those bishops who were in the line of apostolic succession. To not be in communion with the bishop was to be outside the church:

> And this unity we ought firmly to hold and assert, especially those of us that are bishops who preside in the Church, that we may also prove the episcopate itself to be one and undivided. Let no one deceive the brotherhood by a falsehood: let no one corrupt the truth of the faith by perfidious prevarication. The episcopate is one, each part of which is held by each one for the whole.[84]

By logical necessity, Cyprian therefore also had to insist that the efficacy of the sacraments, including the granting of absolution, was bound up

---

[82]W. Weinrich, "Cyprian, Donatism, Augustine, and Augustana VIII: Remarks on the Church and the Validity of Sacraments," *Concordia Theological Quarterly* 55, no. 4 (October 1991): 274.
[83]Cyprian, *Epistles*, 26.
[84]Cyprian, *On the Unity of the Church*, 5.

with the validity of the bishop by whom or in whose name they were administered. Only bishops in true succession could validly administer baptism and the Eucharist—or ordain others to validly administer them—and restore the apostate to communion. In other words, the nature of forgiveness, pardon, and consequent readmission to the church was bound up with the essence of the church's own nature, which was, in turn, dependent on the historic episcopate.[85] Outside of this operative sphere of the Holy Spirit, there could be no effective sacramental ministry and thus no salvation.

What, then, do we take from Cyprian's ecclesiology, particularly with regard to the matter of election, about which, it must be said, Cyprian has very little directly to say? Certainly, the centrality of the bishop was now even more pronounced than it had been in Ignatius's day, and it was more systematically set out. More to the point, episcopal succession was more than simply a sign and pledge of ecclesial unity; it was the very basis of the church's existence and continuing ministry. Cyprianic episcopacy provided for the first time a set of visible criteria by which membership of both the church and the community of the elect could be measured. Anyone who broke communion with the bishop by definition put themselves outside the sphere of the Spirit's activity and thus outside salvation. The boundaries of the church and of the elect were tied narrowly, and inextricably, to the historic episcopate.

Of course, membership within the church was no absolute guarantee of one's election. The church is peopled by those who call themselves Christians but who are, in fact, angels of the enemy.[86] Judas, Cyprian reminds us, was also one of the apostles. Confession, we are told, "does not make a man free from the snares of the devil." It is only "the beginning of glory, not the fullness of the crown."[87] That is to say, Cyprian rejected the Novationist view that the church must be peopled only by

---

[85]Cyprian notes that penance and restoration are to be solemnized by the laying on of the bishop's hands; see *Epistles*, 9-10.
[86]Cyprian, *On the Unity of the Church*, 3.
[87]Cyprian, *On the Unity of the Church*, 21.

the demonstrably pure. It is always possible, insists Cyprian, for people—even the *confessores*—to apostatize away from the church. Indeed, the Holy Spirit himself says that heresies and schisms "are needful" in order to show who has been approved.[88] Nevertheless, baptismal membership of a eucharistic community in which the sacraments were administered episcopally was the minimal requirement. There was no way that election could accrue to anyone outside of it. To separate oneself from the church, insisted Cyprian, would be to cut oneself off from "the womb from which we were born," the "milk by which we are nourished . . . , and her spirit [by which] we are animated."[89] As he would famously say, "He can no longer have God for his Father, who has not the Church for his Mother."[90]

All of this suggests a high degree of individual responsibility. One could choose to abandon the bishop and the church, and thus God himself, or one could persevere through temptations and decide to stay within the holy communion of the mothering church. There is certainly a sense in Cyprian's letters that the *confessores*, the lapsed, the schismatic, and all other corrupted characters had freely chosen their paths. In particular, the lapsed, who now wished to be readmitted to communion, were demonstrating singular freedom of choice. Yet one small comment from Cyprian suggests he is aware that something slightly more complex is going on. "Did he not," says Cyprian, "ordain both for those who deny Him eternal punishments, and for those that confess Him eternal rewards?"[91]

AUGUSTINE'S CHURCH

We could not conclude this chapter without at least briefly considering the contribution to our theme made by St. Augustine. Augustine's doctrine of predestination, as with others considered throughout this chapter, cannot be separated from his ecclesiology. Therefore, to properly comprehend how he understands election, we again need to

---

[88]Cyprian, *On the Unity of the Church*, 10.
[89]Cyprian, *On the Unity of the Church*, 5.
[90]Cyprian, *On the Unity of the Church*, 6.
[91]Cyprian, *On the Lapsed*, 7.

consider what he has to say about the being and limits of the church.

This remarkable and often maligned Father, who was in so many ways the first real "doctor of the church," was the natural heir to Cyprian, whose writings he often refers to in support of his own views. For the bishop of Hippo, as it had been for his North African predecessor, unity within the church was paramount. But there are two crucial differences of context to bear in mind when comparing the ecclesiologies of these two Fathers and indeed what they understood *unity* to imply. First, Augustine had the considerable advantage that between him and Cyprian lay the Council of Nicaea (325). Markers of ecclesial belonging were thus at least doctrinally more certain than they had been in Cyprian's day. To return to Howard Kee's language, many of the most important "boundary questions" had been asked and, for the most part, answered. Bishops, of course, retained a vital role in teaching and sacramental ministry. But they were no longer the sole guarantors of the deposit of faith and the only approved arbiters of orthodoxy; an ecumenical creed could now also play that role. Second, whereas Cyprian's ecclesiology emerged from the context of persecution, Augustine's was informed by his doctrine of original sin. Against the Donatists—who, like the rigorist Novationists nearly two centuries earlier, wished to insist on the necessity of visible ecclesial purity[92]—Augustine argued that original sin makes it impossible for the church to be a congregation of sinless saints, no matter how truly it must also be affirmed as the *sanctorum communio*. On the contrary, the church cannot be anything other than a mixed community, consisting of both good and bad—both corporately and in the lives of its individual members.

Augustine found his scriptural justification for this in Jesus' own teaching in the parable of the wheat and weeds (Mt 13:24-30). The holiness of the church's members is a process and not a status, with perfection made perfect only at the final judgment of all things. Thus, he writes in his *Retractions*,

---

[92]For the Donatists, the bishops were the safeguards of purity more than unity, hence their stress on the personal holiness of all in episcopal orders.

> Whenever . . . I have described the Church as without spot or wrinkle, I
> have not meant to imply that it was already so, but that it should prepare
> itself to be so, at the time when it too will appear in glory. For the present
> time, because of the inexperience and weaknesses of its members it must
> pray every day anew: "Forgive us our trespasses."[93]

This "mixed economy" within the church is precisely analogous to the
relationship between the heavenly city and its earthly counterpart. As
Augustine says in his monumental *De civitate Dei*, the "city of God" and
the "city of man" exist necessarily alongside and even within each other.
Church and state are good and bad simultaneously, with both containing within themselves members of the other sphere.[94]

That this is necessarily the case leads Augustine to refute those who
would censure the church for the presence of the wicked within it.
Some of such people will, he says, repent and thus regain what they had
previously lost by sin. Others, though, will persist in their sins yet also
persist within the church—they are the "tares" who will remain within
God's field until the harvest.[95]

However, Augustine did not stop at simply acknowledging the church's
mixed composition. Noting that there must, by necessity, be an overlap
between the visible institutional church and the invisible authentic
church, with the authentic church of the elect being known, in the end,
only by God, he nonetheless conceded that it is important to distinguish
between notional members of the church and the community of the
righteous. For the Donatists, who wished to enshrine the church as the
spotless virgin bride of Christ, the idea of the church's mixed economy
was anathema, and they invalidated any form of sacramental fellowship
with those whom they declared to be tainted by sin (the *traditores*—those

---

[93] Augustine, *Retractions*, 2.18.
[94] See P. Weithman, "Augustine's Political Philosophy," in *The Cambridge Companion to Augustine*,
ed. D. V. Meconi and E. Stumpe, 2nd ed. (Cambridge: Cambridge University Press, 2014), 236-37.
See also G. W. H. Lampe, "Christian Theology in the Patristic Period," in *A History of Christian
Doctrine*, ed. H. Cunliffe-Jones (Philadelphia: Fortress Press, 1980), 176. Note that, while it is useful shorthand, Augustine does not use this sort of two-kingdom language. Indeed, he insists that
the church is not to be identified with the city of God, nor the state or empire with the earthly city.
[95] Augustine, *Of the Morals of the Catholic Church*, 34.76.

who had "handed over" the Scriptures, and therefore the faith, during the Diocletian persecution of 303–305 CE—being chief among them) and from whom they felt obliged to separate.

Augustine's view raised a more basic question—namely, What is the distinguishing mark of the true church? Whereas for Cyprian the church's existence was guaranteed by the succession of the bishops in their apostolic sees, for Augustine the church is guaranteed by the manifestation of love. The reality of love within the church is in turn proof of the presence of the unifying Holy Spirit, who unites the members of the church both to their head, Christ, as well as to each other. The church, as the visible iteration of the city of God, consists of those who love God and each other rightly. Its members are unified by their common love of God, "a love that rejoices in a common and immutable good: a love, that is, that makes one heart out of many."[96]

As we have noted before with Ignatius, schism and disunity are nothing less than a demonstration of love's absence. They are the inbreaking of the power of the earthly city into the realm of the heavenly. Hence, insofar as this is the negation of the true mark of the church, those who would seek to divide the church (and in Augustine's day that was principally the Donatists) were guilty of denying and destroying the single most decisive aspect that marks the church against the rest of humankind.

Our theme, however, requires us now to ask how this ecclesiology squares with Augustine's doctrine of election. Three points in particular should be made. First, in his mature construct of predestination, Augustine predicates all that he says on the foundational fact that there must be those whom God has called and those whom he has not. Jacob and Esau provide the perfect scriptural paradigm of this truth, just as Cain and Abel supply the genetic paradigm for his two cities: "Though they were not yet born and had done nothing either good or bad, in order that God's purposes of election might continue, not because of

---

[96]Augustine, *City of God*, 15.1.

works but because of his call, she [Rebecca] was told, 'The elder will serve the younger.'"[97]

That is to say, Augustine describes, as two equally real alternatives, an election and a condemnation, both of which lead to (but are not the consequence of) correlative works of merit and impiety, and both of which God decreed before the foundation of creation.[98] This separation of people into two groups is not, however, actualized only eschatologically. On the contrary, insofar as Augustine's church is not entirely identical with the celestial city and is, as we have seen, itself a mixture of good and bad simultaneously, it is also thereby an earthly historical reflection of this predestined duality. That is, the visible church is not by itself or without qualification the community of the elect, but it contains that community within itself as well as those who "may have been called but are not chosen."[99]

Second, this twofold possibility of election and condemnation is not on account of any merit or lack that God foreknew; it is only because of God's grace.[100] As he says, the elect are predestined by God not because they are or will be holy but in order that they may be.[101] Citizens of the city of God are "predestined by grace, elected by grace, by grace a stranger below, and by grace a citizen above."[102] Pride in one's merit as the cause of election thus not only betrays the gospel but also leads to the schismatic destruction of love that constitutes the church.[103] Of course, that some are chosen and others not, and this out of grace instead of merit, begs the question, Why some and not others? To this, Augustine replies simply that, insofar as condemnation is deserved by all, then even if no one was saved we would have no grievance with

---

[97] Augustine, *On the Predestination of the Saints*, 7.

[98] Augustine, *On the Predestination of the Saints*, 7, 35.

[99] Augustine, *On the Predestination of the Saints*, 32-33.

[100] Augustine, *On the Predestination of the Saints*, 7, 11, 16.

[101] Augustine, *On the Predestination of the Saints*, 35.

[102] Augustine, *City of God*, 15.1.

[103] Significantly, in stressing the Cyprianic summary of the gospel—that "we must boast in nothing, since nothing is our own"—Augustine points to the Corinthian divisions (1 Cor 1:12) as illustrating precisely this type of prideful glorying in one's own merit that at once betrays the sufficiency of God's grace and destroys the unity of the church.

God: "But why [faith] is not given to all ought not disturb the believer, who believes that from one all have gone into a condemnation . . . so that even if none were delivered therefrom, there would be no just cause for finding fault with God."[104] That some are saved at all, therefore, is a mercy; that God has made his own choice about who and why is beyond our finding out (Rom 11:33).

Third, however, Augustine's doctrine of election also reflects the opposite pole of his twin-cities typology in that just as the visible church contains those who are not elect, the earthly city contains some who are. That is to say, Augustine holds open the possibility, however remote, that there are members of the elect community outside the ecclesial boundaries. "It is not incongruous," he says, "to believe that even in other nations there may have been men to whom this mystery [of Christ] was revealed, and who were compelled to proclaim it, whether they were partakers of the same grace or had no experience of it, but were taught by bad angels, who, as we know, even confessed the present Christ."[105]

Job "the Idumean" is the classic example of this, but Augustine takes him to be representative of countless others "of other nations" who belong, not by earthly citizenship but by God's grace, to the celestial city of the elect. In this most radical way, Augustine moderates and modifies Cyprian's insistence that salvation is impossible outside the church.

It should be clear, then, that Augustine's doctrine of election cannot be considered apart from his ecclesiology. Within it, he posits an eschatological duality of the elect and the damned, which is proleptically expressed in the mixed economy of the visible church. Predicated on the unsearchable grace of God alone, the community of the elect is indeed within (but in contrast to Cyprian's view also potentially without) the historic church. And, in stark contrast to the Donatists and their Novationist predecessors, the elect, in Augustine's view, are marked by a unifying and embracing love that, paradoxically, excludes

---

[104]Augustine, *On the Predestination of the Saints*, 16.
[105]Augustine, *City of God*, 18.47.

the possibility of being defined by a proud purity that would separate from those deemed impious.

CONCLUSION

From the very earliest days of the church's self-conscious existence in the mid-first century, there had been an evident sense of what constituted the gathered community of the faithful in any given place. This took form, early and notably, through the presence of a bishop around whom the liturgical practices could take place. However, there had been little systematic consideration given to the way in which the church as such was constituted in its membership by the electing will of God. Exclusion from the community could, for a time, be occasioned by moral misdemeanors, the refusal of obedience to the bishop, and the denial of obvious articles of faith, including the triunity of God, Jesus' bodily resurrection, and the necessity of baptism. But this did little more than set out some minimal criteria for membership. What had remained under-developed was any sense of how membership of the earthly community of the church was established by a prior decision of God's freedom in pretemporal eternity.

As we have seen, Ignatius affirmed the eternally elect status of the church but limited its historic actualization to the time after the incarnation. Origen—writing only a very few years before the Decian edict and thus just before Cyprian had to determine his own views—similarly knew the church to have been eternally elected by God, and he recognized it to have taken form at least from the time of Adam. But Origen's emphasis on individual belief as the key marker of ecclesial membership did not provide sufficiently robust indicators that could help identify those who were "truly" Christian. For his part, Cyprian prioritized the role of bishop as the pivotal point around which unity was secured and away from whom no salvation could be had. On the one hand, his recognition that the church was an ark in which good and bad existed expanded the ecclesial membership beyond the ethically pure. On the other hand, his insistence that salvation could be found only in communion with the bishop restricted membership in a way that problematized any possibility of election prior to the church's historic appearance. With Augustine, however, we are presented with a glorious yet realistic portrayal of the church's being. Like Cyprian before him, Augustine's elected community was, in this age, a mixed economy of good and bad together. Indeed, those who, like the Donatists, wished to define the church by visible holiness and thus schismatically separate from all those they deemed to be unworthy proved by that very act that they instead were the ones who lacked the most distinctive marker of elected sociality: love.

For Augustine, election was grounded in God's eternal decision to bestow grace on some and not on others, the reasons for which lie ultimately beyond our understanding. Moreover, Augustine's two-city typology allowed for (indeed, mandated) the possibility that the community of the elect was not only smaller but also in some ways larger than the limits of the visible church. This was a key development in that, whereas the early Fathers tied election to the being of the church (conceiving that also as faithful Israel), Augustine's doctrine incorporated the possibility of asking, as Dietrich Ritschl has done, whether in fact the ecumene might be broader than either church or Israel. As we shall see in the next chapter, however, Augustine's discovery was not taken up in the Middle Ages. On the contrary, whether it was the work of emperors or of popes, the *corpus Christianum* soon came to be identified as being synonymous with the *civitas Dei*.[106]

---

[106]Küng, *Church*, 128.

3

THE MIDDLE AGES

AS WE SAW IN THE LAST CHAPTER, early Christian articulations of the doctrine of election evolved gradually and almost always in close proximity to changing understandings of the being and limits of the church. As the second-century pagan Celsus insightfully recognized, there was a stark differentiation between those who were part of the "Great Church" and those who belonged to various sectarian groups within it. To the extent that the latter were forming factions and thus betraying Christianity's one great attribute, *agape*, they were proving themselves to be apart from the "Great Church."[1] Insofar as ecclesiology was developed to clarify and sharpen the sense of who could rightly lay claim to being part of this new community, the constitution of the ἐκλεκτοί—the "called-out ones," the "elect"—was quite naturally considered within this broader ecclesiological frame and not as a doctrine in its own right. This made eminent sense in a sociopolitical context in which, for the most part, being a Christian was a dangerous undertaking and when the church was qualitatively distinct from the state. Even in Augustine's time, when the empire had been Christianized for a century, election and ecclesiology were written hand in glove, with an overlap but also a distinction being seen between the earthly and the heavenly cities and their respective citizens.

---

[1]Or. *CC*, 3.10, 12.

But this distinction did not last for long. As Hans Küng reminds us, the medieval period saw a hardening of the ecclesio-imperial context. What for Augustine had been a significant though only partial overlap between church and state—that is, that both realms were distinct, neither wholly good nor wholly bad, but each containing elements of the other—was, by the Middle Ages, an almost complete correspondence.[2] As historian R. W. Southern noted, the "history of the Western Church in the Middle Ages is the history of the most elaborate and thoroughly integrated system of religious thought and practice the world has ever known," with the fundamental feature of this time being "the identification of the church with the whole of organized society."[3]

This correspondence did not, of course, forestall conflicts between church and state. Most notably, we might well point to the great struggles for power between the popes and emperors in the eleventh and twelfth centuries, symbolized by but not limited to the so-called Investiture Controversy, which were eventually resolved (for a time at least) more in favor of the church than the state. Consequently, as the emperor's claims to preeminent spiritual legitimacy waned, the "superiority of the sacerdotal element in society" increased.[4] Matthew Levering has argued that it is in this very period, principally with Catherine of Siena, that we see at last the attainment of "the right balance" between the equal weighting of God's unlimited love and humanity's unfettered freedom.[5] "I can and want to and will help whoever wants my help," says God to Catherine.[6] Ironically, however, balance was precisely the element lacking in the religiopolitical context of the day. For all intents and purposes, the *corpus Christianum* was the *civitas Dei*.

---

[2]Küng, *Church*, 128.

[3]R. W. Southern, *Western Society and the Church in the Middle Ages*, Penguin History of the Church 2 (1970; repr., London: Penguin Books, 1990), 2:15-16.

[4]Southern, *Western Society and the Church*, 36-37.

[5]M. Levering, *Predestination: Biblical and Theological Paths* (Oxford: Oxford University Press, 2011), 68.

[6]Catherine of Siena, *The Dialogue*, trans. S. Noffke (New York: Paulist Press, 1980), 78.

In other words, if we are able to understand the development of the doctrine of election until Augustine only in the context of emerging ecclesiologies, so too we must take seriously this new imperial context if we are properly to appreciate the ways in which the doctrine took shape during the Middle Ages. As we shall see, the development of the doctrine of election in this time evolved not so much alongside ecclesiology but rather in tandem with political theology. Elected sociality, as we have come to call it, was defined by membership within the rules of empire. In the opinion of the fourteenth-century jurist Bartolus of Sassoferrato, the distinction between being a good Christian and a citizen of the empire was essentially nonexistent.[7] With the body of Christ thus politicized, citizenship of the empire was determined by adherence to doctrinal orthodoxy, with membership of the elect correspondingly determined and refused by imperial belonging.[8] Jews and Muslims, heretics and pagans were the first, and the easiest, to exclude from the empire. By inevitable consequence, they were also the first and easiest to exclude from the company of the elect and to relegate to the *civitas diaboli*.

In the case of Jews and Muslims, while they were, to greater or lesser extents, granted restricted toleration, both groups were also subject to periodic persecution and almost constant vilification. This is not the place to outline even briefly the colorful and complex histories of Jewish and Muslim engagement within European society. All that can be said here is that, even during times of relative toleration, because

---

[7]C. Fasolt, *The Limits of History* (Chicago: University of Chicago Press, 2013), 172. Note, however, that Bartolus argued this in the context of his broader claim for the emperor's supremacy, not the pope's. It is thus not surprising to note that in Britain, even after the Romans had departed, the British people continued to think of themselves as both Roman *and* Christian, with "both qualities . . . referable to their former status as citizens of the western empire." See T. G. Watkin, *The Legal History of Wales* (Cardiff: University of Wales Press, 2007), 29.

[8]We should note, of course, that the concept of citizenship during the time of the Holy Roman Empire was very different from its expression after the stronger emergence of nation states in the early modern era. In that sense, I am not using the term here to denote specific rights and responsibilities, or even economic activity. Rather, I am using it to denote a particular sense of communal belonging, which accrued to an individual on the basis of the ease with which they were able to identify with the ecclesiopolitical hegemony.

Jews and Muslims were by definition beyond orthodoxy, they could never be members of the *corpus Christianum*, and as such they could never really be full citizens of the empire. John Esposito has said that,

> The European Christian response [to the Islamic incursions into the Christian empire] was, with few exceptions, hostile, intolerant, and belligerent. Muhammad was vilified as an imposter and identified as the anti-Christ. Islam was dismissed as a religion of the sword led by an infidel driven by a lust for power and women.[9]

The reality, of course, was somewhat more nuanced. While the Middle Ages witnessed the Crusades and the *Reconquista* of the Iberian Peninsula from Islamic control, it also saw the flourishing of Islamic culture through the burgeoning intellectual life of medieval universities.[10] Europeans in the Middle Ages encountered Muslims on the battlefield *and* in the academy. Yet it was never an equal meeting; Muslims, and the religion they espoused, were in the last resort seen as dangerous, threatening, and fundamentally opposed to the community of Christian society. Not surprisingly, then, in the early years of the fourteenth century, Dante's *Divine Comedy* depicted Muhammad in the grisliest of fashions, as inhabiting the eighth circle of hell along with all other schismatics:

> Even a wine-cask with the bottom knocked out,
> Does not gape in the way that I saw one,
> Ripped open from the chin to where he farts:
>
> Between his legs, his guts were hanging out;
> His lights appeared, and that disgusting tube
> Which makes shit [*merda*] of what goes down our throats.
>
> While I was all intent on looking at him,
> He looked at me, and his hand opened his chest;
> He said: "Now see how I undo myself!"

---

[9]J. Esposito, *Islam: The Straight Path* (Oxford; Oxford University Press, 1988), 37-67.
[10]See, for example, B. F. Breiner and C. W. Troll, "Christianity and Islam," in *The Oxford Encyclopedia of the Islamic World*, Oxford Islamic Studies Online, www.oxfordislamicstudies.com/article/opr/t236/e0149.

See how mangled Mahomet is:
In front of me, Ali goes weeping,
His face split open from his chin to his forelock.

And all the others you see in this place
Were instigators of scandal and of schism,
When they were alive, and so they are split here.[11]

This portrayal—Muhammad as apostate schismatic—illustrates precisely why Muslims could not in the end be tolerated as full members of the Western body politic; insofar as they represented heterodox religion, the Christian state itself had to exclude them from any sense of ultimate belonging.

As for Europe's Jews, the church did not quite know what to do with them. Jews had been valuable, and often prosperous, members of European society for centuries, providing all manner of services to bishops and the nobility, often as physicians and frequently as artisans. At the same time, they were also feared as strange and corrupting influences within the populace. They were the "eternal strangers"—like Muslims, never really able to belong.

Official church pronouncements reflected this ambiguity, wavering between condemnations of anti-Jewish massacres, on the one hand (such as the papal bulls by Innocent IV in 1247 and Gregory X in 1272), and expulsion orders from cities and towns (such as from Vienna in 1253), on the other. But ecclesial ambiguity was not reflective simply of the church's uncertainty about what to do with the Jews—there was in fact an eschatological necessity to this bifurcated response to them. Church teaching insisted on two things at once: that Jews were "potential Christians," possible members of the remnant of whom the apostle Paul had spoken (Rom 9–11) and who were thus ripe for conversion, but also, in the ossification of their religion and the depredation

---

[11]Dante, *The Divine Comedy*, trans. C. H. Sisson (London: Pan Books, 1981). Inferno, canto xxviii.22-34. Note that, in the tradition of Peter the Venerable (ca. 1092–1156), Dante believed Muhammad to be an apostate from Christianity, with Islam itself being understood as a Christological heresy.

of their lives, witnesses to the fact that God had cast them off, choosing Christians in their place. That is, the church's *adversos Judaeos* teaching required the Jews to be visibly punished for their infidelity, yet also protected as both a testifying artefact and as prospective converts.[12] As Bernard of Clairvaux said, "The Jews are for us the living words of Scripture, for they remind us always of what our Lord suffered. They are dispersed all over the world so that by expiating their crime they may be everywhere the living witnesses of our redemption."[13] That is to say, they were to be protected because their punishment and dispersal served a vital role in God's salvific plan as well as in demonstrating the loss of their election.[14]

The general population, however, was far less vacillating in its attitude. Jews were routinely depicted in art, literature, and popular legends as sorcerers, cannibals, profaners of the eucharistic Host, and even as the corporeal manifestation of Satan himself. Dan Cohn-Sherbok paints a dismal and horrifying picture:

> In the Middle Ages Jews were viewed as the personification of evil. Dabbling in the occult, they were associated with devils and demons. At times, they were depicted as the Devil himself; alternatively, they were seen as intermediaries between the devil and innocent human beings. Given such diabolical attributes, it is not surprising that the Jewish people were relegated to a sub-species of humanity. . . . As the vermin of the earth, they were a contagion in the body of Europe.[15]

Cohn-Sherbok has, in the wake of the Holocaust, read Nazi imagery back into the medieval experience of European Jewry; their being and nature were not understood in terms as simple as he suggests, and certainly the Jewish "threat" was not construed in such pathological

---

[12]J. Y. B. Hood, *Aquinas and the Jews* (Philadelphia: University of Pennsylvania Press, 1995), 28.

[13]Bernard of Clairvaux, "Letter to the People of England," in *Church, State and Jew in the Middle Ages*, ed. R. Chazan (New York: Behrman House, 1980), 103.

[14]S. C. Boguslawski, *Thomas Aquinas on the Jews: Insights into His Commentary on Romans 9–11* (Mahwah, NJ: Paulist Press, 2008), 30-31.

[15]D. Cohn-Sherbok, *The Crucified Jew: Twenty Centuries of Christian Anti-Semitism* (London: Fount, 1993), 55.

ways. Nevertheless, Jews shared with Muslims the common fate of being defined as enemies of both state and church. Exclusion from the one necessarily entailed exclusion from the other.

Of course, other religious and ethnic groups within medieval society fell outside the boundaries of religiopolitical acceptability. The Romani, who migrated into eastern Europe between the eighth and tenth centuries, were at best shunned and at worst put to death; both their German name, *Zigeuner* (roughly, from a Greek word meaning "untouchable"), and their designation in 1322 by the Irish Franciscan Symon Semeonis as "the descendants of Cain," marked them out as irrecoverably alien. The Cathars, too, against whom the Albigensian Crusade was directed in 1209, provide a harrowing example of violent exclusion. During the massacre at Béziers, when the crusading army asked how they should distinguish between the Catholics to be spared and the Cathars who were to be killed, the papal legate who had control of the crusaders is famously reported to have replied, "Kill them all. The Lord knows those who are his."[16] The indiscriminate slaughter at Béziers shows not only how ruthlessly the Augustinian "mixed economy" model of church could be enacted but also how those accused of heresy were understood to have forfeited their rights to both life and election. The Cathars were self-evidently those whom the Lord knew *not* to be his.

Other examples from the Middle Ages abound. The Romani and Cathars, though, along with the instances of Muslim and Jewish exclusion, show how important it is to read the medieval evolution of the doctrine of election through this prism of the *corpus Christianum*, the Christianized body politic. In this context, to be unacceptably alien connoted both a political and a divine judgment, on one's present life and eternal destiny. Only with this in mind can we turn now to a more detailed exploration of two of the most significant medieval contributors to our theme.

---

[16]"*Caedite eos. Novit enim Dominus qui sunt eius.*"

THOMAS AQUINAS

We begin our consideration by looking at the views of the "angelic Doctor," St. Thomas Aquinas (1225–1274). The thirteenth century into which Thomas was born was the high-water mark of the ecclesiastical supremacy to which we have just referred, marked most noticeably by the excommunication of Frederick II and Innocent IV's crusade against the imperial Hohenstaufen dynasty. Thomas was not entirely quarantined from these conflicts. In 1239 fighting between Frederick II and Gregory IX spilled over into the Benedictine abbey in Monte Cassino— of which Thomas's uncle was abbot and in which Thomas had begun his education—forcing his family to transfer him to the newly established *studium generale* (university) in Naples.[17] It was here that Thomas most likely first encountered the works of Islamic scholars such as Averroës and those of Aristotle, which were to become so formative for his own views.

Thomas himself represented the high point of scholastic theology. Of course, as is widely recognized, Thomas's influence within his own lifetime was not nearly as great as it was in the centuries after his death. Just three years after he died, the bishop of Paris, Étienne Tempier, and the archbishop of Canterbury, Robert Kilwardby, both raised questions about his orthodoxy. That particular issue was settled, in Thomas's favor, only in 1324 and only after much heated discussion.[18] Nevertheless, and notwithstanding the raised eyebrows his work produced

---

[17]See B. Davies, *Thomas Aquinas's Summa Theologiae: A Guide and Commentary* (Oxford: Oxford University Press, 2014), 3.

[18]P. van Geest, H. Goris, and C. Leget, eds., introduction to *Aquinas as Authority: A Collection of Essays; A Collection of Studies Presented at the Second Conference of the Thomas Instituut te Utrecht, December 14–16, 2000* (Leuven: Peeters, 2002), vii. It has been suggested that Thomas's free use of the "pagan" Aristotle was largely responsible for the controversies that surrounded him. However, the fact that the hitherto-dominant Augustinian tradition was predicated on a neo-Platonism that was surely just as pagan in origin renders this a somewhat spurious argument against him. What is more likely is that it was not so much Thomas's Aristotelianism per se that was problematic for his detractors but the fact that his synthetic approach was seen to undermine the emphasis on God's free sovereignty that was championed by neo-Platonic Augustinianism. See J. T. Slotemaker and U. Zahnd, "Thomas and Scholasticism to 1870," in *The Oxford Handbook of Catholic Theology*, ed. L. Ayres and M-A. Volpe (Oxford: Oxford University Press, 2015).

among some of his contemporaries, Thomas ranks indisputably as the foremost theologian of the age, in a time when the church was the foremost power in European life. Given the church's dominant place in medieval society, and Thomas's preeminent place within the church, we therefore ought to ask how his views aligned with broader socioreligious attitudes. More particularly, if Küng and Southern are right, that in Thomas's day the *corpus Christianum* was directly identifiable with the *civitas Dei*—the Christianized body politic and temporal manifestation of the elect community—in what ways, if at all, did Thomas's doctrine of election either inform or mirror that equation?

Thomas's great pedagogical distinction was in his use of Aristotelian philosophy in his conception of and methodological approach to theology. This sounded an entirely new philosophical voice to the neo-Platonic Augustinianism that had dominated Western theology for a millennium. To be sure, Thomas was not the only one, nor even the first, to give voice to Aristotle—Odo Rigaud (d. 1275) attempted to construct a synthesis of Aristotle's logic and scientific theology, while St. Bonaventure (d. 1274) had also adjusted his theological method along Aristotelian lines. Nevertheless, it was Aquinas who gave fullest expression to a systematic articulation of Christian doctrine using Aristotle as his guide.[19] The great irony, then, is that Thomas sided with Augustine in his doctrine of election, even while employing an utterly different philosophical approach to theological construction.

This becomes evident when we consider Thomas's discussion of predestination and election in his last and probably greatest work, the *Summa Theologiae*.[20] Located within his doctrine of God and immediately after the section on providence, with which it is inextricably connected, Thomas's exploration of predestination inquires into eight specific questions: (1) whether predestination can be attributed to God

[19]S. F. Brown, "Medieval Theology," in *The Blackwell Companion to Modern Theology*, ed. Gareth Jones (Oxford: Blackwell, 2004), 137-40.
[20]Note that *predestination* is Thomas's primary term here. Election is the logical precondition of predestination, such that the predestined are objects of God's electing will. *Summa*, Ia, q.23, a.4.

at all, (2) what predestination in fact is, (3) whether reprobation also belongs to God, (4) whether predestination and election are identical, (5) what role human works or merits play in the determination for election or reprobation, (6) whether predestination is infallibly assured, (7) whether the number of the predestined is fixed, and (8) whether saintly intercession can help. In answering these questions, Thomas takes his lead from both Augustine and Aristotle.

The Augustinian influence is immediately apparent in Thomas's first answer, in which he insists on God's free sovereignty. God's providence, to which all created things are subject, directs them to their two ends: the first is proportionate to nature and is therefore attainable by the creature's own efforts, and the second, eternal life, is disproportionate to nature and made possible by God alone, having its only preexistent cause in God's will.[21] Similarly, the action of predestination is an action of its Subject and not of the one who is predestined—thus it affects but does not "place anything in" the one who is the object of the divine action, such that that thing could be viewed as a causative merit.[22]

Later in the *Summa*, Thomas also insists on the necessary Christological aspect of our predestination. Having argued for the predestination of Jesus Christ to be the Son of God, he proceeds to show that two things follow in consequence: first, that it was by one and the same eternal act that God predestined both Jesus and all others who are predestined in him, and second, that Jesus' predestination is the first act of predestination, of which ours is a (logically but not temporally) subsequent copy.[23] That is to say, predestination to eternal life is decreed in eternity by God for some, in the same act by which Jesus Christ is predestined to be the cause and accomplishment *ex tempore* of our salvation.

---

[21] Aquinas, *Summa*, Ia, q.23, a.1. By this, Thomas also excludes implicitly what he later excludes explicitly (contra Origen and the Pelagians)—namely, that God's foreknowledge of human merit is the cause of anyone's predestination. "The use of grace foreknown by God is not the cause of conferring grace." *Summa*, Ia, q.23, a.5.

[22] Aquinas, *Summa*, Ia, q.23, a.2.

[23] Aquinas, *Summa*, IIIa, q.24, a.3-4. Note that it is Christ in his human nature who is predestined to be united to the Word of God.

At the same time, there appears to be more than a hint of divine caprice in Thomas's depiction of God's freedom. Providence, he says, allows for the possibility of certain defects (*aliquem defectum*) in the things that are subject to it. Thus, insofar as some people are ordained to eternal life through God's providential care, that same providence also allows others to fall away from that end and thus into reprobation.[24] Yet to locate this in God's capriciousness would be a grave error. On the contrary, it is God's radical transcendence and distinction from his creatures—his "simplicity"[25]—that compels Thomas to say that God's providential love entails different endings toward which people are directed.[26] For Thomas, the perfection of God's love is that he does not wish every type of good to every person (*non tamen quodcumque bonum vult omnibus*), and so, within the dynamics of his love, he chooses not to wish to some the good of eternal life.[27] Precisely as *different manifestations of the same divine love*, God spares those whom in his mercy he has predestined, and he punishes others whom he has reprobated.

All this, insists Thomas, is part of God's divine goodness that must, by necessity, be manifested in various ways within his creation.[28] Why? Because creation bears within itself an incapacity for the simplicity that is intrinsic to God's own being. In other words, the utter otherness of creation from its creative God, by which it lacks the unified integrity of essence and existence that is proper to God, means that God must demonstrate his one and the same love in a multitude of ways that, although appearing unequal, are in fact simply various expressions of

---

[24]Aquinas, *Summa*, Ia, q.23, a.3.

[25]Aquinas, *Summa*, I a.3.

[26]In commenting on this aspect of Thomas's understanding of God, Katherine Sonderegger says that, in her view, "Nothing in the contemporary theological doctrine of God . . . outstrips the radicality of Thomas's doctrine here." This God of whom Thomas speaks possesses, in Sonderegger's words, "sheer Reality." K. Sonderegger, *Systematic Theology: Volume 1, The Doctrine of God* (Minneapolis: Fortress Press, 2015), 35.

[27]Aquinas, *Summa*, Ia, q.23, a.3. In this context, Thomas's distinction between God's "antecedent" and "consequent" wills is also important. Antecedently, and as the eternal giver of both being and salvation, God wills that all people be saved. Consequently, in which God wills "simply," he adjudges people as and how they act in themselves, in consideration of which punishment is justly bestowed on those who sin. *Summa*, Ia, q.19, a.6; q.23, a.4.

[28]"*Necesse est autem quod divina bonitas . . . multiformiter repraesentetur in rebus.*"

the same divine goodness.[29] Thus predestination and reprobation are both parts of God's providence—the former including the will of God to confer grace on some, the latter including the will of the same God to permit others to fall into sin and thus to suffer the punishment of damnation on account of that sin into which he has let them fall.

We may well ask, along with St. Paul (Rom 9:14), how this squares with divine justice. Is it not unjust "that unequal things be given to equals"? As we have already seen, however, reprobation and predestination are, in a certain sense for Thomas, not different things at all but simply different expressions of the same thing: God's goodness. Nonetheless, insofar as the effects are different and cause us to ask why, Thomas refers us back to the inexplicable divine will that remains shrouded in mystery: there is "no reason, except the divine will."[30] In any case, insofar as predestination is granted gratuitously and without regard to merit or worth, the giver is free to dispense with as much or as little as he likes, without any damage to the principle of justice.[31]

Notwithstanding the heavy emphasis on God's providential sovereignty in his treatment of this topic, Aquinas does not ignore the importance of human decision-making. The reason for this is the distinction between primary and proximate causation. Reprobation and predestination, he says, differ in their respective causalities. Whereas predestination is primarily and proximately the cause of both the eternal life to come *and* the grace that is received in this life, reprobation is not the proximate cause of sin in this present life *but only* of the eternal punishment that is received in the next. The reprobate are not divested of their power to choose by reason of their reprobation and so are able to—and do!—freely choose the sins for which their eventual damnation is just reward. "Guilt proceeds from the free will of the person who is reprobated."[32] Therefore, says Thomas, the reprobate are

[29] Aquinas, *Summa*, Ia, q.23, a.5.
[30] *"Non habet rationem nisi divinam voluntatem."* Aquinas, *Summa*, Ia, q.23, a.5.
[31] Aquinas, *Summa*, Ia, q.23, a.5.
[32] *"Sed culpa provenit ex libero arbitrio eius qui reprobatur."* Aquinas, *Summa*, Ia, q.23, a.3.

such because God in the multiple manifestations of his divine goodness
has chosen them to be such, but the sins they commit for which they
receive their eternal punishment are nonetheless imputed to them as
guilt.[33] Similarly, the certainty of predestination does not nullify the
effectual significance of free will. In this regard, Thomas refers us to
ideas of necessity (*necessitas*) and contingency (*contigentiam*) within
God's providence. While predestination "most certainly and infallibly
takes effect," the effect itself is not thereby necessitated but remains
contingent on free will. In this way, "God's infinite power can effect with
infallible certainty both that an action should take place and that it shall
be a free action."[34] As Steven Boguslawski says, "Predestination considered as an effect in individuals does not obliterate human free will
from which it contingently issues."[35]

Aquinas thus gives a thoroughly Augustinian account of predestination, insofar as both God's sovereignty and humanity's freedom are
accorded significance if not ultimately equal weighting. Moreover, he
does so by consistently affirming an Aristotelian emphasis on divine
simplicity and God's identity as transcendent causality (albeit a causality that does not destroy contingent causalities that are brought
about in time by human free will).

Nevertheless, there is an enduring, troubling aspect to Thomas's doctrine. While never advocating the sort of "double predestination" that
would come to typify seventeenth-century Reformed theology—
primarily because to do so would make God both the ultimate and
proximate cause of reprobation, thus undermining his insistence of the
reprobate's freely chosen culpability—he depicts God's actions with
regard to the reprobate as being fundamentally at odds with his actions
on behalf of the elect. For example, "not all sins are taken away" by
Christ's atoning death, not because Jesus' death is not sufficient but

[33] Aquinas, *Summa*, Ia, q.23, a.3.
[34] D. Knowles, "The Middle Ages," in *A History of Christian Doctrine*, ed. H. Cunliffe-Jones (Philadelphia: Fortress Press, 1980), 275.
[35] Boguslawski, *Thomas Aquinas on the Jews*, 59.

because of the sins of those "who do not adhere" to him.[36] Human fault
thus limits the efficacy of Christ's atonement—yet, as we have seen, it
is because of God's eternal decision that these people be reprobated that
they commit the sins by which the atoning death of Christ loses its ef-
fectiveness for them. Similarly, with respect to Jesus' prayer for unity
(Jn 17:20-21), Thomas avers that Christ did and does not pray for all
people, or even for all believers, but "only for those who were predestined to obtain eternal life through him."[37] That is, the damned do not
act evilly despite being treated in exactly the same way as the elect; on
the contrary, they are treated differently by God in this present life in
such a way that one might justifiably question whether culpability
really accrues only to them.[38]

Such, then, is Thomas's account of predestination. But how does this
engage with or mirror the wider context in which he was writing and
which we have already said is the necessary backdrop for the medieval
doctrine of election? We can inquire into this through particular attention to Thomas's theology of Israel, noting that Europe's Jews were
chief among those who were by definition marginalized from the po-
liticoreligious community of Thomas's day and whose eternal acceptability to God was parsed through the proxy of political toleration. It
should be remembered that traditional church teaching framed Jews
in a unique theological space—they were the only ones of whom it
could be said that the promises of covenant and election had originally
been given; they were the ones from whom the prophets had come; yet
they were also the ones who had rejected and killed Jesus. Thus, the
Jews were guilty of particular culpability: the elect, from whom election
had been stripped. Nor was there any sophisticated nuancing of this
designation. Jews, both biblical and postbiblical, were alike in their
infidelity and guilt. Collective Jewish guilt was assumed, and officially
taught, from the time of St. John Chrysostom in the fourth century

---

[36]Aquinas, *Summa*, IIIa, q.1, a.4.
[37]Aquinas, *Summa*, IIIa, q.21, a.4.
[38]See Levering, *Predestination*, 83.

until the promulgation of *Nostra Aetate* in 1965. Yet, remarkably, this is not quite what we see in Thomas's construal of Jewish election.

According to John Hood, Thomas Aquinas was no different than all other medieval theologians. He simply accepted that the Jewish crucifixion of Jesus signaled the end of the legitimacy of the Hebrew religion and that the Jews themselves were "infidels . . . unworthy of toleration."[39] Hood argues that, while Thomas recognized that guilt for Jesus' death could not be attributed entirely evenly—the *majores* and *princepes*, by which he meant the religious elite of first-century Palestine, were willfully culpable; the *minores* (that is, the ignorant "rest of Jewish society") were led astray because of their blind ignorance—he nonetheless concluded that, whether by intent or spiritual blindness, Jews as a whole had been and remained collectively guilty.[40] To return to an earlier theme, Hood relies on the idea of differentiated causation: God has determined the Jews for ultimate reprobation, but they remain proximately responsible for their choices of unbelief, for which their damnation is just punishment.

But Thomas's Israel theology can be read in a different way. Steven Boguslawski provides a somewhat more positive interpretation in his exploration of texts from both the *Summa Theologiae* and Thomas's contemporaneous commentary on Romans. In his view, Thomas refuses to regard Jews as an alien group within society because Christianity both derives from and is dependent on them, historically and eschatologically. That is to say, the church cannot exist in and of itself but only in its inseparable relationship to Israel.[41] Boguslawski rightly notes that this inseparability is not an intrinsically positive statement about Israel; as we have seen with Bernard of Clairvaux, the necessity of Israel's witness can be parsed in fundamentally judgmental ways. Nonetheless, Jewish existence does not seem to carry quite the same negative determinism for Thomas as it did for most of his contemporaries.

---

[39]Hood, *Aquinas and the Jews*, 62.
[40]Hood, *Aquinas and the Jews*, 62-75.
[41]Boguslawski, *Thomas Aquinas on the Jews*, 38.

For one thing, he avers that Jewish worship practices (not only within the pages of Scripture but even in his own day) cannot be disparaged as mere idolatry. Whereas the rites of non-Jewish unbelievers "are neither truthful nor profitable [and] are by no means to be tolerated," the rites of the Jews "foreshadowed the truth of the faith which we hold," and thus the Christian faith "is represented in [this] figure."[42] This is the case, suggests Boguslawski, because Thomas further regards the Jews as occupying a midpoint in the hierarchy of *infidelitas*. In its most grievous form, unbelief is the denial of faith after having accepted it. In its least aberrant form, unbelief is the mark of the heathen who have not believed because they have never heard. Between these two extremes lies the unbelief of the Jews:

> In this way the unbelief of heretics, who confess their belief in the Gospel, and resist that faith by corrupting it, is a more grievous sin than that of the Jews, who have never accepted the Gospel faith. Since, however, they accepted the figure of that faith in the Old Law, which they corrupt by their false interpretations, their unbelief is a more grievous sin than that of the heathen, because the latter have not accepted the Gospel faith in any way at all.[43]

As Boguslawski puts it, for Thomas, "it is better to be a confessing Jew than a heretical Christian."[44]

In his exploration of Thomas's Romans commentary, Boguslawski goes even further. His reading of this expository work leads him to argue that for Thomas, being a Jew is not *the worst* thing one can be; indeed, salvation ultimately accrues to the Jews as well. Routinely accustomed to speaking of Israel historically and not spiritually, in his Romans exposition Thomas boldly claims a final salvific hope for the Jews as such: "Israel shall be saved, not in a manner individually, but universally."[45] As he says regarding the irrevocability of God's decision (Rom 11:29),

---

[42]Aquinas, *Summa*, IIa-IIae, q.10, a.11.

[43]Aquinas, *Summa*, IIa-IIae, q.10, a.6.

[44]Boguslawski, *Thomas Aquinas on the Jews*, 39.

[45]Aquinas, *Commentary on Romans*, §916. Cited in Boguslawski, *Thomas Aquinas on the Jews*, 97.

For someone would be able to say by opposing this that the Jews, if formerly they were most beloved . . . on account of the fathers, nevertheless, the hostility which they employed against the Gospel prohibits [it] lest in the future they be saved. But this the Apostle asserts to be false, saying for the gifts and the call of God are without repentance since concerning this God does not repent.[46]

According to Boguslawski, Thomas not only has good things to say about Jewish ritual dignity but indeed fully anticipates their eventual redemption. The inclusion of the Gentiles into God's redemptive plan does not undermine the Jews' own salvation; rather, it is the Jews' continuing election—from which their fall is only temporary—that is the seedbed of Gentile inclusion.[47] That this would be the conclusion of someone as surrounded by social anti-Semitism as Thomas is remarkable. It illustrates that even in the midst of the pervasive exclusionary *corpus Christianum*, Thomas was able to apply his doctrine of predestination in an ultimately affirming and sympathetic manner to that group within Christianized society that had, for centuries, been resolutely excluded from elected sociality. In turning now to arguably the "second most significant" theologian of the Middle Ages,[48] Duns Scotus, we will be able to see whether and to what extent Thomas really was a lone voice.

DUNS SCOTUS

If Thomas Aquinas was the "angelic doctor," then John Duns Scotus (ca. 1266–1308) was, by common acclaim, the "subtle doctor." This would

---

[46]Aquinas, *Commentary on Romans*, §924. Cited in Boguslawski, *Thomas Aquinas on the Jews*, 101. This perhaps accords with Thomas's insistence that a person's predestination is certain if, in fact, they have been predestined. ("*Unde non oportet dicere quod Deus possit non praedestinare quem praedestinavit.*") *Summa* Ia, q.23, a.7.

[47]Holly Taylor Coolman draws a similar conclusion to Boguslawski, noting that Thomas's Israel theology can be used as a positive tool for contemporary dialogue between Jews and Christians. See H. T. Coolman, "Romans 9–11: Rereading Aquinas on the Jews," in *Reading Romans with Aquinas*, ed. M. Levering and M. Dauphinais (Washington, DC: Catholic University of America Press, 2012), 104-11.

[48]R. Cross, *Duns Scotus*, Great Medieval Thinkers, ed. B. Davies (Oxford: Oxford University Press, 1999), ix.

seem to be an entirely reasonable honorific so long as subtlety, in respect to Scotus, is understood in terms of sophisticated nuance rather than implying some sort of veiled obscurity. Certainly, as Richard Cross has ably shown, Scotus's theology was, at the very least, complex. But two things ought to be said about this complexity. First, the intricacy of Scotus's theology, forced on it by its very subject matter, was compounded by his intentionally uneven continuation of his predecessors' heritage. It would be a mistake to assume that, while they were all "medieval theologians," Scotus occupied the same world of both politics and theology as did the great intellectual protagonists of the thirteenth century. Although working only slightly less than two generations after both Aquinas and his own confrère, Bonaventure, Scotus inhabited a theological space that was nonetheless significantly different in tone and context. Cross notes that, while naturally familiar with the works of Aquinas and Bonaventure, Scotus himself engaged more deliberately with his closer contemporaries, in particular with Henry of Ghent (ca. 1217–1293), whose theological system was distinguished by its synthesis of Augustinianism, Aristotelian epistemology, and Avicennian ontology.[49] Indeed, Henry of Ghent was "the one thinker more than any other [who provided] Scotus with material for discussion."[50] That his more immediate interlocutors are these days less familiar to us than his more famous forebears makes it even harder to penetrate what he has to say from subject to subject.

Second, the complexity of his thought notwithstanding, Scotus's message was, on one reading at least, remarkably simple. Notwithstanding his genius "for original and subtle philosophical analysis," his semantic precision served a greater purpose than mere logical profundity. On the contrary, his thought was "not motivated by a love for the abstract or technical as such" but was rather compelled toward technical abstraction as the necessary tool for the "vindication of that

---

[49]Cross, *Duns Scotus*, 5. See also P. Porro, "Henry of Ghent," in *Stanford Encyclopedia of Philosophy*, ed. Edward N. Zalta (Fall 2014), http://plato.stanford.edu/archives/fall2014/entries/henry-ghent/.
[50]R. Cross, *Duns Scotus on God* (Aldershot, UK: Ashgate, 2005), 6.

which move[d] his thought more than anything else: the love of God."[51] To put it otherwise, in Scotus's ethical ontology of God there is "an infinite love" that proceeds from God and which originates with necessity in God's eternal will.[52] The nuanced finessing of terms like *necessity*, *contingency*, and *voluntarism* are not used simply to serve their own rhetorical sophistication but are instead vital means through which Scotus seeks to elucidate the infinite quantum of divine loving. We shall come to see how this frames Scotus's theology of election in due course. First, however, we ought to orient ourselves to the particulars of his own context (geographical and therefore sociopolitical), different as it was from that of Aquinas.

Scotus was born in the Scottish borderlands, most probably in the town of Duns. As a birthplace, Duns was hardly an inspiration. Its first documentary mention was as late as 1179—less than one hundred years before Scotus's birth—at which time a certain Hugo de Duns witnessed a charter that granted the benefice of a church to Kelso Abbey, some sixteen miles away. Over the next few centuries, Duns became far better known for its strategic importance as a mustering place for battle in the frequent skirmishes between the Scots and the English. It seems never to have been what one might call a center of learning, and so it is hardly surprising that Scotus's own time there is shrouded in doubt. Indeed, that he was even born there, though now the scholarly consensus, is in fact a matter more of speculation than of well-attested fact.[53]

Having entered the Convent Church of Our Lady in Dumfries as a young teenager in or around 1279, Scotus received the Franciscan habit and shortly thereafter was moved to Oxford, where he began his formal studies. Precisely when he commenced his Oxford studentship is unknown, although 1288 is a reasonable guess. We do know he was ordained to the priesthood at St. Andrew's Priory, Northampton, in the

---

[51]A. Vos, H. Veldhuis, E. Dekker, N. W. den Bok, and A. J. Beck, eds., *Duns Scotus on Divine Love: Texts and Commentary on Goodness and Freedom, God and Humans* (Aldershot, UK: Ashgate, 2003), 1.

[52]Vos et al., *Duns Scotus on Divine Love*, 10.

[53]Cross, *Duns Scotus on God*, 1.

Diocese of Lincoln in March 1291. Given that Oxford was in the Lincoln Diocese at this time, it is not unlikely that Scotus was in Oxford for about three years before his ordination, during which time he would have started his formal priestly training. The final stages of his academic life in Oxford are better attested. The Franciscan provincial, Hugh of Hertilpole, requested in July 1300 that Scotus be licensed to hear confessions in the Franciscan church in Oxford, implying that the provincial, at least, assumed that Scotus would be in Oxford for at least the rest of that year. In the academic year of 1300–1301, Scotus participated in a disputation in Oxford with the Franciscan master Philip Bridlington. Thus, it would appear that Scotus was a student in Oxford for about thirteen years, from sometime in 1288 to the end of the academic year in 1301.[54] By 1302, he was lecturing on Peter Lombard's *Sentences* at the University of Paris, where he stayed until 1307. In the final year of his life, and on the orders of the Franciscan Minister-General, Gonsalvus Hispanus (ca. 1255–1313), Scotus moved to Cologne, dying there in November 1308.

While his life may have been short, it was not lived narrowly. Indeed, one of the most striking aspects of Scotus's scholarship is his evident willingness to learn—somewhat idiosyncratically—from a wide variety of sources, experts, and authorities. Yet this preparedness to learn from others was never uncritical. As was mentioned earlier, Henry of Ghent may have been Scotus's favored interlocutor, but the engagement was one of "critical reaction" *against* Henry's ideas rather than a holus-bolus acceptance of them.[55] The Islamic scholar Avicenna (ca. 980–1037) also loomed large in helping to shape Scotus's thought, although, again, not without qualification.[56]

---

[54] See T. Williams, "Introduction: The Life and Works of John Duns the Scot," in *The Cambridge Companion to Duns Scotus*, ed. T. Williams (Cambridge: Cambridge University Press, 2003), 1-3; Cross, *Duns Scotus*, 3-4; Cross, *Duns Scotus on God*, 1-2; and Vos et al., *Duns Scotus on Divine Love*, 3-4.

[55] S. D. Dumont, "Duns Scotus, John (c.1266–1308)," in *The Routledge Encyclopedia of Philosophy*, (London: Taylor and Francis, 1988), www.rep.routledge.com/articles/biographical/duns-scotus-john-c-1266-1308/v-1.

[56] See M. B. Ingham and M. Dreyer, *The Philosophical Vision of John Duns Scotus: An Introduction*,

Similarly, and notwithstanding the prevailing Aristotelianism that permeated the universities of both Oxford and Paris, Scotus was heavily critical of Aristotle as well as of Thomas Aquinas's attempt to reconcile Christian dogma with Aristotelian principles.[57] We have already noted that Aquinas himself was condemned by Bishop Tempier for his advocacy of various Aristotelian themes. More significantly for our purposes, Richard Cross has also demonstrated that Scotus sided with Tempier against the "Aristotelians," including Aquinas.[58] In particular, Scotus was concerned about the limitations that the condemned propositions seemed to place on God's sovereign potentiality, the possibility of contingency, and the freedom of the individual.[59] Each of these looms large in his understanding of election, in which we see him proposing his particular views in opposition to such Aristotelian logic.

In discussing Scotus's teaching on election, it is important to note at the outset that he speaks of this in the context of eternal life as something that one gains rather than as a bifurcated fixed identity that one is arbitrarily assigned in pretemporal eternity.[60] Hence, in the first instance, election must be parsed with reference to a gift of eternal life that one "earns" (what "earning" this gift means we will consider below). In this context, there are four main themes to address, each of which bears on Scotus's conclusions in very particular ways. These are (1) the nature of "merit," (2) the distinction and relationship between disposition and will, (3) causation, and (4) contingency.

To begin with the question of merit, Scotus takes for granted, as did most of his medieval contemporaries, that while humans cannot do anything autonomous to deserve eternal life, they must nonetheless

---

(Washington, DC: Catholic University of America Press, 2004), 55n7. See also R. Cross, *The Physics of Duns Scotus: The Scientific Context of a Theological Vision* (Oxford: Clarendon Press, 1998), 39, 71, 87, 95, 261.

[57] L. W. B. Brockliss, *The University of Oxford: A History* (Oxford: Oxford University Press, 2016), 99.

[58] Cross, *Duns Scotus on God*, 4. Cross notes, however, that the views condemned as Aristotelian were in fact more accurately to be found in Aristotle's Islamic exegete, Averroës, than in Aristotle himself.

[59] Scotus's passionate insistence on the freedom of the will, over and above the importance of the intellect, was itself very un-Augustinian. Brockliss, *University of Oxford*, 99.

[60] It should also be noted that Scotus's preferred term is *praedestinatio* rather than election.

do *something*. Eternal life is indeed a gift freely given by God through grace, but it is not given for *nothing*. Rather, it is a gift given for a very particular thing. What the "thing" is for which the gift is given is the first matter of contention.

Scotus would have us understand that the merit, for which anyone receives eternal life, must be an act that is done by us and not just done in us. It is for that reason that he rejects the view of Peter Lombard, who, in book one of his *Sentences*, argues that the "merit" is the work of the Holy Spirit within a person.[61] Scotus insists that if that were the case, then no merit would in fact accrue to the person receiving eternal life, but only to the Spirit of God, who surely does not need it! Rather, the "merit" that tends to eternal life must be a work that is done by the person; it must be a human act. Indeed, one can now say that it must be both a human *act* (that is, *something* must be done) and a *human* act (that is, the thing that is done must be done by a person and not by God). Of course, we have already noted that Scotus rejects the semi-Pelagian idea that the act that is done can be an autonomously human act.[62] God must be involved somehow, and for Scotus the divine involvement is through the gift of God that disposes the person toward love. Thus, we can say that the meritorious act that tends to eternal life is the act that arises from the disposition to love. This, argues Scotus, is not generated purely from within someone but only as and how the Holy Spirit gives this disposition to the person.[63]

Having thus defined what Scotus means by a merit by which a person receives eternal life, we come to the second theme—namely, the way in which Scotus relates and distinguishes between disposition and will. The Scot insists that, if the merit is an act, then it must be the consequence

---

[61]This is evident specifically in Lombard's Distinction I 16, "De missione Spiritus Sancti." Lombard uses Augustine as his authority on this, insofar as Augustine speaks of the Spirit as "the love of the Father and the Son, by which they love each other and us." *De Trinitate* 15.18.32. See also *De fide et symbol* 9.19. See D. Coffey, "The Holy Spirit as the Mutual Love of the Father and the Son," *Theological Studies* 51 (1990): 193-229.

[62]See A. Vos, *The Theology of John Duns Scotus*, Studies in Reformed Theology 34 (Leiden: Brill, 2018), 245-46.

[63]See Scotus, *Lectura* I 17 §§1-55.

of the actualization of the will. The disposition, which is granted as a gift by God, is not in itself the enactment of the act but only the tendency toward it. The will of the person must be enacted to make that disposition an act. Only when the will is thus engaged to turn the disposition to love into action can this become an act of love that is, itself, the merit.

This leads us to our third theme, in which Scotus posits the distinction between two types of causality, both of which are needed to actualize the will. There are, he says, two agents that concur in an act, "the first one of which is free [*liberum*] and the second natural [*naturale*]." By a natural cause, or agent, Scotus means something that must, by definition, tend toward its proper end (*semper inclinat in finem*). In this case, the natural agent is the disposition to love. Love cannot but tend toward love if it is to remain loving. Conversely, the will is the "free agent" that has no such necessity. It can choose to be enacted or not.[64]

Thus, Scotus demonstrates the importance of co-causality but is then required to show that these causes are not equal in their causation. He argues that if the disposition to love was the first or primary agent in the actualization of that disposition into meritorious act, then as a natural agent that *must* tend toward its proper end there would be an inbuilt necessity to the act that would nullify its meritoriousness: "If the will were moved by love, the activity of the will would not be free. For when the second agent is moved by the principal agent which moves naturally, it is not moved freely."[65] Consequently, the primary causal agent must be the will. As a *free* cause, any actualization of the will by the disposition to love will be free and unnecessary, and therefore meritorious. Both the disposition to love and the will constitute the actualization of the meritorious act; both are causal within their own terms. The will causes the enactment of the act to be free, while the disposition causes the act to be loving.

---

[64]Scotus, *Lectura* I 17 §§71-81.
[65]"*Quia si voluntas moveretur a carite, actio voluntatis non esset libera, quia quando secundum agens movetur ab agente principali movente naturaliter, non movetur libere.*" Scotus, *Lectura* I 17 §73.

To this point, Scotus has shown how an act may be enacted that allows it to be both free and loving, and therefore meritorious. His emphasis, however, has been on the human subject of the action. Yet the primary determinant of any act's meritoriousness is not the human subject of the act but the God to whom the act is offered. That is, in and alongside the human enactment of the loving act, it must be equally true that the merit of the act exists not intrinsically within the act itself but only because God, as the one to whom the act is offered, is prepared to *accept* it as such. Meritoriousness, from God's side, is bestowed *extrinsically* on the act that is done and does not belong to it inherently.[66] So, asks Scotus, what are the grounds by which God accepts such an act as meritorious? Again, we are faced with primary and secondary causality, although in the case of God's acceptance of the act relative to the person's enactment of it, the order is reversed. The act must primarily be characterized by the lovingness of its disposition in order to be accepted as a meritorious act. Only once this has been established is it important (indeed, necessary) that the will has been engaged freely to enact that disposition. As Scotus puts it, "The act comes from both the will and from love . . . [but] the act of love is accepted not so much because of the will as because of love the disposition tending to its object."[67]

In sum, to the question of what someone must do to gain eternal life (to be, as it were, elect), Scotus gives the following answer. There must be a merit, something that is done and that is subsequently accepted by God as merit. But this meritorious act must at the same time be something that is freely willed by the doer yet is an act of love, corresponding

---

[66]Scotus, *Lectura* I 17 §90.

[67]Scotus, *Lectura* I 17 §§90, 92. As a curious side point, Scotus does note that the fact that God has decided to accept a loving act as a meritorious act to eternal life implies an alternative choice whereby he could have chosen not to accept such an act. This is the distinction between God's ordained power (*de potentia ordinata*—what God *has* chosen) and his absolute power (*de potentia absoluta*—what God *could have* chosen.) Similarly, God could have chosen to accept an act that was not an act of love to be the meritorious act toward eternal life. Against this, however, we need to note that for Scotus, loving God is a necessary ethical truth. Therefore, love is not just requested but required. As an ethical necessity, the implication is clearly that God would require this type of loving act not just in this world but in every possible world that he could have made. *Lectura* I 17 §§102-3.

to the requirement of loving God. In other words, God gives the disposition to act in a loving way, but the free will of the human causes (or not) that disposition to be actualized. Thus, humans must consent to be saved, on the one hand, and God must consent to accept their loving act as a meritorious act, on the other.

True to his appellation, Scotus as the "subtle doctor" is not yet finished with the topic. Having shown the nature of the merit that is repaid with eternal life and the free actualization of the disposition to love by which it is caused, Scotus proceeds in *Lectura* I 40-41 to ask whether those whose election has been illustrated by their loving merit can in the end be dispossessed of their reward. In other words, can you lose your election?

This is hardly a new question, nor are the alternatives surprising. If the answer is yes, then God's will can be changed. If the answer is no, then no room is left for the freedom of human choice. On the first, and notwithstanding his hesitation about Aristotelian "proofs" of divine immutability, Scotus rejects the view that God could change his mind. Divine simplicity, according to which God cannot be the subject of, or moved by, accidents ("changes that a persisting subject undergoes during its existing," which might then include the changing of one's mind) renders it impossible that God could decide against something he has already chosen.[68] As to the second, given that we have already noted Scotus's insistence on the freedom of the will as the primary cause or agent of the meritorious act, we can hardly expect him to answer in the negative. How, then, does he resolve the dilemma?

In answering this, we are brought to the fourth of the themes mentioned above, (synchronic) contingency. For Scotus, the solution to this perennial problem is to argue that God's decree for election is immutable but not necessary. In claiming this, he points to two distinct freedoms, both of which must be observed. On the human side, an elected person can be condemned because she has free choice to continue sinning

---

[68]Cross, *Duns Scotus on God*, 119.

(*potest peccare per liberum arbitrium*). If the elect uses her free choice badly in that way—that is, by continuing to sin—then she is not justified and thus cannot be elect.[69]

For God, similarly, an elect person can be condemned on the basis of the freedom of God's will from temporal necessity. Referring to the concept of synchronic contingency that he develops more fully in distinction I 39—that is, that at any one moment in time there exists a true alternative to the state of affairs that actually exists—he argues here that, if God wills something at a certain point in time, he can also will its opposite at the same moment. Because God is a purely free agent, he has the "synchronic power of opposites"—the capacity to will both a and $-a$ in the same eternally timeless instant, even if only one of the alternatives is in fact realized. Therefore, an *actual* object of will coexists with the simultaneous *possibility* of its opposite.[70] The two things do not actually exist at the same time—that would be a contradiction. But the *possibility* of the opposite exists. In this case, being elect is a synchronically contingent reality, existing alongside the possibility of the same person also being condemned—a synchronic that is real but not realized.[71]

The final question that we must address (because Scotus himself asks it) is whether election or reprobation can ever properly be deserved. It has already been seen that, with respect to election (that is, the gaining of eternal life), Scotus insists that there must be a merit. There must be an act that is freely done by the person and that is subsequently accepted by God as sufficiently meritorious in character to warrant the gift of eternal life. The gift is indeed gracious, but it is not given for nothing. But what of reprobation? Is it equally true that, in order to justly warrant reprobation, a person must similarly *do something*? To answer this, we must recognize one final distinction that Scotus makes.

---

[69]Scotus, *Lectura* I 40 §5. Note that for Scotus, justification is not explicitly delineated from sanctification, such that to be justified carries the same meaning as "not persevering in sin."
[70]Cross, *Duns Scotus*, 57-58.
[71]Scotus, *Lectura* I 40 §6.

For him, the question can be answered only with respect to what he calls the "grounds" (*ratio*) of election, on the one hand, and reprobation, on the other. By this Scotus means not the logical or sequential *basis* of reprobation or election but their respective end points, their *teloi*. That is to say, while both election and reprobation are acts of will, they nonetheless also have their own particular grounds; they are done with specific purposes in mind, because the ground for willing something in the first instance is its *finis*.[72] With this in mind, Scotus argues that the ground of election is that the elect ones are brought into communion with the God who wills them to be elected. In other words, the *ratio* of someone's election is not so much their own meritorious act or even God's willing them to be elected but rather their participation by that election in the divine community.

This, however, is not true of reprobation. Whereas there is no merit on any person's part that establishes the *ratio* (purpose) of their election, there is a merit for reprobation. Because, in Scotus's view, God does not wish anyone to be reprobated, there must be something that someone *does* to deserve it.[73] There must be a ground of reprobation, which for Scotus is to be identified not with *any* sin but only with "ultimate sin" or "sinning to the end" (*peccatum finale*). Emphasizing God's superabundantly loving disposition, Scotus insists that God cannot, and will not, reject anyone unless that person deserves it through the (continuing) act of ultimate sin. In consequence, he is compelled to the view that there must indeed be a merit done by someone that constitutes the ground of reprobation.[74]

We must come to the conclusion, then, that Scotus treats both reprobation and election qualitatively differently. Whereas there can be no human *ratio* for election, there must be a human *ratio* for reprobation, otherwise God would never will it. In which case, it is clear that the

---

[72]Vos et al., *Duns Scotus on Divine Love*, 160.

[73]Note that in identifying God's wish not to reprobate anyone, Scotus is following Augustine's commentary on Genesis. "God is not an avenger before the other is a sinner." See Scotus, *Lectura* I 41 §26.

[74]Vos et al., *Duns Scotus on Divine Love*, 162.

occasion of loving is not the cause of God's decision to elect, but the occasion of sinning is the cause of God's decision for reprobation. Oddly, then, Scotus's theology of election is supralapsarian but his theology of reprobation is infralapsarian.[75]

This, then, is the overall shape of Scotus's doctrine of election. It is quite plainly of a different order entirely to that which had been proposed by Aquinas not too many years beforehand. But what resonance, if any, did it have within the broader sociopolitical context in which it was developed? Here, too, if we consider Scotus's attitudes toward the Jews, as we did with Aquinas, we will find considerable alignment between his construal of election and the refusal of that elect status to those most obvious enemies of the *corpus Christianum*.

At the outset, it is worth noting that, while Scotus may have been sheltered from many of the troubles that beset Continental Europe until his own relocation there in the early fourteenth century, England itself was one of the more aggressively anti-Semitic societies of the day. Just ten years before Scotus's birth and in the same diocese in which he was ordained, eighteen Jews were executed for allegedly murdering nine-year-old Hugh of Lincoln in a ritual sacrifice. The fact that the story was soon disproved mattered little. The ensuing accusations and subsequent convictions—the first time that the English civil magistracy had ever handed down a capital sentence for ritual murder charges— nonetheless gave vent to an outpouring of anti-Jewish hatred throughout the country.[76] Later in 1279, just before Scotus entered the Northampton

---

[75]Vos et al., *Duns Scotus on Divine Love*, 161.

[76]The chronicler, Matthew Paris, described the murder and Jewish conspiracy behind it in the following way: "This year [1255] about the feast of the apostles Peter and Paul [July 27], the Jews of Lincoln stole a boy called Hugh, who was about eight years old. After shutting him up in a secret chamber, where they fed him on milk and other childish food, they sent to almost all the cities of England in which there were Jews, and summoned some of their sect from each city to be present at a sacrifice to take place at Lincoln, in contumely and insult of Jesus Christ. For, as they said, they had a boy concealed for the purpose of being crucified; so a great number of them assembled at Lincoln, and then they appointed a Jew of Lincoln judge, to take the place of Pilate, by whose sentence, and with the concurrence of all, the boy was subjected to various tortures. They scourged him till the blood flowed, they crowned him with thorns, mocked him, and spat upon him; each of them also pierced him with a knife, and they made him drink gall, and scoffed at him with blasphemous insults, and kept gnashing their teeth and calling him Jesus, the false

Priory, another group of Jews was executed in that very town, also for allegedly crucifying a Christian youth.[77] It was during this same period that, on the orders of Edward I, England's Jews were accused of widespread financial fraud (including counterfeiting and "coin-clipping"[78]), with more than three thousand Jews imprisoned throughout the country, three hundred of whom were later executed. In 1290, Edward's hostility to the Jews culminated in their forcible expulsion from all English lands. From then until 1655, there was no legal record of any Jew living in England. It was within this context that Scotus's theological opinions of Jews were shaped.

Yet, despite this heatedly anti-Semitic environment in which Scotus was formed, he was not simplistically anti-Jewish himself. Echoing Aquinas, and indeed much of standard Christian teaching, Scotus honored the Old Testament rites as true, if unintended, prefigurations of Christ's advent. Judaism itself was understood by him to be the proper religious tradition that had been ordained by God in and for the pre-Christian age.[79] Rituals and ceremonies performed under this tradition, in a time when God wished to be worshiped in that fashion, were, says Scotus, proper, blessed, and meritorious. Old Testament rituals, including circumcision, when done out of love for and obedience to God, should be rightly understood as sacramental.[80] Moreover, the meritorious efficacy of these rites was not annulled precisely at the coming of Christ but rather continued into the early decades of the

---

prophet. And after tormenting him in divers [sic] ways they crucified him, and pierced him to the heart with a spear. When the boy was dead, they took the body down from the cross, and for some reason disemboweled it; it is said for the purpose of their magic arts." See G. Bennet, *Bodies: Sex, Violence, Disease and Death in Contemporary Legend* (Jackson: University of Mississippi Press, 2005), 263-64.

[77]N. L. Turner, "Jewish Witness, Forced Conversion and Island Living: John Duns Scotus on Jews and Judaism," in *Christian Attitudes Towards the Jews in the Middle Ages: A Casebook*, ed. M. Frassetto (New York: Routledge, 2007), 184.

[78]Coin clipping, where slivers of a coin's precious metal were shaved off the edge in order to melt down into bullion, was a common practice but was nonetheless illegal and often ascribed to "greedy" Jews.

[79]See Turner, "Jewish Witness, Forced Conversion and Island Living," 184.

[80]Scotus, *In Sententias* 4, d.1, q.6. Cited in Turner, "Jewish Witness, Forced Conversion and Island Living," 186.

church's existence, as demonstrated by Paul's circumcising of Timothy and Peter's allegiance to the law in Jerusalem.[81]

Scotus demonstrates, therefore, an evident and genuine respect for Hebrew religious practice throughout the period of the Old Testament and even into the start of the New. However, he did not look so kindly on Jews themselves. As people, he says, they are selfish, violent, and barbarous, prone to idolatry and fatal legalism.[82] As Nancy Turner puts it, Scotus was singly scathing of Jews "in any context in which their devotion to the Law is not the central focus."[83] But the Jews are more than merely morally wrong—they are *collectively* and *criminally* wrong. Repudiating the Thomistic distinction between the *majores* and the *minores*, Scotus judges *all* Jews—leaders and laity alike—to be knowingly culpable for Jesus' death. It is merely an extension of the same logic when he argues for the forcible conversion of all Jews.

We saw in an earlier part of this chapter that Thomas Aquinas held out hope for the eventual redemption of Jews as such, and that this was not inconsistent with his doctrine of predestination. Scotus, however, notwithstanding his emphasis on God's superabundant love that tends toward election and not reprobation, refused to countenance the Jews in such a sympathetic manner. Indeed, he seems to have been deeply influenced by the pervading anti-Semitism of his native homeland. Jews were intrinsically inimical to the body of Christ and thus to the *corpus Christianum*; as Jews, they could only ever be outsiders. Jewishness as such counted as the "sin unto the end" that, as we have seen, was the one *ratio* necessary for meriting reprobation. Only by forcible conversion and baptism, at the point of the sword if necessary, could that Jewishness—that ultimate sin against both God and the Christian body politic—be sufficiently expunged.

---

[81]For Scotus, of course, the old law does soon pass into irrelevancy, being merely a shadow of the truth that came in Christ. Thus, for postbiblical Jews to continue to live according to its precepts is both foolhardy, pointless, and proof of Jewish obstinacy.

[82]Scotus, *In Sententias* 1, d.2, q.3. Cited in Turner, "Jewish Witness, Forced Conversion and Island Living," 189.

[83]Turner, "Jewish Witness, Forced Conversion and Island Living," 189.

CONCLUSION

We began this chapter by noting that the age of medieval Christianity coincided with an almost complete overlapping of the boundaries of church and state. Being a "good believer" in one was virtually synonymous with being a "good citizen" in the other. Or at least, if one was excluded from the community of the church for any reason, it was nearly impossible to be a fully participatory member of the empire. Thus, insofar as the doctrine of election found concrete expression in the composition of the church, and insofar as church and state were largely coterminous, the identification of God's elect—and, in consequence, the designation of the reprobate—was inherently politicized. If European Jews and Muslims were the most obvious victims of this politicization of doctrine, they did not remain the only ones. As European Christendom stumbled its way into the angry years of the Reformation, the church began to turn in on itself. No longer was the church as such the visible bearer of election; rather, one's elect status began to depend on the *part* of a now-divided church to which one belonged.

4

THE REFORMATION AND EARLY
POST-REFORMATION CONTROVERSIES

THE FIVE HUNDREDTH ANNIVERSARY of the purported beginnings of the "Reformation" in 2017 quite naturally stimulated a fresh
interest in the life and theology of Martin Luther.[1] In the course of this
renewed focus, Luther's reputation and legacy were again tied inextricably to his doctrine of justification and correlative attack on the abuse
of indulgences. There was, of course, nothing improper in this way of
recounting history. Nevertheless, no matter how important Luther's

---

[1] The suggestion that the tumultuous period of social, political, and religious upheaval in sixteenth-century Europe can be brought together under the singular term *Reformation* is now
rejected by most scholars. As Eamon Duffy has said, "The Reformation" is a particularly "unsat-
isfactory designation" that conceals a "battery of value judgments" and implies a singularity of
purpose in crushing papal power and heralding modernity. Far from being a "confessional mo-
nopoly," reformist agendas were evident throughout the various branches of Roman Catholicism
as well as under the banner of a variety of Protestant groups, ranging from Lutheran orthodoxy
to Calvinist theocracy, from Anabaptist pacifism to Thomas Müntzer's violent apocalypticism.
See E. Duffy, *Reformation Divided: Catholics, Protestants and the Conversion of England* (London:
Bloomsbury, 2017), 2. In other words, there was, as Diarmaid MacCulloch has pointed out, a
plurality of "Protestantisms" and a diversity of "Reformations." See D. MacCulloch, *Reformation:
Europe's House Divided, 1490–1700* (London: The Folio Society, 2003). Even the most unqualified
history will at least recognize a chronological sequence of reforming movements. Such narratives
typically begin with the so-called Magisterial Reformation—so called because of its reliance on
the princes and other instruments of statecraft for its implementation—beginning in 1517 and
largely identifiable with Luther, Melanchthon, and Calvin, before moving on to the "Catholic
Reformation" of the 1520s, the "Radical," or "Left Wing of the Reformation" from around 1525,
and then finally the prolonged English reforms from the 1530s. While it would be churlish to say
that this narrative is entirely wrong, it does nonetheless amplify the problem to which I have
already alluded: the notion that "the Reformation" (no matter how many segments you want to
divide it into) began in 1517 with the posting of Luther's Ninety-Five Theses and that it was thus
a cataclysmic but ultimately inevitable turn of events, the origins of which can be neatly named,
located, and even today visited.

"discovering of the gospel of pure grace" was,[2] it was hardly the only thing characterizing either Luther himself or those reforming years, nor the only moment of doctrinal import. For if, alongside Luther's *iustitia fidei*, there is one other piece of theological shorthand to have emerged from the religious life of sixteenth-century Europe, it would be the preoccupation with John Calvin's understanding of election and predestination and the manner in which his doctrine has for so long and by so many been naively read as a proxy for the entire Reformed tradition. That this may or may not be fair to him is not really the question. The fact is, Calvin's very particular views on this topic, regardless of whether the topic itself was determinative for him, have aroused such fractious debate that the centrality of the doctrine, to Calvin and to Reformed theology generally, has become something of an automatic assumption. In this chapter, then, we will focus our attention squarely on the debates within the Reformed tradition that arose in connection with this doctrine between 1537 and 1619. Our gaze will therefore be concentrated mostly on Calvin, his successor Theodore Beza, and the maverick Jakob Arminius. Before getting there, though, it would be remiss to entirely overlook Martin Luther's own thoughts on the doctrine of election.

LUTHER ON ELECTION

In 1525 Luther published a major treatise that, in 1537, he would later describe as one of his best works.[3] *The Bondage of the Will* was his lengthy retort to Erasmus of Rotterdam's semi-Pelagian essay of the year before, "Discussion Concerning Free Will." In that pamphlet, Erasmus had argued that, the problem of sin notwithstanding, human free will remained and people were in fact capable of willing the good. This was in stark contrast to the traditional Augustinian view (with which Luther agreed) that free will was incapable of anything but sin, that it was not

---

[2] D. Bonhoeffer, *DBWE* 4:49.

[3] "*Nullum enim agnosco meum iustum librum, nisi forte de Servo arbitrio et Catechismum.*" (None of my works is worth anything, except *de Servo Arbitrio* and the Catechism.) M. Luther, letter to W. Capito, July 9, 1537, *WA BR* 8:99.

possible not to sin (*non posse non peccare*). Luther's reply to Erasmus—
pointedly titled *De Servo arbitrio* ("On Enslaved Choice")—was a mul-
tifaceted repetition of precisely this Augustinian point: "God knows
nothing by contingency, but . . . he foresees, purposes, and does all things
according to his immutable, eternal, and infallible will. By this thun-
derbolt, 'Free-will' is thrown prostrate, and utterly dashed to pieces."[4]

For Luther, this was not simply a rebuttal of the type of vacuous mo-
rality that he believed Erasmus was advocating. "You draw up for us . . .
a 'Form' of those things which you consider 'necessary unto Christian
piety' . . . [but] of Christ you make no mention."[5] Much more than that,
it was—precisely in its denial of free will—a claim for salvific certainty.
As Martin Brecht reminds us, Luther's experiences in the monastery had
proven to him the vanity of trying to please God through his own meritorious works. Now, however—having recognized that salvation was
utterly separate from his will and was God's concern alone—he could
rest in God's faithfulness and cease worrying about his own failings.[6]

Despite his scathing denunciation of (what he believed to be) Erasmus's Christless piety and his repudiation of the salvific worth of human
behavior, Luther was not principally indisposed to the question of
moral life. His perspective on it, however, not only differed sharply from
Erasmus's but also informed his understanding of election. Fulfilling
God's will was, of course, good and right. But only the elect could do so,
and they not by their own capacity but only by God's work within them.
"'Who (you will say) will endeavor to amend his life?'—I answer, No
man! *No man can* . . . But the Elect, and those that fear God will be
amended by the Holy Spirit; the rest will perish unamended."[7] For
Luther, recognition of one's impotence in this regard was both the necessary precursor to faith and a consequent source of comfort to the elect,

---

[4]M. Luther, *The Bondage of the Will*, trans. H. Cole (Grand Rapids: Eerdmans, 1931), 38.

[5]Luther, *Bondage of the Will*, 29-30.

[6]M. Brecht, *Martin Luther: Shaping and Defining the Reformation, 1521–1532*, trans. J. L. Schaaf
(Minneapolis: Fortress Press, 1990), 234.

[7]Luther, *Bondage of the Will*, 67. Emphasis added. Luther goes on to make the same point about
belief: no one can believe save the elect, who do so only through the Spirit. *Bondage of the Will*, 70.

from whom the burden of works-righteousness was thus lifted. By the same token, however, if nothing we do can merit salvation, then neither can anything we do determine our reprobation. In both cases, human agency and will are rendered salvifically superfluous, with God the sole author of election and reprobation.[8]

It should be evident, then, that Luther's *Bondage of the Will* was not, primarily, a treatise on the doctrine of election. Rather, it was his "great exposition of [his] doctrine of God, of man [*sic*], and of the relationship between [them]."[9] Pivoting on the fundamental issue of the justification of the sinner, this treatise dealt most explicitly with the question of human free will. Insofar as it did, though, it had necessarily also to consider, at least tangentially, the merits—or, more precisely, the lack thereof—of the elect. It cannot be said that Luther advanced the development of our doctrine in any evident way. Nor, however, can it be claimed that he entirely ignored it.

CONTESTING CALVIN

The methodological function of the doctrine of election in John Calvin's theology has been, over time, both assumed and contested. In the second half of the nineteenth century, for example, the father-and-son team of Albrecht and Otto Ritschl departed from orthodox wisdom by disputing the centrality of the doctrine for Calvin's overall program.[10] Theirs were not, however, lone voices. Bruce McCormack has ably demonstrated that their claims were taken up, and then strengthened, by Wilhelm Niesel, "who [was the] first [to] succeed . . . in marginalizing Calvin's doctrine of predestination vis-à-vis his theology as a whole."[11] That it was Niesel who

---

[8] Brecht, *Martin Luther*, 229.

[9] Brecht, *Martin Luther*, 235.

[10] According to Otto Ritschl, Calvin is to be censured for not making predestination as central as Calvin's own theo-logic suggests it ought to have been. See *Dogmengeschichte des Protestantismus*, vol. 3 (Göttingen, 1926). See also A. Ritschl, "Geschichtliche Studien zur christlichen Lehre von Gott," *Jahrbuch für deutsche Theologie*, Bd.13 (1868).

[11] B. L. McCormack, "The Sum of the Gospel: The Doctrine of Election in the Theologies of Alexander Schweizer and Karl Barth," in *Orthodox and Modern: Studies in the Theology of Karl Barth*, ed. B. L. McCormack (Grand Rapids: Baker Academic, 2008), 48.

did this should perhaps not be surprising; he had been a student of Karl Barth's in Göttingen and would likely have heard Barth's own lectures on Calvin, in which Barth also shied away from any unequivocal assertion of the doctrine's overarching significance for the French reformer (although he later revised this view). While Calvin "championed [it] relentlessly," seeing in the doctrine of double predestination the "core and lodestar" of the doctrine of God, Barth also insists in these Göttingen lectures that for Calvin this doctrine was simply "*one* characteristic feature" that in fact took only a secondary and corrective rather than primary and constitutive place in his concept of God.[12] In more recent years, Alister McGrath has tried to split the difference. Election was not, says McGrath, "central" for Calvin, but it was fundamental.[13]

Alexander Schweizer and F. C. Baur, however, epitomize what has long been the more popular view, both that this doctrine stood at the heart of Calvin's theology and that his systematic exposition of the Christian faith is thereby incomprehensible without it.[14] One would be hard pressed these days to defend the view that election was inconsequential to Calvin (which, in any case, is not what either Barth, Niesel, or the Ritschls ever claimed). Yet simply to affirm its importance is hardly satisfactory either. Any nuanced understanding of Calvin's theology of election must recognize that it occupied differing levels of significance for him at different times of his career and therefore also in the various iterations of his *Institutes* as well as in various other works. Moreover, we cannot easily set aside François Wendel's claim that the doctrine of election's increasing importance for Calvin had more to do with ecclesial politics and pastoral observations than

---

[12]K. Barth, *The Theology of John Calvin*, trans. G. W. Bromiley (Grand Rapids: Eerdmans, 1995), 55, 78, 119. Emphasis added.

[13]A. E. McGrath, *Reformation Thought: An Introduction* (Oxford: Blackwell, 1993), 125. See also R. A. Beinert, "The Meaning and Practice of Conversion: A Comparison of Calvin's and Luther's Theologies," *Lutheran Theological Review* 22 (2009–2010); B. Gerrish, "The Place of Calvin in Christian Theology," in *The Cambridge Companion to John Calvin*, ed. D. L. McKim (Cambridge: Cambridge University Press, 2004), 300.

[14]A. Schweizer, *Die Glaubenslehre der evangelish-reformierten Kirche* (Zurich: Oreil, Füssli, 1844); F. C. Baur, *Lehrbuch der christlichen Dogmengeschichte* (1847).

dogmatic necessity.[15] We will explore further the history of interpreting Calvin's doctrine later in the chapter, in which it will also become clear how important it is to differentiate between Calvin's own doctrine of election and the way in which it was adopted by later Calvinists. In the first instance, though, we must return to the approach we have taken throughout this book. That is to say, in order to understand Calvin's doctrine, we must seek to understand it contextually.

CONTEXTUALIZING CALVIN

Born in July 1509 in the strategically significant town of Noyon,[16] Jean (John) Calvin was born into privilege, upward mobility, and social connectedness. His father, Gerard Cauvin, was secretary to the local bishop, attorney to the cathedral chapter, and close friends with the region's leading family, the de Hangests (with whose sons John would go to school). Initially favoring an ecclesiastical career for his son, Gerard sent John to the University of Paris sometime between 1520 and 1521. Strengthening the suggestion that John was, at least at this time, destined by his father for a churchly career, we can note that his education was largely paid for by the benefice of La Gésine, which had been bestowed on John in May 1521 as a "down payment" for his anticipated priestly service.

It is not entirely clear which college John was associated with while in Paris, although it seems likely that he began his education at the Collège de la Marche before transferring to the Collège de Montaigu in 1523. There his primary education was in those subjects that formed the backbone of the bachelor of arts curriculum—logic, metaphysics, ethics, natural sciences, and rhetoric[17]—after which, in about 1527–1528, he

---

[15]F. Wendel, *Calvin: The Origins and Development of His Religious Thought*, trans. P. Mairet (London: Collins, 1980), 264. See also I. John Hesselink, "Calvin's Theology," in McKim, *Cambridge Companion to John Calvin*, 83.

[16]Noyon had long been an important site of intellectual and religious activity. It was made an episcopal see in 531 and, in 768, was the location for Charlemagne's coronation as King of the Franks. Just seven years after John's birth, Noyon hosted the signing of a treaty between Francis I and Charles V, by which France resigned its claim on Naples.

[17]See T. H. L. Parker, *John Calvin: A Biography* (Louisville: Westminster John Knox Press, 2007), 21-28.

became eligible to pursue studies in one of the three professional disciplines of theology, law, and medicine. Notwithstanding his earlier plans, in 1528 Gerard Cauvin ordered John's relocation from Paris to Bourges and Orléans so that John could study law instead of theology. Quite why Gerard made this decision is uncertain, although it may be because of the allegations against him of financial mismanagement of the cathedral chapter for which he was the attorney, which in turn provoked inevitable hostility between Cauvin and the church authorities. In any event, Calvin spent the next five years in and around these two cities, graduating from law in 1533.

The significance of this narrative of planning and re-planning, of movement and upheaval at his father's behest, can be seen in the way Calvin's various relocations, first to Paris and then to Bourges and Orléans, brought him into contact with the diverse intellectual traditions that inevitably influenced him. Paris, for example, and in particular the Collège de Montaigu in which Calvin more than likely spent most of his time until 1528, was typified by the type of conservative Catholicism that was in decline in many other parts of Europe.[18] Aristotelianism and nominalist scholasticism (the so-called *via moderna*), both of which were waning elsewhere, continued to be dominant in Paris. Consistent with this intellectual conservatism, and noting that Luther had turned his back on the semi-Pelagian tendencies of the *via moderna* that was still evident in Paris, it is no wonder that Luther himself was declared a heretic by the theological faculty in April 1521, just as Calvin was arriving in Paris to study.[19]

Yet Paris was not entirely Romanized. Stirrings of reformist sentiment were obvious throughout the city during Calvin's student days there, notably but not only through the sponsorship of the king's sister,

---

[18]G. Haas, *The Concept of Equity in Calvin's Ethics* (Carlisle, UK: Paternoster, 1997), 9.

[19]This, of course, was after Leo X's papal bull *Exsurge Domine* (June 1520), but it was in fact the culmination of the Leipzig Disputation in 1519, which resulted in the universities of Paris and Erfurt being asked to adjudicate between Luther and Eck. The condemnation from Paris was not, therefore, simply a belated rubber-stamping of the pope's decree but rather the consequence of a separate, if not entirely distinct, process.

Marguerite d'Angoulême, and the humanist influences of Jacques Lefèvre d'Étaples. The burning of the Augustinian monk Jean Vallière—France's first Protestant martyr—in a Parisian pig market in August 1523 no doubt also provoked simmering tensions within the city. What Calvin may have thought of all this is unknown. Did he leave Paris in 1528 with Lutheran, or at least reformist, inclinations in mind? That we do not know for certain, but it seems improbable, given that he was a regular preacher in parishes around Bourges through the late 1520s, something that would have been unlikely had his Roman orthodoxy been at all in doubt. Nonetheless, as a profoundly intelligent young scholar, the notion that he was unaware of, or unaffected by, the controversies in Paris between conservative Catholicism and moderate Lutheran reformism is unlikely in the extreme.

But alongside Catholic conservatism, Calvin was also exposed to that other great intellectual trend of the day: humanism. Indeed, once ensconced in his legal studies south of the capital, Calvin found himself in a humanist stronghold. As a distinct pedagogy, humanist methodology had found its way into French law schools primarily through the scholarship of Guillaume Budé. By the time Calvin arrived at Orlèans, humanism had become the most significant intellectual influence there and would make an indelible impression on him, as it did on his friends—professor of Greek Melchior Wolmar, the jurist Nicholas Duchemin, and fellow law student François Daniel. Even a cursory glance through Calvin's commentary from 1532 on Seneca's *De Clementia*, filled with references to classical Greek and Latin writers while citing Scripture itself only three times, illustrates how deeply the humanist impulse had affected him.[20]

Circumstances changed rapidly for Calvin in 1531. The death of his now-excommunicant father and the termination of his legal studies led

---

[20]William Bouwsma puts it this way: "Between 1527 and 1534, and in a more general sense all his life, Calvin inhabited the Erasmian world of thought and breathed its spiritual atmosphere; he remained in major ways always a humanist of the late Renaissance." W. J. Bouwsma, *John Calvin: A Sixteenth-Century Portrait* (Oxford: Oxford University Press, 1988), 13.

him by various means back to Paris as the best place to further his humanist career. But the Paris of 1531–1533 was very different from the Paris he had left in 1528. The evangelically minded Marguerite was now more influential than ever over her brother the king, a turn of events that had in turn strained relations between the court and the Faculty of Theology, particularly as it was represented by its arch-conservative dean, Noel Bédier.[21] There is no direct evidence that Calvin himself became "Protestant" at this time.[22] Nonetheless, he was increasingly associating with known evangelical reformers, among whom were the popular preacher Gérard Roussel, whose sermons Bédier had denounced as heretical, and Nicolas Cop, who, in late 1533, was appointed rector of the University of Paris.[23]

Indeed, Calvin's friendship with Cop was to have far-reaching consequences. In the wake of Cop's infamous commencement lecture of November 1533, both men were forced to flee from Paris to escape, at best, arrest and trial.[24] Having thus fled the city in which he had lived for most of the previous eleven years, and after various detours through places like Basel and then back to Noyon to resign his benefice, Calvin found himself in mid-1536 heading to Strasbourg, the home of Martin Bucer, with whom Calvin had already been in correspondence.[25] Yet he would not arrive there for another two years. Either unluckily or providentially, the war between Francis I and Charles V intervened, forcing Calvin to break his journey in Geneva. From July 1536 on (except for a brief exile, coincidentally in Strasbourg between 1538 and 1541), Geneva was to remain Calvin's home until his death in 1564.

---

[21]See A. Ganoczy, "Calvin's Life," in McKim, *Cambridge Companion to John Calvin*, 4.

[22]Indeed, the timing of his "conversion" remains ambiguous and contested, with scholars variously dating it from 1527 to 1534.

[23]In a letter to his friend François Daniel in October 1533, Calvin spoke warmly of both the queen, Roussel (whom he refers to as Megæra), and Cop. See J. Calvin, letter to Daniel (October 1533), in *The Letters of John Calvin*, ed. J. Bonnet (Eugene, OR: Wipf & Stock, 2007), 1:36-40.

[24]Cop used his inaugural address as rector of the university to urge theological and structural reform within the church along evangelical lines. The backlash against this was so strong that Cop was immediately removed as rector and forced to flee the city. Calvin himself was implicated as he was widely believed responsible for the text of the lecture.

[25]Calvin had written to Bucer from Noyon in early September 1532.

These, then, were the contours of Calvin's early life, by which his adulthood, and his maturing theology, would be decisively shaped. Calvin had begun his life in the bosom of a respectable family that had close connections to the Roman Catholic Church, with the presumption that he would be ordained. But the threads of Calvin's life took him on a much different journey: from a break with the church that was occasioned more by his father's problems than his own, to a career change from ministry to law, to a youthfully exuberant association with Parisian Protestant "troublemakers," and, finally, to the founding of the Genevan reforms. Having thus oriented ourselves to Calvin's historical context, we can now turn our attention to the material content of his theology, particularly his (evolving) doctrine of election.

CALVIN'S CATECHESIS (1537)

With Geneva being his home for the second half of his life, it is no surprise that Calvin produced his most substantial and significant works in that city.[26] Most importantly, of course, this was to include a revision and enlargement of his *Institutes of the Christian Religion*, which had first been written in Basel in 1535 and was then reworked three times before its final iteration in 1559.[27] Predicated on the (false) assumption that this is where Calvin's most sophisticated views on election and predestination can be found, many have turned their attention only to this source. To be sure, we will need to look there shortly. However, Calvin's theology of election is found not only there but indeed in many of his shorter, and even pastoral, pieces. Given that Calvin occupied a teaching office in the city's cathedral from the very start of his time in Geneva, it should not

---

[26]Wulfert de Greef has provided an excellent introductory study of Calvin's major publications, in which he shows that, with the exception of *De Clementia* (1532), the Cop sermon (1533) into which he likely had at least some input, and a handful of forewords to Bible translations, the vast majority of Calvin's published works date from 1536—*after* he had arrived in Geneva. See W. de Greef, *The Writings of John Calvin: An Introductory Guide*, expanded ed., trans. L. D. Bierma (Louisville: Westminster John Knox Press, 2008), 64-68.

[27]In 1539, Calvin enlarged the *Institutes* from six to seventeen chapters, adding a section on the Trinity and on the vital Reformation doctrine of justification by faith alone. In 1543, the work was further expanded to twenty-three chapters, notably with the inclusion of a section on ecclesiology. The changes in 1550 were largely to do with formatting for clarity and ease of use.

be surprising that this theme appears in his sermons, lectures, and catechetical devices. And so, before embarking on a consideration of his treatment of election in the *Institutes*, we will begin by looking briefly at how he tackled the problem in some of these other sources.

One of the first texts produced by Calvin for the Genevan people was his *Instruction in Faith* of 1537. A "clear, serene, and even pleasant statement" of Protestant faith, this short booklet provides some of the first clues to how Calvin was later to develop his doctrine of election.[28] In it he expresses an unequivocal belief in the utter depravity of all humankind. The human heart, he says, "is totally imbued with the poison of sin [and] can emit nothing but the fruits of sin."[29] Nonetheless, while we in our sinfulness "pile upon ourselves an ever heavier judgment," we are not left without the "unspeakable benignity" of "our merciful Father."[30] Of course, there is a catch, a dialectical inequality between sin and salvation. For the mercy to which Calvin refers does not extend effectually to all, even though all are subject to sin. Rather, those who are recalled "from error to the right way, from death to life, from ruin to salvation" are only those *whom [God] pleases* to re-establish as heirs to eternal life."[31] This suggestion of divine foreordination is developed further on in the text when Calvin treats explicitly, albeit very briefly, the subjects of election and predestination.

As he will do in his *Institutes*, Calvin discusses these matters in the broader context of the Christian life rather than as a constituent part of his doctrine of God. He begins by noting the "contrast of attitudes" between believers and unbelievers, which in the section immediately prior he has said is manifested in joyful participation in Christ, on the one hand, and blind rejection of Christ, on the other.[32] As he has hinted

---

[28]J. Leith, "Foreword to the 1992 Edition," in J. Calvin, *Instruction in Faith*, trans. and ed. P. T. Furhmann (Louisville: Westminster John Knox Press, 1992), 13.

[29]Calvin, *Instruction in Faith*, 25.

[30]Calvin, *Instruction in Faith*, 26-27.

[31]Calvin, *Instruction in Faith*, 27. Emphasis added.

[32]Calvin, *Instruction in Faith*, 37-38. Note that those who are numbered among the unbelievers are, for Calvin, to be counted as *plurimi*, a Latin word that is best defined in the superlative as "the greatest number." See *CO* 22:46n34.

earlier, Calvin now makes explicit that both those who have been pre-destined to election, and those who have been rejected, have been so preordained by one and the same eternal counsel (*par mesme conseil*) of God before the world's foundation. How and why this should be the case is, he says, *le grand secret* that we are forbidden to investigate. Rather, we ought to be content in the knowledge that the dispensation of mercy to some is caused by God's goodness alone and that the rejection of the many to God's wrath is entirely just and good, and would still be just and good if there were none who were saved.[33] Indeed, Calvin's emphasis in this short section is on the need for us humbly to accept God's sovereign decision instead of trying to "penetrate the very interior of heaven" in order to understand God's eternal will—a venture that can result only in "miserable distress [*angoisse*] and perturbation."[34]

In other words, Calvin's first catechism does not shy away from declaring a sharp and eternally fixed distinction between two groups of people—the elect (the few) and the reprobate (the many, *plurimi*). He displays no interest in exploring the ins and outs of God's decree any further than this. This reticence is only partly explained by the catechetical context. More important is Calvin's conviction that the eternal decision of God remains rightly veiled from our minds, a veiling that leaves us free to rejoice in our election and so, in our lives, to follow Christ in peaceful assurance.

CALVIN ON ROMANS (1540)

Three years later, while in exile in Strasbourg, Calvin wrote his first exegetical commentary, predictably perhaps on St. Paul's epistle to the Romans.[35] Notwithstanding his intention to write with "lucid brevity,"[36]

---

[33]Calvin, *Instruction in Faith*, 38; CO 22:46.

[34]Calvin, *Instruction in Faith*, 39; CO 22:47.

[35]The commentary was completed in or around October 1539 and published in 1540. John Hesselink has noted that in the decade prior to Calvin's own commentary, no fewer than thirty-five other commentaries on Romans had been published, including those by Bucer, Bullinger, and Melanchthon. See I. John Hesselink, "Calvin on the Relation of the Church and Israel Based Largely on His Interpretation of Romans 9–11," in *Calvin as Exegete*, ed. P. de Klerk (Grand Rapids: Calvin Studies Society, 1995), 98.

[36]John Calvin, "Letter to Simon Grynaeus," in *C-Rom1*, xxiii.

Calvin goes into far greater detail about God's eternal predestining will here than he did in his *Instruction in Faith*. Of more significance than simply the respective lengths of treatment, though, is the fact that in his Romans commentary Calvin seeks to underscore the *continuity* between God's pretemporal decisions and the subsequent unfolding of those promissory decisions through history. As John Haroutunian has put it, Calvin's understanding of predestination is inseparable from his observation of the past and current sufferings of the church. A church under persecution, as Calvin himself had experienced, "had nothing to sustain them except the promises of God." Thus, Calvin sought to direct the faithful to a recognition that their present sufferings were neither the result of unfettered human caprice nor accidental but rather—in conformity to the experiences of the prophets, apostles, and other martyrs, and in particular conformity to Christ himself—had been predestined by God according to the divine purpose.[37] This in turn means that the wickedness of those who persecute the true church is ultimately also within the eternal purpose of God. Like Pharaoh, the enemies of the church, be they within or without it, have been ordained by God *for this very* purpose. Their eventual and justified judgment is thus not only *proximately* caused by their wickedness but *primarily* caused by God's sovereign will. Only by remembering this hermeneutic of continuity between time and eternity can Calvin's doctrine of predestination, as expressed in this commentary, be rightly understood.

Calvin begins his commentary with a summary of Paul's argument that, unsurprisingly, is centered on the doctrine of justification by faith: "The only righteousness available to humankind is the mercy of God in Christ which, offered to us through the gospel, is apprehended by faith."[38] But this subject matter is then parsed by Calvin with particular reference to the distinction between Jews and Gentiles. While, following the

---

[37]J. Haroutunian, "General Introduction," in *C-Rom2*, 41-42.
[38]"*Unica esse hominibus iustitism, Dei misericordiam in Christo: dum, per evangelium oblata, fide apprehenditur.*" CO 49:2. AT.

apostle, the entire commentary is written with this theme in mind, we will focus our attention primarily on the key passages in Romans 9–11.[39]

Uncontroversially, Calvin highlights Paul's own words that the gift of righteousness is neither a consequence of belonging to any particular bloodline nor of lacking that bloodline. Jews and non-Jews stand equal in their sin before God. While this may prompt some to argue that Israel as such therefore has no perpetual significance *post-Christum*, this is not in fact what Calvin says. God's covenant with Israel remains in force because it depends, in the end, not on the faithfulness of any ethnic or religious community but solely on the graciousness of God. "Although they were unbelievers and had broken His covenant, yet their perfidy had not rendered the faithfulness of God void."[40]

Nonetheless, the retention of the covenant's validity does not imply a guarantee of salvation to all within the covenantal bond. While the covenant is made with Abraham and all his descendants, not all of them enjoy the benefits or receive the inheritance of the covenantal promises.[41] Calvin insists there remains a distinction, within both Israel and the church, between the "generally elect" and the "particularly elect." God's general election of those to whom he has bound himself in inviolable covenant sits as the outer perimeter of a more limited "secret election." That is, there is an election of the entire people of Israel (and by extension, the whole of the visible church), which is itself a manifestly gracious act. Yet this general election does not prevent God from also choosing "by his secret counsel" a smaller subset of those "whom he pleases." There is, as Hesselink puts it, an *ecclesiola in ecclesia*, with the promise and gift of election to life subsisting finally only in that "little church."[42]

---

[39]The point here is not to concentrate on Calvin's understanding of the relationship between Israel and the church, or even what he thought Paul's understanding of that relationship was. Rather, it is to glean from this context the pertinent comments about God's election.

[40]CO 49:172. "*Non tamen eorum perfidia exinanitam esse Dei fidem.*"

[41]C-Rom1, 344-46.

[42]Hesselink, "Calvin on the Relation of the Church and Israel," 103. Interestingly, David Martyn Lloyd-Jones explicitly rejects the idea that Calvin ever had a theology of *ecclesiola in ecclesia* but says that Luther did. However, Lloyd-Jones argues this from the perspective of Calvin's views on schism from the corrupted church, not as a function of his doctrine of election. See D. M. Lloyd-Jones, "Ecclesiola in Ecclesia," paper presented at the Puritan and Westminster Conference, 1965.

The recipients of this secret election are characterized by their faith—
that, of course, remains the necessary condition—but that they possess
such faith in the first place is a consequence of their having been predestined by God's secret counsel before their adoption. Faith is thus the
evidence of a person's particular or secret election but not its ground.
To put it otherwise, Calvin gives no account to works or merit: "False,
then, is the dogma, and contrary to God's word,—that he elects or rejects, as he foresees each to be worthy or unworthy of his favor."[43] On
the contrary, whereas faith is the proximate cause of election, and sin
(or unbelief) the proximate cause of reprobation, both faith and sin
(and therefore also election and rejection) have God's eternal will as
their primary cause. "Before [either] are born," says Calvin, "they are
destined to their lot."[44] God's will is not simply part of the reason for
anyone's destiny—it is the only reason. As Calvin puts it, commenting
on Romans 11:32, "There is nothing in any[one] why he should be preferred to others, apart from the mere favor of God; and that God in the
dispensation of his grace is under no restraint that he should not grant
it to whom he pleases."[45]

CALVIN ON MICAH (1550–1551)

Later during his tenure in Geneva, when his authority was being seriously questioned by the city council, Calvin returned to the subject of
election. This time, however, he laid greater emphasis on human culpability. Calvin's Micah sermons, which he delivered between November 1550 and January 1551, are replete with references to God's
wrath and judgment. But they are also full of references to the individual's responsibility for her own end. It is within this context that we
see Calvin speak of the elect and the reprobate. As John Haroutunian
has rightly pointed out, Calvin is at pains to note that the affliction of
God's punishment is experienced by both the reprobate *and* God's own

---

[43]*C-Rom1*, 351.
[44]*C-Rom1*, 370. "*Nunc vero significat, antequam nascantur, iam suae sorti addictos esse.*" CO 49:188.
[45]*C-Rom1*, 443.

people alike. Yet while believers experience this as God's efforts to "reclaim us for himself" and thus turn back in repentance, the reprobate—those "rebellious and incorrigible evildoers"—understand such afflictions to be nothing of any consequence, do not therefore repent, and so store up for themselves their eternal damnation.[46] Their eventual judgment is brought about by their own decisions. The world, in fact, "elects to oppose [God]," propelling itself toward its own damnation.[47] That is to say, in these sermons Calvin does indeed bifurcate humanity into two distinct groups of elect and reprobate, but—more so than he did in the Romans commentary—he pictures them as being at least in part responsible for their own categorization.

Who, then, are the reprobates, whose determination to sin propels them toward their own damnable end? Commenting on Micah 3, Calvin suggests they can be identified, at least in part, with those who were "previously ordained" and called by God but, as a consequence of their falsifying the gospel, are blinded by God and "consign[ed] to the ranks of the reprobate."[48] Not simply unbelievers, the reprobate in this context are those who were once ordained into God's service but who have turned their backs on him.

For Calvin, though, human decisions never trump God's decision. The weight of causation is not purely on the side of humanity's chosen wickedness. That is to say, those who are chosen for rejection and perdition are not so simply by virtue of their actions and unbelief. Were this to be so, then one might reasonably argue the opposite: that merit, works, and worthiness are at least in part causative of election. This, of course, Calvin cannot allow. On the contrary, while it is true that in these sermons there is a greater role accorded to a person's own will and decision as a proximate cause of one's eventual end than is evident in Calvin's Romans commentary, this is not the final word. Rather—as a

[46]J. Calvin, *Sermons on the Book of Micah*, ed. and trans. B. W. Farley (Phillipsburg, NJ: P&R Publishing, 2003), 83.
[47]Calvin, *Micah*, 370-71.
[48]Calvin, *Micah*, 158.

reiteration, in fact, of what he had learned from St. Paul's epistle—Calvin returns to his insistence on the primacy of *God's* will: that he, in accordance with his own righteousness, "has placed them in [that] state."[49]

THE *INSTITUTES* (1559)

We come finally to Calvin's magnum opus, his monumental apology for the Christian faith, the *Institutes of the Christian Religion*. It should first be noted that the final edition of Calvin's *Institutes*—the one we tend to read today—was in fact its fourth iteration, with three earlier versions going back originally to a short primer of only six chapters, which Calvin had published in 1536.[50]

Notwithstanding that the *Institutes* itself has a "biography" and, insofar as it evolved was thus a work of dynamic reflection rather than a static system,[51] it is to the fourth and final edition from 1559 that most people turn in their efforts to discover what Calvin has to say about election and predestination. As we have seen, it was hardly the first time he had treated these themes, having done so repeatedly and intentionally in both catechesis and exegesis over the previous twenty-three years. Likewise, predestination is hardly the most dominating feature of the work. Tucked away in chapters twenty-one to twenty-four of book three—amounting to a mere 5 percent of the total number of chapters and only about 9 percent of the total page count—Calvin's treatment of election is materially slight. However, McCormack is right in his caution that, while predestination may not be the systematic center of Calvin's thinking (indeed, there may not have been any center, as such), we ought not marginalize it as thoroughly as Niesel once did.[52]

---

[49]Calvin, *Micah*, 412.

[50]Work on the first iteration of the *Institutes* went back to at least 1535, with Karl Barth suggesting that the beginnings of that first edition dated from Calvin's short stay in Angoulême in 1534. Barth, *Theology of John Calvin*, 160.

[51]See, for example, B. Gordon, *John Calvin's Institutes of the Christian Religion: A Biography* (Princeton, NJ: Princeton University Press, 2016). Gordon argues that "Calvin would have hated the designation of his *Institutes* as a book of academic theology. That was precisely what it was not." On the contrary, "Calvin knew the faces of those for whom he wrote" and intended the book to be for them, pastorally, as "a book to be lived." See Gordon, xii, xiii.

[52]McCormack, "Sum of the Gospel," 49.

Calvin prefaces all he has to say on this subject by an appeal to Scripture. Acknowledging the inherent difficulties of the subject—a subject that can be categorized only as a "mystery of salvation"—Calvin cautions against metaphysical speculation and instead points enquirers to the witness of the Bible.[53] On that ground, he stakes a claim for his defining argument:

> We shall never feel persuaded as we ought that our salvation flows from the free mercy of God as its fountain, until we are made acquainted with his eternal election, the grace of God being illustrated by the contrast—viz. that he does not adopt promiscuously to the hope of salvation, but gives to some what he denies to others.[54]

Anticipating what will become even more forcefully stated in years to come, Calvin thus admits into the discussion the notion of a double predestination. Christian Link is not incorrect when he says that, for Calvin, the assuredness of election in Christ was a cause for "joyous certainty." Nevertheless, Calvin was also deeply conscious of the shadow side of God's electing decree. There is, as Link puts it, an inevitable "separation of the elected from the condemned" that is proposed in this part of the *Institutes*, such that whatever joyous certainty may be found is felt only by those within the church.[55]

That joy and fear, hope and despair are thus equally possible responses to the fact of God's predestining will is made even more obviously the case when we recognize that, for Calvin, the only basis on which all human merit can be removed from the soteriological equation is if the divine decision to elect or reject is to be found solely in God's freedom.[56] Moreover, this is not the only thing determined in God's freedom. God, writes Calvin, "not only foresaw the fall of the first man . . . ; but also *at his own pleasure* arranged it."[57]

---

[53]*Inst* 3.21.1, 3.23.9.
[54]*Inst* 3.21.1.
[55]C. Link, "Election and Predestination," in *John Calvin's Impact on Church and Society, 1509–2009*, ed. M. E. Hirzel and Martin Sallmann (Grand Rapids: Eerdmans, 2009), 108.
[56]*Inst* 3.21.5.
[57]"C'est que Dieu non seulement a preveu la cheute du premier homme . . . , mais qu'il l'a ainsi

What, then, are we to say? That God freely wishes and actively arranges both the unmerited election of some and the merited reprobation of the many? Yes and no. Certainly, that a small number of God's human creation should attain salvation is due *only* to the sovereign freedom in which God chooses them for life and not death. In contrast, says Calvin, to the opinions of Ambrose, Jerome, and Aquinas, grace is not dispensed by God according to his foreknowledge of the good for which it will be used. The actions of the elect are not in any way meritorious for salvation.[58] But is the rejection of the many solely on account of the sin by which they—and in fact, all—fall under God's wrath? While human sinfulness may indeed be the proximate cause of our rightful punishment, Calvin refuses to allow that human sin is the result merely of God's *permissive* will. On the contrary, it is not the case "that man brought death upon himself" as the sole author of his own fate; rather, this is the consequence of God's own ordination. That is to say, the reprobation of the many is "for no other cause than that [God] is pleased to exclude them from the inheritance which he predestines to his children."[59] This, Calvin insists, does not excuse the sin or the sinner. We remain culpable for all our acts, even those explicitly ordained by God. Yet as Matthew Levering shows, it is here that we reach the nub of the problem: God's permission to allow evil and sin to take place is not separable from his eternal will. "He fully and freely wills this order . . . in which some are left out from union with God."[60]

This, in a nutshell, is Calvin's mature doctrine of election: a doctrine in which everything rests on the eternally free decision of God to order a world in which sin flourishes, in which some are undeservedly rescued, and in which the many are propelled to their destruction by the sins for which they are responsible but which were, in pretemporal eternity, ordained by God for them to do. And in a final, strange irony, whereas

---

voulu." *Inst* 3.23.7.
[58]*Inst* 3.22.8-9.
[59]*Inst* 3.23.1.
[60]M. Levering, *Predestination: Biblical and Theological Paths* (Oxford: Oxford University Press, 2011), 106.

Calvin's pastoral observations by which his consideration of this doctrine was initiated—the observation that some among his flock heard and responded to the gospel, while the majority turned a blind eye and a deaf ear—were predicated on an assumption of human agency, his final iteration of the doctrine rendered effectual *only* the agency of God.

We ought not, however, leave Calvin quite yet, for there is one more significant point that needs to be made, specifically the doctrinal location in which Calvin places election. As we have seen, this doctrine does not take center stage in the 1559 *Institutes*; rather, it is tucked away toward the end of book three. More importantly, it is situated between Calvin's discussion of justification and his ecclesiology. It is, therefore, a doctrine primarily to be preached to those who are indeed elect. As we have seen above, of course, both election and reprobation are deliberate acts of the divine will. In other words, they are both intentional decisions of God, not merely passive permissions. Yet the location of this entire discussion, bookended as it is by justification and ecclesiology, means that the two poles of election and reprobation are unequally weighted. Calvin's emphasis falls more toward God's mercy than his judgment.[61]

As we saw at the start of the chapter, Calvin's life was never without controversy, and neither was this article of his theology. Less than sixty years after the publication of the *Institutes*, it was precisely this doctrine that came under scrutiny—not by Calvin's Lutheran or Catholic opponents but by his own followers.

THE CALVINISTIC CENTRALITY OF PREDESTINATION

In the opening part of this chapter, it was suggested that the pivotal role played by the doctrine of election in Calvin's overall theological architecture has been, paradoxically, both assumed and contested. David Congdon has reminded us that "while it is not inaccurate to see Calvin as a proto-Calvinist," the Calvinist typology of salvation by which Calvin himself is so frequently characterized "often loses contact with

---

[61]D. C. Steinmetz, *Reformers in the Wings: From Geiler von Kaysersberg to Theodore Beza*, 2nd ed. (Oxford: Oxford University Press, 2001), 119.

[Calvin's] actual writings."[62] And as Mark Thompson has said, Calvin
has been "a victim of caricature and misunderstanding." In recent times,
says Thompson, there has even been a "robust industry of 'anti-
Calvinism.'"[63] While Thompson might be right, his comments simply
beg the question: What in fact *is* the relationship between Calvin and
Calvinism? To what extent can the two be identified with each other?

There is, of course, a long and conflicted history to the interpretation
of Calvinism, with much of the historical debate turning on the twofold
question of whether (a) the doctrine of predestination was as central to
Calvin as it was for his followers, and (b) if it was, whether there is a
direct continuity between the two modes of its articulation. Throughout
the nineteenth century, the typical answer to both was yes. As Bruce
McCormack has shown, the foremost advocate of this view was Schleiermacher's pupil, Alexander Schweizer. For Schweizer, one of the two
foundational differences between the Lutheran and Reformed traditions was that, whereas the primary question for the former was *anthro-
pological* (How does humankind receive God's blessing? By faith, not
works), the Reformed tradition begins with a *theological* question (*Who*
blesses or withholds blessing? God alone does).[64] Doctrinally, argued
Schweizer, this theological starting point was articulated through the
doctrine of predestination, with this being the key material principle.
That this was true for later Calvinism is because it had already been true
of the father of Reformed theology, John Calvin.

It has already been noted in this chapter, though, that Schweizer's
views have lost much of their credibility throughout the twentieth
century. Thus, new interpretations have emerged that seek to recast the
relationship between Calvin and Calvinism. In deliberate contrast to
Schweizer, one line of interpretation has sought to highlight the distinc-
tions and differences between Calvin, on the one hand, and Zwingli's

---

[62]D. Congdon, *The God Who Saves: A Dogmatic Sketch* (Eugene, OR: Cascade Books, 2016), 5.
[63]M. D. Thompson, ed., *Engaging with Calvin: Aspects of the Reformer's Legacy for Today* (Nottingham, UK: Apollos, 2009), 11-12.
[64]McCormack, "Sum of the Gospel," 41-42.

successor in Zurich, Heinrich Bullinger, on the other. Or, to put it slightly differently, the interpretive emphasis is placed on the purported differences between a Genevan theology of testamentary covenant and a Rhineland Reformed theology that maintained the conditionality of God's covenant.[65] Some scholars, chief among whom was Thomas Torrance, have deliberately pitted Calvin against the later Calvinists to argue that the seventeenth-century predestinarianism was a radical departure from Calvin's own views.[66] Yet a fourth interpretive strand has sought to find the beginnings of Reformed theology elsewhere than Calvin, in the writings of people such as Theodore Beza (Calvin's successor in Geneva) and Peter Martyr Vermigli. Frank James, for example, argues that the so-called Calvinist doctrine of double predestination owes its origins more to Vermigli—and through him to Gregory of Rimini—than to Calvin himself.[67] In other words, the answer to the twofold question we posed above is not now nearly as clear-cut as it had been for Schweizer. In the last half of this chapter, we will explore this question through two very different Reformed personalities: Theodore Beza and his sometime student, Jakob Arminius.

THEODORE BEZA: THE B BETWEEN A(RMINIUS) AND C(ALVIN)

Born into a French Catholic patrician family, Theodore Beza (1519–1605) rose to rapid prominence following his conversion to Protestantism in 1548. Often cited as Calvin's successor, his biography mirrored that of his more famous colleague in a number of significant ways. Like Calvin, Beza first studied law at Orléans before turning his mind and career to the church and finding a home in Geneva. Both brilliant and prolific, Beza should be regarded more properly as Calvin's coworker, not merely his successor. Although he lived for a further forty years after Calvin's

---

[65]See, for example, L. J. Trinterud, "The Origins of Puritanism," *Church History* 20, no. 1 (1951): 37-57.

[66]See for example, T. F. Torrance, *Scottish Theology from John Knox to John MacLeod Campbell* (Edinburgh: T&T Clark, 1996); and D. Macleod, "Dr T. F. Torrance and Scottish Theology: A Review Article," *The Evangelical Quarterly* 72, no. 1 (2000): 57-72.

[67]F. A. James, *Peter Martyr Vermigli and Predestination: The Augustinian Inheritance of an Italian Reformer* (Oxford: Clarendon Press, 1998).

death, many of his most significant contributions were made during Calvin's lifetime.[68] Some have argued that Beza was theologically more derivative than Calvin, intending less to provide doctrinal advances than to faithfully expound the views of his teacher. Consequently, says David Steinmetz, it has been the assumption of (too) many scholars that Beza's own theology was "nothing more than an echo of Calvin's."[69]

Nonetheless, neither as coworker nor successor was Beza merely a clone of his more famous colleague. There are loci in which significant differences between the two can be identified. For our purposes, the principal place of distinction was in their respective theologies of election. According to Steinmetz, one of the reasons why Calvin's version of this doctrine has so frequently been viewed as both centrally important and unwaveringly harsh is that it has been read through the lens of Beza's theology.[70] Yet the two were quite distinct. In the first place, Beza made much more than Calvin did of the distinction between God's eternal decrees and his subsequent execution of them. This had two important consequences. First, it short-circuited speculation on the act of the eternal willing itself and instead focused attention on the "here and now" enactment of that willed decree in the history of salvation. Second, by positing a strict distinction between the decree and its execution, the notion of a capricious, arbitrary God (whom we can identify in Calvin's thought) is replaced by an emphasis on the sinner, not the willing God, as the proximate cause of reprobation.[71]

> Although he destined those whom he pleased to hatred and destruction by his own mere will from eternity, without regard for any unworthiness of their own, yet he actually hates and destroys only those who deserve hatred and destruction by their own corruption or unrestrained obstinacy.[72]

---

[68]Steinmetz, *Reformers in the Wings*, 114.

[69]Steinmetz, *Reformers in the Wings*, 117.

[70]Steinmetz, *Reformers in the Wings*, 118.

[71]D. Sinnema, "God's Eternal Decree and Its Temporal Execution: The Role of This Distinction in Theodore Beza's Theology," in *Adaptations of Calvinism in Reformation Europe: Essays in Honor of Brian G. Armstrong*, ed. M. P. Holt (Aldershot, UK: Ashgate, 2007), 59.

[72]T. Beza, *Tractationes Theologicae* (Geneva, 1582), 3:438. Cited in Sinnema, "God's Eternal Decree," 61.

In the second place, Calvin, as we have seen, located predestination between the doctrines of justification and ecclesiology as part of his much larger theology of the Christian life. Beza, however, moved it back to its more traditional place within and proceeding from the doctrine of God.[73] This so-called high predestinarianism took shape in the form of a supralapsarian vision of God's eternal willing; that is, God determined the composition of the elect and the damned before envisaging Adam's sin. Materially, the consequence of this move was that the logic of election *must* follow the logic that derives from the attributes of God. Therefore, if God is both righteous and merciful, then predestination must as a necessary consequence be expressed and experienced in both righteous and merciful ways—the bifurcation mapping on to two separate groups of people. The entire drama of salvation flows out according to this pattern, as little more than "philosophical determinism."[74] Structurally and materially, therefore, Beza's theology of election diverged markedly from Calvin's. Significantly, it was Beza's version of predestination that Jakob Arminius learned and subsequently repudiated.

JAKOB ARMINIUS

Jakob Arminius, born and orphaned early in Utrecht, was not, in the first instance, an especially likely controversialist. His initial studies were, we might say these days, broadly ecumenical, in that at Leiden he encountered not only solidly Reformed theology but also advocates of Luther, Zwingli, and the Anabaptists. This, indeed, is an important point to register because—contrary to those who have been (or are) predisposed to reject Arminius out of hand as simply "un-Calvinist"— the reality is that there were at least two distinct camps within the Dutch Reformed church in Arminius's time. Some favored "a form of Erastianism and toleration toward Lutherans and Anabaptists," these typically being the laity (including the lay magistracy). Yet a sizeable portion

---

[73]P. Benedict, *Christ's Churches Purely Reformed: A Social History of Calvinism* (New Haven, CT: Yale University Press, 2002), 302.
[74]Steinmetz, *Reformers in the Wings*, 119.

of the clergy insisted on a far stricter Calvinism, both in theology and polity.[75] Arminius evidently thrived in such an atmosphere. He proved himself so adept in his studies that the powerful merchants' guild of Amsterdam agreed to fund the final three years of his education.

Theodore Beza's first encounter with Arminius was in 1582, when the young Dutch student moved to Geneva to attend its recently established academy, of which Beza had been the inaugural rector. Initially, Beza was highly commendatory, recommending him for a pastoral role in Amsterdam. Indeed, it has long been assumed that Arminius was, at first, a devotee of Beza's own supralapsarian doctrine of predestination. The story goes that he was, as a faithful follower of Beza, tasked by Amsterdam's ecclesiastical court to prepare a defense of Beza's position against "certain good brethren who belonged to the Church of Delft"[76] as well as the humanist Dirck Coornhert, who together had proposed an infralapsarian view, specifically in opposition to Beza. Upon studying their ideas, Arminius found himself so convinced by them that he was unable to write the rebuttal he had been charged with producing.

More recently, however, Carl Bangs has significantly undermined this narrative, arguing instead that the story of his "conversion" is little more than a somewhat clumsy fabrication, the flaws of which have been increasingly overlooked the more it has been handed down as fact.[77] On the contrary, Bangs argues, Arminius had never been enamored with Beza's predestinarianism and had thus never experienced a "conversion" away from it. Most probably, suggests Bangs, Arminius had always held to what Stanglin and McCall refer to as "a sort of conditional predestination."[78]

---

[75]J. M. Pinson, "Jacobus Arminius: Reformed and Always Reforming," in *Grace for All: The Arminian Dynamics of Salvation*, ed. J. D. Wagner and C. H. Pinnock (Eugene, OR: Resource Publications, 2015), 154. The consequence of this should be obvious: there simply was no consensus among Reformed theologians on the nature of predestination or election.

[76]"Funeral Oration," in *The Works of James Arminius DD* (London, 1825), 1:30. Cited in C. Bangs, *Arminius: A Study in the Dutch Reformation* (Grand Rapids: Zondervan, 1985), 138.

[77]Bangs, *Arminius*, 138-41. See also K. D. Stanglin and T. H. McCall, *Jacob Arminius: Theologian of Grace* (Oxford: Oxford University Press, 2012), 28-29.

[78]Stanglin and McCall, *Jacob Arminius*, 29.

What, then, did Arminius teach about predestination that caused so much consternation? Certainly the popular reception of his teachings, that he was simply and self-evidently an "anti-Calvinist" proponent of free will, will not do. The picture is filled with far more color and texture than that. Matthew Pinson, for example, has demonstrated that Arminius's theology was more properly "a further development of Reformed theology rather than a departure from it."[79] However, before delving into Arminius's doctrine of predestination itself, we need to set it in its doctrinal context.

Following his teacher Beza, and contrary to Calvin, Arminius locates predestination within the doctrine of God and alongside creation as the arena in which the objects of predestination engage with God's salvific purposes. Insofar as they are, to that extent, doctrinal "twins," Arminius is adamant that neither predestination nor creation can be at odds with one another. That is, if creation is the exercise of God's sovereign freedom to establish, in love, something that is of him and for him, and therefore intrinsically good (Gen 1:31), then there can be no other action or will of God that would be purposed toward evil, sin, and destruction. This is his most basic objection to the supralapsarian position, according to which God decrees certain members of his creation to an end that is decidedly *not* good (reprobation).[80] Moreover, the fact that supralapsarianism logically entails that such a determination is taken prior to any act of or decree for creation means that God becomes one who condemns *possible* people, not only before they actually sin but even before he decrees that they will sin. This, says Arminius, cannot be considered to be in any way just.[81]

---

[79]Pinson goes on to say, "By focusing on Arminius's doctrine of predestination and its differences with both Calvin and post-Dort Calvinism, people have tended to emphasize Arminius's differences with Calvin and the Reformed tradition rather than his similarities with them. Both Arminians and Calvinists have thought of Arminius's theology as essentially a reaction against Reformed theology rather than the self-consciously Reformed theology that it is." Pinson, "Jacob Arminius," 148.

[80]This, of course, is contrary to Thomas's view that even damnation must be a demonstration of God's love.

[81]Stanglin and McCall, *Jacob Arminius*, 104-5, 108, 112.

This critique of the fundamental inconsistency of the supralapsarian doctrine led Arminius, after lengthy and long-standing debates with his opponents, to a final, mature statement of the doctrine in 1608, which sought to give appropriate (if not equal) weight to both divine foreknowledge, on the one hand, and human freedom, on the other.[82] According to Carl Bangs, Arminius's *Declaration of Sentiments* set out the necessary parameters of a proper doctrine of predestination: (a) it is comprehensible only Christologically; (b) it must be based on Scripture and the historical teachings of the church (namely, the first six centuries and the Reformed confessions of the sixteenth century); and (c) it must preserve both God's innocence from the authorship of sin and his sole authorship of salvation.[83] Within and conforming to these limitations, Arminius's articulation of predestination takes shape in the form of four *logical* (but not chronological) decrees.[84]

The first such decree insists that there is no object of election other than Jesus Christ. In Arminius's own words, "The first specific and absolute decree of God for effecting the salvation of sinful humanity is that he has determined to appoint his Son, Jesus Christ . . . to destroy sin by his own death, to obtain the lost salvation through his obedience, and to communicate it by his power."[85] It is important, for reasons we shall come to shortly, to note that this first decree already assumes the prior determination to create the world and to permit sin. The good creation and the moral autonomy of humanity to sin or not (*potuit . . . non peccare*)[86] are, in other words, the logical antecedents to the first of

---

[82]See J. Arminius, *Arminius and His Declaration of Sentiments: An Annotated Translation with Introduction and Theological Commentary*, trans. W. S. Gunter (Waco, TX: Baylor University Press, 2012).

[83]Bangs, *Arminius*, 350.

[84]The first two are absolute (that is, unconditional), antecedent, and reflective of God's general will; the third is "mechanistic" (in that it provides the effectual *means*); and the fourth is conditional and specific.

[85]Arminius and Gunter, *Arminius and His Declaration of Sentiments*, 135.

[86]Arminius insists that Adam was not preordained to an inevitable fall into sinfulness (he could, in freedom, have chosen not to sin), nor does God take the opportunity presented by Adam's sin to turn his back on humanity and in so doing make sin inevitable in human historical perpetuity. The reason for this is simple: if humans are predetermined to sin (that is, they are incapable of not sinning), then culpability for that sin lies not with humans but with the one who so predetermined

God's absolute decrees. Therefore, it is by definition opposed to the supralapsarian *ordo decretorum*, in which creation and the divine permission to sin are subsequent to a logical prior decree.[87]

The second Arminian decree posits a derivative object of the decree, the community of those who are "in Christ" and who have persevered in faith. This same decree argues also that there are others who, unrepentant and unbelieving, remain in sin and under the judgment of God. Clearly this is a decree of "corporate salvation" and "corporate condemnation" in which the objects of the twofold decree are not individuals but classes of people.[88] Bangs reminds us that the absoluteness—the unconditionality—of this decree is at issue, insofar as the form of this decree begs the question of whether faith and repentance are causal to election and, subsequently, whether unbelief and unrepentance are thus causal of God's wrath. In Bangs's view, both questions must be answered in the negative. On the contrary, faith and repentance are proximate *characteristics* of the elect but not meritorious works: "We give the name of 'believers' not to those who would be such by their own merits or strength, but to those who by the gratuitous and peculiar kindness of God would believe in Christ."[89]

Third, in the first of the two conditional decrees, God has provided the sufficient and necessary means for repentance and faith. In effecting what the first two establish as God's will, this third decree does two things. In the first place, it affirms Christ's place as the executor of the electing will; he is its ground but also its administrator. Second, it denies

---

them—that is, God. Arminius steadfastly refuses to countenance any idea that tends this way, and so the *possibility* of not sinning remains, at least theoretically, on the table for him.

[87] One might be tempted to perceive a preemptive hint of Karl Barth's Christological grounding of election in this decree, insofar as Arminius's position could be, and at Dort was, summarized in this way: *Christus mediator non est solum executor electionis, sed ipsius decreti electionis fundamentum* (*CD* II/2, 67). Yet, as we shall see, Arminius neglected what was key to Barth's doctrine—namely, that Jesus Christ is not only not a decree but the Son of God, and he is the *subject* of election as much as its proper object. Barth himself refused the similarities with the Arminian position. "We cannot unfortunately find much cause for pleasure in such a statement. . . . The general tenor of the Remonstrant theology was so bad . . . [that it can be understood only] in light of the persistence of medieval semi-Pelagianism." *CD* II/2, 67.

[88] Stanglin and McCall, *Jacob Arminius*, 135.

[89] J. Arminius, "Disputation XV: On Divine Predestination," in *The Works of James Arminius, DD*, ed. J. Nichols (London: Longman, Rees, Orme, Brown & Green, 1828), 228.

any notion that the damned are cursed purely on account of God's caprice. Rather, even they have had access to the "necessary and sufficient" means of repentance, so their reprobation is a consequence of their own disobedience *in the face of* what they have received but nonetheless refused. Just as in his reversal of the supralapsarian ordering of the decrees, here too Arminius is determined to protect God from any charge of culpability for sin and to assign the blame solely to the free disobedience of those who refuse the means of salvation. Whereas Calvin would have the reprobate damned proximately by their own sin but eternally by God who so orders the world that they do by necessity sin unto their own destruction, Arminius insists that the end of God's good creation must be good, so he could not with consistency eternally will what is bad.

The fourth and final Arminian decree, and the one by which he is most clearly distanced from his Reformed colleagues, concerns the election of "certain particular persons" and the damnation of particular others. Unlike the second decree, this last treats the ultimate fate of individuals, not anonymous classes. As Arminius puts it, "God decreed to save and condemn certain specific persons." On the face of it, there is nothing greatly controversial about this. Yet it is precisely at this point that Arminius falls into difficulty, for it is in relation to this decree that the problem of divine foreknowledge arises. It is, he insists, "in the foreknowledge of God, by which he knew from eternity . . . which persons . . . through his prevenient grace would believe and through prevenient grace would persevere, and also who would not believe and persevere."[90] That is to say, Arminius reverses the order preferred by both supra- and infralapsarianism, to make God's eternal willing a consequence of his (logically) prior knowledge. To put it slightly differently, God, already armed with the knowledge of who will accept his grace, consequently chooses to elect them.[91]

---

[90]Cited in Stanglin and McCall, *Jacob Arminius*, 135.
[91]Pinson says that "for Arminius, the primary problem with . . . [both the] supralapsarian [and] infralapsarian [positions] was that they did not root predestination in the mediatorial work of Christ. It was as though Christ and his work were an afterthought. In both supralapsarianism and infralapsarianism, God decreed first which individuals would be elected and which would be reprobated.

In summary, these four decrees constitute the structure and content of Arminius's mature doctrine of predestination. In its most basic form, it says this: God wills the election and salvation of all people but, in his eternal foreknowledge, recognizes those who will accept his grace through faith, and in logical subsequence he predestines them specifically for election to life. Faith is thus a precondition of election but is not thereby a meritorious work. Indeed, contrary to the accusations of his contemporary and subsequent detractors, Arminius repudiates all forms of Pelagianism. While the autonomy of human will and the potential to not sin loom large in Arminius's thinking, they are not causal of election and, by themselves, are incapable of moving anyone Godward. Human nature, says Arminius, which is utterly "destitute of grace and God's spirit . . . tends directly downward to those things that are earthly."[92] The freedom of the human will notwithstanding, fallen humanity needs the "prevenient, internal operation of God's grace" in order to be able to come to faith and thus accept salvation.[93] As Robert E. Picirilli has put it, "The unconditionality of God's sovereign 'decisions' . . . does not necessarily mean that all the ends God has purposed are achieved unconditionally or necessarily." Rather, the point is that God *unconditionally* decrees that election and reprobation are *conditioned* on the belief or unbelief of the individual concerned.[94]

Throughout this overview of Arminius's mature statement on predestination, we have noted the tension between the freedom of God's volition and divine knowledge, and also the freedom of the *human* will to believe or not believe. As hinted above, Arminius's capacity to retain this tension with doctrinal integrity was due in large part to his conversation with certain extra-confessional—that is, Roman Catholic—

Only then did he decree to appoint Christ as mediator for the salvation of the elect. This is backward, Arminius argued. It 'inverts the order of the gospel.'" Pinson, "Jacob Arminius," 158.

[92]J. Arminius, "Apology Against Thirty-One Articles," article 15, in Nichols, *Works of James Arminius*, 15.

[93]Stanglin and McCall, *Jacob Arminius*, 161.

[94]R. E. Picirilli, *Grace, Faith, Free Will: Contrasting Views of Salvation—Calvinism and Arminianism* (Nashville: Randall House, 2002), 45.

contemporaries. Eef Dekker, for example, has shown that significant elements of the Arminian conclusion are drawn from—if not in fact made possible by—the theory of so-called "middle knowledge" (*scientia media*), as proposed by the sixteenth century Spanish Jesuit, Luis de Molina.

Medieval theories of divine knowledge presupposed two types of knowledge available to God: *scientia naturalis* (natural knowledge), which is God's knowledge of Godself, and of the totality of all other possibilities outside of God's being; and *scientia liberalis* (free knowledge), which is God's knowledge of actualized reality, that is, of those possibilities—and only those possibilities—that God has, in the freedom of his own willing, chosen to bring into being. The content of God's free knowledge is thus a sub-set of the content of God's natural knowledge. As Dekker has shown, however, the potential difficulty with this model is that human freedom of will is left unaccounted for. If God determines which out of the totality of all possibilities are to be realized, then included in this sub-set of actualized possibilities are all human acts of will.[95]

Molina's solution was to propose a "middle knowledge" "by which [God] . . . saw in his own essence what each such faculty would do with its innate freedom were it to be placed in this or in that or, indeed, in infinitely many orders of things."[96] In other words, before freely deciding what sub-set of all possibilities will be actualized, it is open to God to know what individual humans will freely choose to do, given certain particular circumstances: "By creating specific circumstances, God infallibly knows what a human being will freely do; for instance, whether or not he will reject God's grace."[97]

Arminius was not only aware of this distinction proposed by Molina, he employed it. In one of his *Public Disputations*, he defines *scientia*

---

[95]E. Dekker, 'Was Arminius a Molinist?', in *Sixteenth Century Journal* XXVII, no. 2 (1996): 339.
[96]L. de Molina, *On Divine Foreknowledge: Part IV of the Concordia*, trans. A.J. Freddoso (Ithaca: Cornell University Press, 1988), 4.52.9. See Dekker, 'Was Arminius a Molinist?', 339.
[97]Dekker, 'Was Arminius a Molinist?', 339.

media as "that by which [God] knows that if *this* happens, *that* will take place." This last form of knowledge, he goes on to say, "precedes the free act of [human] will, but sees something future by hypothesis."[98] In other words, by appropriating Molina's *scientia media*, Arminius was able to affirm unequivocally the sovereignty of God to choose certain possibilities for realization, and at the same time to affirm, equally without qualification, the freedom of individuals nonetheless to decide this way or that—for belief or unbelief. How? Because the realized possibilities freely chosen by God already include within themselves God's knowledge of what people will freely choose in whichever circumstances they (by God's free choice) happen to find themselves.

As should be clear by now, Arminius's doctrine was at odds with what both Beza and Calvin had to say on the subject. Nevertheless, Arminius insisted that Reformed confessional statements, and indeed the majority of doctrinal history, were on his side. The "Papists, Anabaptists, and Lutherans" were, he said, as vehemently opposed to any supralapsarian view as he, and one would search in vain for any supralapsarian comfort in any patristic work before Augustine.[99] No matter how much he pleaded his own orthodoxy, however, Arminius died knowing that his opponents were stronger than he. Merely a decade after his death, the Arminian-influenced Remonstrants were condemned at the Synod of Dort, with the most outspoken of them exiled to other lands. While the Canons of Dort did not explicitly anathematize either the Remonstrant party or Arminius himself, they nevertheless codified a "hard Calvinism"—(too) often depicted in its expurgated caricature, TULIP—which in the centuries since has become, if not entirely accurately, almost synonymous with the post-Reformation Reformed tradition.[100]

---

[98]J. Arminius, *Public Disputation*, 'On the Nature of God', 4.43.

[99]Stanglin and McCall, *Jacob Arminius*, 111, 131.

[100]Richard Muller helpfully reminds us that the TULIP acronym (that "acronym of questionable pedigree"!) can be associated only anachronistically with the Canons of Dort. There is no evidence, says Muller, that the acronym was endorsed or even mooted as a concise summary of Calvinism prior to the nineteenth century. Furthermore, the Canons of Dort were not intended to be a timeless summary of Reformed orthodoxy but rather more modestly as an "interpretive codicil" to the already existing confessional documents, with specific reference to Remonstrant

We have seen through this chapter that the doctrine of election was the site of some of the most vigorous debates during the hundred or so years of Continental reform. Of course, other points of controversy sparked their own interconfessional hostilities. Most obviously, debates around justification and sacramental belief drove wedges between Protestants and Rome, and even between the different Protestant factions. With regard to election, however, while the arguments were no less acrimonious, they were located primarily within the Reformed wing of Protestantism. Instead of this doctrine causing rifts *between* confessional traditions, it was a cause of division within one tradition.

Naturally, all of these Reformation-era debates took place within a deeply contested religious context. As we shift gears to explore the doctrine of election in the nineteenth century, however, we will find that it was no longer primarily *confessional* differences that formed the background of its articulation but rather the emergence of increasingly strong nationalisms.

---

ideas only. (That is, the five Canons of Dort corresponded to the Five Articles of Remonstrance.) Thus, to employ TULIP as an accurate shorthand for the totality of Calvinism per se is both historically nonsensical and theologically naive. R. A. Muller, *Calvin and the Reformed Tradition: On the Work of Christ and the Order of Salvation* (Grand Rapids: Baker Academic, 2012), 55, 58-59.

PUBLIC AND PRIVATE ELECTION
IN THE NINETEENTH CENTURY

IN A LETTER FROM THE SUMMER OF 1944, the German pastor-martyr Dietrich Bonhoeffer wrote from his prison cell in Tegel that the future of theology—indeed, the future of every person before God—was to seek ways of speaking and being *etsi deus non daretur*, "as if there were no God."[1] In truth, though, that future was not something for only a postwar world; it had in fact been true from the start of the seventeenth century as the archetypal characteristic of "modernity." Through the years of Enlightenment, social and industrial unrest, and political revolution, European society had gradually learned to establish new cultural norms and forms on foundations other than ecclesiastical and religious authorities.[2] Alec Vidler has expressed it well. Taking the French Revolution as his starting point rather than the *Aufklärung*, he nonetheless makes the same point that the whole tumultuous period, between the Remonstrant controversy and the close of the eighteenth century, was the "great dividing-line in the political

---

[1] D. Bonhoeffer to E. Bethge, 16 July 1944. Cited in *DBWE* 8:476. The phrase comes originally from the seventeenth-century Dutch jurist Hugo Grotius (1583–1645), although Reinhold Seeberg finds a similar expression in Martin Luther's model of statecraft—namely, that the temporal authorities should govern *"als were keyn Gott da."* See Luther's sermon on Ps 127 from 1524, in *WA* 15:373. For a recent essay on Bonhoeffer's particular use of Grotius's maxim, see Kevin Lenehan, *"Etsi deus non daretur*: Bonhoeffer's Useful Misuse of Grotius' Maxim and Its Implications for Evangelisation in the World Come of Age," *Australasian Journal of Bonhoeffer Studies* 1, no. 1 (2013): 34-60.

[2] G. Green, "Modernity," in *The Blackwell Companion to Modern Theology*, ed. G. Jones (Oxford: Blackwell, 2004), 163.

history of Europe, the sign of the downfall of the *ancien régime*, a sort
of atomic bomb of which the fallout is still at work." Vidler goes on to
say that it was "a beginning as well as an end: the beginning of a still
continuing series of attempts to build new structures to take the place
of the system that had collapsed" and of which the church had been an
integral part.[3] Of course, one of the foundations of this newly conceived society was the determination to live *etsi deus non daretur*.

It can hardly be a surprise, then, to read that European religious
thought in the nineteenth century, when understood in the context of
these new social norms, has been described as "a curious puzzle." How
could it not have been, when the combined force of the political and
intellectual revolutions over the previous century or so had rendered
even the *possibility* of theology, of "God-talk," deeply problematic?[4] If
one was to live—even live religiously—in these times, as though there
were no God, then religious speech about God was inevitably conflicted and confusing. One consequence of this "possibility problem,"
however, was that, rather than theology and religious thought more
generally tailing away into obscurity, the nineteenth century witnessed
a remarkable burgeoning of theological ideas. Some of these ideas were
hailed as "creative breakthroughs" or as "temporary detours from the
true line of [doctrinal] development," while others were repudiated as
"expressions of infidelity and apostasy."[5] With ecclesial authority no
longer strong enough to dictate confessional obedience, and with

---

[3]A. Vidler, *The Church in an Age of Revolution*, Penguin History of the Church 5 (1961; repr.,
London: Penguin Books, 1990), 11.
[4]C. Welch, *Protestant Thought in the Nineteenth Century*, vol. 1, *1799–1870* (New Haven, CT: Yale
University Press, 1972), 1, 5.
[5]Welch, *Protestant Thought*, 1. There was also, of course, the substantial influence of Pietism, by
which Lutheranism and eventually the Reformed traditions were deeply touched. In the brief
overview that follows, while there is a sense of "earthy naturalness" to the religious philosophies
of people like Schelling, Fichte, Schlegel, and others, this ought not be understood as the polar
opposite of Pietism, despite the "supranaturalism" by which the latter was distinguished. On the
contrary, without wishing to draw or even imply a direct and unbroken line between Pietism and
racist nationalism, it was nonetheless Pietism's emphasis on both the possibility and necessity of
divine revelation that, when stripped of its Christological content, could be and was transposed
onto new forms of revelation through media such as "blood," *Kultur*, and an ethnic-national
"essence" (e.g., *Volkstum*).

Scripture itself unshackled from its uncritical canonicity and regarded, instead, as an artifact of *wissenschaftlich* curiosity, Continental theology ranged into diverse, uncharted, and sometimes bizarre territory.

Doctrine was also impacted by the political upheavals of the day, not least in the context of notions of "belonging." It is hardly a coincidence that the diversification of theological thought in this period we have been discussing coincided with the rapid emergence of the European nation-states, from around the time of the Peace of Westphalia (1648).[6] The more clearly national boundaries became etched on maps, the more strongly was the idea of distinct national identities impressed into peoples' consciousness as a marker of both belonging together and, correspondingly, separating from others. If, as we have noted in earlier chapters, the medieval *corpus Christianum* was, to all extents and purposes, contiguous with the geography of Christian Europe, by the nineteenth century the identity of "true Christians" was being defined more explicitly by ideas of nationalistic patriotism, the special sanctity of particular lands, and the assumption of collective national characteristics. As Hugh McLeod has said, in different ways and throughout different countries,

> nationalism and Christianity came to be intertwined in nineteenth-century Europe. National identities were to an important degree defined by reference to specific Christian traditions, their history, their forms of worship, and their heroic figures. At the same time nationalism often came to be seen as an integral part of Christianity.[7]

---

[6]The Peace of Westphalia has long been regarded as the origin of the modern state system, at least in terms of international diplomatic and trade relations. See, for example, G. Poggi, *The Development of the Modern State: A Sociological Introduction* (Stanford, CA: Stanford University Press, 1978), 89; and H. J. Morgenthau, "The Problem of Sovereignty Reconsidered," *Columbia Law Review* 48, no. 3 (1948): 341. More recently, this status has been called into question. S. Beaulac, "The Westphalian Model in Defining International Law: Challenging the Myth," *Australian Journal of Legal History* 8, no. 2 (2004): 181-214; D. Croxton, "The Peace of Westphalia of 1648 and the Origins of Sovereignty," *The International History Review* 21, no. 3 (1999): 569. Nevertheless, whether or not the Peace of Westphalia was itself the originator of modern state theory, the emergence of European nation-states can be dated with reasonable accuracy to the general period.
[7]H. McLeod, "Christianity and Nationalism in Nineteenth-Century Europe," *International Journal for the Study of the Christian Church* 15, no. 1 (2015): 7.

France vividly encapsulated this mood in its "La Marseillaise" from 1792 by calling on its citizens, in their "sacred love of the Fatherland" (*la Patrie*), to take up arms lest the "impure blood" of foreigners should "soak [their] fields."[8] Indeed, the religious mythology of French nationalism sanctioned—and sanctified—the repelling of such defilement on the basis that France was, at least since the time of King Clovis, the "First Daughter of the Church."[9] In England, too, national destiny and a theology of divine mission coincided. "The rise of the United Kingdom as a world power was connected to the religion of its people," the British Empire being nothing less than "God's instrument for the great work of spreading His gospel throughout the world."[10]

This odd confluence of ardent nationalistic singularity and Romantic Christianity was no more clearly demonstrated than in the divinization of the Germanic *Volkstum* from the early 1800s. In an unfinished poem by Friedrich Schiller from 1801, "Deutsche Größe," Schiller spoke with evangelical zeal of the mission to spread the blessings of Germanic culture to the ends of the earth. The German, he said, is "the core of humanity" and "has been chosen [*erwählt*] by the world spirit to work on the eternal edifice of the development of humanity."[11]

Just a few years later in 1808, in an extended paean of praise to the Germanic people and language, Johann Fichte similarly endowed German-ness with a unique divine merit. Putting aside the irony that, at this point, Germany as a single nation did not exist, Fichte nonetheless proclaimed that the German people were the *Urvolk* who "bore

[8]The invading foreigners of "impure blood" were, at the time in which the song was written, from Austria and Prussia.
[9]According to legend, the Frankish king Clovis (ca. 466–511), who was converted from paganism by his Christian bride Clotilde, was baptized and crowned by St. Remigius in the cathedral at Rheims, the chrism having been delivered to Remigius by the Holy Spirit himself. This one event became chronicled as both the foundation of the French nation, the establishment of its monarchy, and the proof of the monarchy's sacredness.
[10]S. Brown, *Providence and Empire: Religion, Politics and Society in the United Kingdom, 1815–1914* (2008; repr., London: Routledge, 2013), 3.
[11]F. von Schiller, "Deutsche Größe," in *Schillers Werke. Nationalausgabe*, 2 I, 431-36. Cited in M. Oergel, *Culture and Identity: Historicity in German Literature and Thought, 1770–1815* (Berlin: Walter de Gruyter, 2006), 149.

in themselves a pledge of eternity."[12] It followed that true patriotism lay in accepting the premise that the German people were both eternal and supreme: "Among all modern peoples it is in you that the seed of human perfectibility most decidedly lies, and to whom the lead in its development is assigned."[13]

Were the German people to fail in their task, he said, they would take with them "the hope of the entire human race, of any salvation from the depths of its misery."[14] Of course, Fichte knew his Kantian universalism too well to lapse into a "naively chauvinistic" nationalism. Rather, his adulation of German-ness was based on his teleological philosophy of history. Germanic eternality meant that it was the German people "who were to usher in a new epoch in history by creating a new, more spiritual world." In due course, then, "the proper manifestation of [that] new spiritual world [would be] the German nation."[15]

Fichte's more famous contemporary, Georg Hegel, expressed the same sentiments a decade later when, in his *Philosophy of Right* (1820), he grandly declared the sovereignty of the historically absolute state as an "earthly divinity" (*Irdisch-Göttliches*).[16] While in these lectures he did not single out Germany for particular praise—on the contrary, he attacked the musings of German constitutional theorists as "the most vapid" of all[17]—his *Lectures on the Philosophy of History* (1822–1823) struck a different tone and extolled German virtue with Fichtean excess: "The German Spirit is the Spirit of the New World. Its aim is the realization of absolute Truth as the self-determination of Freedom . . . The destiny of the German people is, to be the bearers of the Christian principle."[18]

---

[12]W. Steed, preface to A. Kolnai, *The War Against the West* (New York: Viking Press, 1938), 8.

[13]J. G. Fichte, *Addresses to the German Nation*, trans. I. Nahkimovsky, B. Kapossy, and K. Tribe (Indianapolis: Hackett Publishing, 2013), 187.

[14]Fichte, *Addresses to the German Nation*, 188.

[15]A. Fiala, "Fichte and the *Ursprache*," in *After Jena: New Essays on Fichte's Later Philosophy*, ed. D. Breazeale and T. Rockmore (Evanston, IL: Northwestern University Press, 2008), 188-89.

[16]G. F. W. Hegel, *The Philosophy of Right*, trans. H. B. Nisbet (Cambridge: Cambridge University Press, 1991), §272 (Addition), 307.

[17]Hegel, *Philosophy of Right*, §272, 305.

[18]G. F. W. Hegel, *Lectures on the Philosophy of History*, trans. J. Sibree (London: G. Bell & Sons, 1914), 354.

That the German people had a divine destiny was inextricably connected with a widespread sense of having been, in Schiller's own words, "elected." As the poet and political historian Peter Viereck put it, Hegel was outlining the "possibility of a new Chosen People to replace the Jews, whose mission [was] *passé*," and he was even bold enough to predict that "the Germanic peoples would now be the teleological agents of the God of History."[19]

It was into this context of social upheaval, intellectual and industrial revolution, and, most importantly from our perspective, nationalistic Christianity that arguably the greatest of all theologians in the nineteenth century, Friedrich Schleiermacher, was to speak and leave his indelible mark. As we turn now to consider his particular contribution to our theme, we ought to ask ourselves how, and to what extent, this mood of nationalized predestination shaped his own understanding of election.

FRIEDRICH SCHLEIERMACHER

Born in 1768 in the eastern Prussian city of Breslau,[20] Schleiermacher was educated initially at the Moravian school in Niesky before continuing his seminary training in the town of Barby, three hundred kilometers to the west.[21] On the whole, his years in Niesky were happy; his time at Barby

---

[19]P. Viereck, *Meta-Politics: The Roots of the Nazi Mind* (New York: Capricorn Books, 1965), 288. See also my *Covenanted Solidarity: The Theological Basis of Karl Barth's Opposition to Nazi Antisemitism and the Holocaust* (New York: Peter Lang, 2001), 64. The German historian Hartmut Lehmann puts it this way: "During and after the Franco-Prussian war, many German Protestants came to believe not only that God had granted them a victory over their archenemy, but also that by doing so God had significantly elevated them. In the years that followed, the notion of a new covenant between God and the German people was . . . filled with considerations of power politics, and it was closely linked to considerations rooted in Darwinism. After the 1880s . . . the belief in a new covenant gradually gave way to ideas of German uniqueness and German superiority based on power and race." See H. Lehmann, "'God Our Old Ally': The Chosen People Theme in Late Nineteenth- and Early Twentieth-Century German Nationalism," in *Many Are Chosen: Divine Election and Western Nationalism*, ed. W. R. Hutchison and H. Lehmann (Minneapolis: Fortress Press, 1994), 104.

[20]Breslau, along with most of the rest of Silesia, had been annexed by Prussia in the War of the Austrian Succession in the 1740s. Under the terms of the Potsdam Agreement of 1945, Breslau was placed under Polish administration and its name changed officially to Wrocław.

[21]The connection between Niesky and the Moravian Brethren was intimate, the town having been founded in 1742 by Moravians fleeing Roman Catholic persecution. It was also close to Herrnhut

was far less so. According to Thandeka, at Niesky Schleiermacher was captivated by the Moravians' combination of deep piety and their humanist-flavored education, by which his "mind and heart were given the grace to be one." In Barby, however, that "unity between head and heart was sundered."[22] Yet in both places he found himself confronted and repelled by some of the harsher Brethren doctrines. Schleiermacher himself noted that he had been plagued by a fear of eternal punishment from the age of eleven, and he suggested in his autobiography that, on commencing at Barby, he was immediately exercised not only by that division between mind and spirit of which Thandeka speaks but also by an internal conflict between sin and damnation:

> Now commenced another struggle generated by the views held among the United Brethren relative to the doctrines of the natural corruption of man and of the supernatural means of grace. . . . My own experience furnished me with abundant evidence in favor of the truth of the first of these two chief pillars of the mystic-ascetic system, and at length I came to look upon every good action as suspicious. . . . I was thus in that state of torture . . . , my belief in the moral faculty of man having been taken from me.[23]

Two years later, his fearful preoccupation with human corruption was replaced by a more hopeful—but for that reason more controversial—sense of God's will. In a letter to his father, he announced that he could no longer believe that Christ's death was "a vicarious atonement," not only because Jesus himself never declared it to be so but also because it was inconsistent with God's creative design: "I cannot believe [a vicarious atoning death] to have been necessary, because God, who evidently did not create men for perfection, but for the pursuit of it, cannot possibly intend to punish them eternally, [just] because they have not

---

—only forty-five kilometers away—where, in 1722, Ludwig von Zinzendorf had granted the Moravian Brethren land. That is, Niesky was barely thirty years old when Schleiermacher went there as a young student.

[22]Thandeka, *The Embodied Self: Friedrich Schleiermacher's Solution to Kant's Problem of the Empirical Self* (Albany: State University of New York Press, 1995).

[23]F. D. E. Schleiermacher, "Autobiography," in *The Life of Schleiermacher, as Unfolded in His Autobiography and Letters*, vol. 1, ed. F. Rowan (London: Smith, Elder & Co., 1860), 6-7.

attained it."[24] As we shall see, the placement of creation, justification, and election alongside each other in this letter is not coincidental. On the contrary, it contributes to Schleiermacher's understanding of God's predestining will.

In his *Glaubenslehre*, Schleiermacher pivots his doctrine of justification on the insistence that the divine act of redemption is in every case initiated by the miraculous activity of Christ: "[The] whole process is Christ's efficacious action. . . . Thus all these workings of divine grace are supernatural insofar as they rest on God's being in the person of Christ and also actually proceed from this source."[25] Nonetheless—and despite the all-too-frequent assumption that his signature motif, *Gefühl*, can be reducible to a naive inwardness—there remains a necessary worldliness, or better, historicity, to this divine activity. "All these workings of divine grace are also historical and history-forming, thus natural."[26] As Kevin Vander Schel has said, redemption both originates from Christ's divine will and work and is "conditioned by the ongoing development of the natural and historical world."[27] In other words, the *Wunder* of Christ's appearance is the unity of God's activity and its actualization in a very specific geotemporal context.

The point that Schleiermacher is trying to make here, and that he had earlier tried to make to his father, is that the moments of creation and justification are not separable either from each other or from God's eternal willing. He says that in God "there is no difference between decision and activity" and that "the divine activity [by which Schleiermacher means the uniting of divinity and humanity in the incarnation] is only decree, and, as such, it is already identical with God's decree of humanity's creation, and it is contained in that decree.[28] The consequence of this is that

---

[24]F. Schleiermacher to J. G. Schleiermacher, 21 January 1787. Cited in Rowan, *Life of Schleiermacher*, 46-47.

[25]*CF*, §108.5, 706.

[26]*CF*, §108.5, 706.

[27]K. Vander Schel, *Embedded Grace: Christ, History, and Reign of God in Schleiermacher's Dogmatics* (Minneapolis: Fortress Press, 2013), 117.

[28]*CF*, §97.2, 594.

there is only one eternal and general divine decree regarding justification ... [which is], in turn, the same thing as Christ's mission [*Sendung*].... In addition, this decree, in turn, is also simply at one with that decree regarding the creation of the human race, inasmuch as the human race first reaches its perfect end in Christ. Moreover, since in God thinking and willing, willing and doing are functions not to be divided, all of this ensuing process is simply comprised of *one* divine act for the purpose of altering our relationship with God, the temporal manifestation of which is begun in Christ's existence as a human being and from which the collective new creation of humanity proceeds.[29]

Schleiermacher does not, therefore, reject the Reformed notion of an eternal decree of election. What he does, though, is refuse to buy into the supralapsarian/infralapsarian debates regarding the proper ordering of the divine decrees. Unlike Arminius, who took issue with both lapsarian positions but did not deny that there was an ordering of multiple decrees, Schleiermacher insists on the *singularity* of the decree that in itself encompasses creation, election, incarnation, and redemption. As Gockel puts it, according to Schleiermacher, "one can speak of God's intention in the singular but not in the plural."[30] Moreover, far from being a *decretum horibile* (Calvin's "terrifying decree"), this decree is nothing more or less than the expression of God's "divine good pleasure" (*das göttlich Wohlgefallen*). While in and of itself this good pleasure is value neutral—it could, that is to say, simply express in theoretical terms what God might want, be that good or bad, creation or destruction, election or reprobation—Schleiermacher parses it in a distinctly positive fashion, as indeed he is compelled to by the logic of its singularity. In other words, this divine good pleasure, which is itself the substance of the eternal decree, is ontologically (but not, of course, temporally) the simultaneity of the reign of God, the ongoing act of creation and its sustenance (what Schleiermacher calls "the development of the natural world"), and the fullness

---

[29]*CF*, §109.3, 718-19.
[30]M. Gockel, *Karl Barth and Schleiermacher on the Doctrine of Election: A Systematic-Theological Comparison* (Oxford: Oxford University Press, 2007), 23.

of Christ's redemptive work through both the incarnation and the mission of the Holy Spirit:

> Just as the entire world is ordered by God in such a way that God could say, "it is all good" . . . , so too, if we consider the reign of God as a whole that is complete in itself, we can say only that it is determined as it is solely by the divine good pleasure. That being the case, everything that belongs to Christ's being as he is, on the one hand, and the entire internal multiplicity of the human race in time and space, from which multiplicity the reign of God is formed through Christ, being as it is . . . , are both determined by the divine good pleasure.[31]

The fact that God's kingdom and the redemptive activity of Christ are self-evidently good and that creation and its historical progression—and specifically the creation of humanity—are ordered with them by the same eternal decree of divine good pleasure entails an essential goodness of creation as such that is neither ultimately nor eternally determined for destruction. As Vander Schel words it, this decree of divine good pleasure is "all-inclusive" and "all-encompassing," connecting all of God's activity—in heaven, on earth, and under the earth—together in the singularity of God's eternally loving will.[32] Insofar as God has united himself to humanity through Christ, the effects of this union are such that the end of Christ's redemptive work extends "to the regeneration of the whole human race."[33]

Having in mind, therefore, this unity and interconnectedness of decree and action, and the foundation of both in the goodness of God's good pleasure, we can ask, How, then, did Schleiermacher understand the traditional bifurcation of humanity into two distinct groups of elect and reprobate? Or to return to a theme from the earlier part of this chapter, in the midst of increasingly nationalistic expressions of election and mission, belonging and segregation, how did Schleiermacher articulate a theology of eternal identity?

---

[31]*CF*, §120.3, 790-91.
[32]Vander Schel, *Embedded Grace*, 132-33.
[33]*CF*, §118.1, 772.

ELECTION IN THE GLAUBENSLEHRE

Consideration of a doctrine of election is, for Schleiermacher, necessarily embedded within the doctrine of the church and has as its twin the doctrine of the communication of the Holy Spirit. The "concept of election through the emergence of the church," says Schleiermacher, is "a matter of the divine government of the world." In this context, election is a backward glance to the world out of which, in order to "fashion the church," its members have come; the communication of Spirit, meanwhile, is the enabling of those church members to keep working together in the constantly new task of that churchly fashioning.[34]

Insofar, then, as Schleiermacher draws an explicit connection between church, election, and Spirit (and noting at the outset that the church consists of those who have been separated from the world), he distinguishes between those in what he calls the "outer circle," the "locus for the preparatory workings of grace," and those who inhabit the "inner circle," "from which these preparatory workings proceed." Schleiermacher affirms that those who populate the outer circle of preparation are indeed called, but it remains the case that only those who have subsequently been introduced into the inner circle can rightly be termed the elect.[35] This, he hastens to add, is not on the basis of any difference in worthiness, because we all "have wholly the same status . . . of common sinfulness."[36]

But exactly who are the people in these two circles? Importantly, the people of the outer circle are not the sum of all non-Christians, for Schleiermacher insists that not all non-Christians are called. Rather, the composition of that outer circle is those who have been drawn near the church's community after having heard the proclamation of the gospel and who are thus able to be moved, or influenced, by those in the inner circle who have in turn been regenerated by the Holy Spirit. That is, the "outer circle" people are, we might say, "nearly Christian," or

---

[34]*CF*, §116.1, 763.
[35]*CF*, §116.1-2, 764.
[36]*CF*, §116.2, 764.

"*becoming* Christian," in that they exist in the realm where the initial outworkings of grace start to have their regenerative effect. In other words, calling and election are two modes of human existence that are lived proximately to the church—the one on the outer side, the other on the inner side—and not a general bifurcation of the whole of humanity. Nevertheless, there is a more general bifurcation to which Schleiermacher addresses himself, which returns us first to the nexus between election and divine government and second to that between the divine willing and its natural manifestation in the created order.

Schleiermacher posits the uncontroversial thesis that "[for] as long as the human race continues to exist on the earth it can never be the case that all persons living at any given time can be uniformly taken up into the reign of God."[37] Notwithstanding the fact that one could counter this thesis by proposing a (hypothetical) situation in which God *did* will and enact precisely such a globally simultaneous "taking up," what Schleiermacher means by this is simply what can be naturally observed—namely, that the proclamation of the gospel extends throughout the world and down through the generations only ever unequally. The inequality of this evangelistic expansion is in part due to the many different sociological contexts in which the church operates and by which it is variously assisted or hindered in its proclamation, partly by the "mysterious" ways in which individuals are either attracted to or repelled by the gospel and partly also by the simple fact that God so orders peoples' lives that many die before having heard it.

Therefore, there is an inequality in the effecting of regeneration among people and thus the timeliness with which each individual encounters, first, the outer circle of preparatory grace and then the inner circle of the elect. Schleiermacher argues, though, that this ought not to be understood as a negative inequality. Because of the relationship between the natural order that is itself ordered by God's willing and his

---

[37]*CF*, §117, 766-67.

redemptive decree in Christ, we must conclude that God has "definitely and unconditionally willed this" unequal way in which people are "taken up" into God's reign. Had he not so willed it, "God would have arranged either a different natural order for human life or a different order of salvation for the human spirit."[38] Moreover, this divinely ordered inequity is not the last word; it has, we might say, only penultimate significance. That is, Schleiermacher refuses to countenance the "irresolvable dissonance" that would inevitably result if we, presupposing the continuation of life after death, "were to think of a portion of the human race as entirely excluded from this community [i.e., of the elect, the church]." Given that we do, or at least Schleiermacher does, presuppose that continuity of postmortem life, the choice is either an intolerable dissonance or the final inclusion of the whole of humanity in the communion of salvation. In the next three sections of his *Glaubenslehre*, we find Schleiermacher's answer to why the choice must be for the second of these alternatives.

It is self-evident that some people are consciously aware of both their sin and their unmerited reception of grace, while others are conscious of neither. Yet Schleiermacher says we ought not regard this as a sign that some particular (greater or lesser) portion of humanity—those, that is, who lack such awareness—is thus destined forever to be excluded from "the divine efficacious action of Christ." On the contrary, he says, we would be more correct to see this present and self-evident inequality between people as nothing other than "the natural form that divine activity ... take[s] in its historical appearance." As mentioned above, the timeliness with which some people enter into that self-consciousness of sin and grace, and the delay in the same that is experienced by others, is merely a temporary contrast between people that is "in process of vanishing at every particular point."[39]

More to the point, though, Schleiermacher argues that a strict dichotomy between the blessed and the lost (an eternal distinction

---

[38]*CF*, §117, 771.
[39]*CF*, §118, 771-72.

between the saved and the damned) is possible only if we accept the proposition that God's attributes are divisible from one another—that is to say, if we separate God's mercy as one thing, and his justice as something else, both of which can be directed to their human objects independently of the other. Rather, says Schleiermacher, "It is not to be conceded that there is a divided revelation of divine attributes . . . Instead, justice and mercy must not be exclusive of each other," with God's mercy thus being shown also to those who experience his justice.[40] The consequence of all this is the unthinkability of a permanent exclusion of some people from Christ's blessedness, and so we must reckon with the fact that "everyone who is now still outside this blessed community [will] at some time or other be within it."[41]

In explaining this further, Schleiermacher returns to an earlier theme, that of the difference in time in which people come to their consciousness of sin and grace compared to others. That the affective work of regeneration occurs at different moments for different people means that any individual's separation from Christ's community can only be understood as true at a given time, and not as true for *all* time. According to Schleiermacher, there are "always some people in whom divine predestination has *not yet* reached its goal." In fact, at any given moment, "it is always proper to say that most people are *not yet* thought of as among the elect."[42] But he insists this is the perspective only from our present moment. Such people as are outside the community of the church are simply where the church itself once was; thus, the coming to light within them of divine predestination is not something that will never happen for them, but merely a matter of the temporal progression of the ordering and outworking of God's decree.[43] Even death must not be understood as a person's "last chance," for such a proposition presumes that Christ is Lord of the living only and not also of the dead

---

[40]*CF*, §118, 776.
[41]*CF*, §118, 772.
[42]*CF*, §119, 781. Italics added.
[43]*CF*, §119, 782.

(cf. Rom 14:9), that his jurisdiction stops at the grave.[44] This Schleiermacher is not prepared to countenance.

It is regrettably true to say that, thanks largely to Karl Barth's much-publicized love/hate relationship with Schleiermacher, the legacy of this great nineteenth-century theologian has been frequently neglected and even more often misunderstood. Opinion is still divided as to whether his placement of the doctrine of the Trinity at the conclusion of the *Glaubenslehre* signified an astonishing marginalization of this pivotal locus or, alternatively, set it as the crowning glory of Schleiermacher's entire theological enterprise.[45] Similarly, his formulation of the doctrine of election causes some readers to reject the God who is therein envisaged. "It is practically impossible," says Sung-Sup Kim, "to accept Schleiermacher's God, whose answer to our prayer we cannot expect and who is incapable of wrath or mercy, as the God who loves and cares for us."[46]

One thing that is clear, though, is that in Schleiermacher's interpretation of God's eternal decree, *all people*, according to the ordering of the progressive affectivity of that decree within history and nature—and importantly, given his context, irrespective of race or nationality—are in the end predestined to participate in the community of Christ.

J. N. DARBY AND THE EXCLUSIVIST PROPOSITION

It would be hard to find someone as far removed from Schleiermacher as John Nelson Darby (1800–1882). Born not into Moravian pietism but rather the establishment of the Church of Ireland, Darby came from a

---

[44]*CF*, §119, 773-74.

[45]For the traditional view, see D. M. Meeks, "Trinitarian Theology: A Review Article," *Theology Today* 38 (1982); C. Axt-Piscalar, *Der Grund des Glaubens: Eine theologiegeschichtliche Untersuchung zum Verhältnis von Glauben und Trinität in der Theologie Isaak August Dorners* (Tübingen: Mohr, 1990). For alternative readings that regard Schleiermacher's trinitarianism to be more fundamental, see, for example, F. Schüssler Fiorenza, "Schleiermacher's Understanding of God as Triune," in *The Cambridge Companion to Friedrich Schleiermacher*, ed. J. Mariña (Cambridge: Cambridge University Press, 2005), 171-88; and S. M. Poe, *Essential Trinitarianism: Schleiermacher as Trinitarian Theologian* (London: Bloomsbury T&T Clark, 2017).

[46]S-S. Kim, *Deus providebit: Calvin, Schleiermacher, and Barth on the Doctrine of Providence* (Minneapolis: Augsburg Fortress, 2014), 209.

privileged pedigree, with even his middle name—given in honor of his godfather, Horatio Lord Nelson—a testament to his landed connections. Whereas Schleiermacher's life was decisively influenced by both Enlightenment and Romantic sensibilities as well as by the myriad revolutions of late-eighteenth-century Europe, Darby's was shaped more by Anglo-Irish politics and his rebellion against modernity. Yet it is precisely Darby's distance from Schleiermacher that makes him such a curious counterpoint, not least because of his millenarian vision of "the elect."

Darby's early life and schooling were unremarkable, albeit well-heeled. As with his brothers, he attended the elite Westminster School—in his day, and until the Public Schools Act of 1868, formally joined to Westminster Abbey—but seemingly went through his early education largely unnoticed. Darby's headmaster, William Carey (later, bishop of Exeter), could apparently remember nothing of him, even after Darby had achieved some modest international renown.[47] The situation was different, however, once Darby matriculated at Trinity College Dublin. There he excelled, graduating in 1819 as Gold Medalist in classics. From classical education, Darby turned initially to law. It would seem that he was first admitted to the Irish bar, probably the Court of Chancery, in January 1821. Some biographers, notably Max Weremchuk, have suggested that he began his legal career at London's Lincoln's Inn, at the same time as John Henry (later Cardinal) Newman.[48] However, the Inn's *Black Books* contain no mention of a John Darby, although there is a George Darby, who is listed as having been called to the bar on November 21, 1821.[49] In any event, the law held no long-term interest for him, and following some sort of religious conversion in 1822, Darby sought ordination in the Church of Ireland. According to Timothy Stunt, Darby was a "tireless" priest in

---

[47]W. G. Turner, *John Nelson Darby* (London, 1990), 14. Cited in M. A. Clarke, "A Critical Examination of the Ecclesiology of John Nelson Darby" (unpublished PhD diss., 2009), 47.

[48]M. Weremchuk, *John Nelson Darby* (Neptune, NJ: Loiseaux, 1992), 32.

[49]*The Records of the Honorable Society of Lincoln's Inn. The Black Books*, vol. 4, *From AD 1776 to AD 1845* (Lincoln's Inn, 1902). Whether this "George" was in fact John is impossible to determine from the evidence of the *Black Books* alone.

County Wicklow, exemplifying the type of exact churchmanship favored by Irish sacramentalists.[50] He was, in fact, of a Tractarian mind, following its precepts "years before Dr Newman . . . thought on the subject, and when Dr Pusey was not heard of."[51]

But it was the specifically *Irish* aspect of Darby's religiosity that became his prime motivator. As Grayson Carter has noted, it was the disaffected Irish evangelicals who constituted the seedbed of the later Darbyite Brethren.[52] Of particular significance for Darby was the 1801 Act of Union, by which inter alia the Church of Ireland was united with the Church of England. This was troubling to Darby for three reasons. First, the "substitution of the despotic authority of the English Crown for that of the Pope was highly provocative" and offended his Irish sensibilities.[53] Second, it offended his evangelistic zeal. In 1822, Archbishop William Magee had issued a requirement that, consistent with the Union, converts from Catholicism were to swear allegiance to the English Crown. In Darby's view, this set up a stumbling block in the way of the conversion of Irish Catholics, for whom loyalty to an English king was anathema. Indeed, he complained that Magee's insistence virtually stopped Catholic conversion in its tracks.[54] Third, it reified an

---

[50]T. Stunt, "John Nelson Darby: Contexts and Perceptions," in *Protestant Millennialism, Evangelicalism and Irish Society, 1790–2005*, ed. C. Gribben and A. R. Holmes (Basingstoke, UK: Palgrave Macmillan, 2006), 84.

[51]J. N. Darby, "Analysis of Dr Newman's *Apologia pro Vita Sua*: With a Glance at the History of Popes, Councils, and the Church," in *The Collected Writings of J.N. Darby*, ed. W. Kelly (Kingston-on-Thames, UK: Snow Hill, n.d.), xviii, 146, 156.

[52]As Carter says, "The dissatisfaction of Dublin Evangelicals with the state of their own Church, their fears for the future of the Protestant ascendancy in Ireland, and their yearning for voluntary association in religious activities outside the Church, were caused in part by a conviction that the structures of the Established religion were rigid and immobile, hindering evangelism, and preventing the formation of new congregations where needed. There was also anxiety at the exclusion of the Evangelical clergy from many Irish parishes, or even entire dioceses. This informal Evangelical network—prosperous, lay-dominated, gathered into coteries outside the control of the Anglican hierarchy, and often bitterly critical of the worldliness of the Irish Church—were a propitious environment for separatism." G. Carter, *Anglican Evangelicals: Protestant Secessions from the Via Media, c. 1800–1850* (Oxford: Oxford University Press, 2001), 198-99.

[53]Carter, *Anglican Evangelicals*, 213.

[54]J. N. Darby *Considerations Addressed to the Archbishop of Dublin* (1827), in *Collected Writings* (Winschoten, Netherlands: H. L. Heijkoop, 1971), 1:1.

Erastian settlement between church and (English) state that, to Darby, was scripturally unjustifiable.

In short, it was a matter of time before Darby left the established Irish church, seeing it as a moribund artefact of English supremacy that enjoyed neither logical nor scriptural support. As he was to write in later years,

> I find no such thing as a national church in Scripture. Is the Church of England—was it ever—God's assembly in England? I say, then, that her constitution is worldly, because she contemplates by her constitution—it is her boast—the population, not the saints. The man who would say that the Church of England is a gathering of saints must be a very odd man, or a very bold one. All the parishioners are bound to attend, by her principles. It was not the details of the sacramental and priestly system which drove me from the Establishment, deadly as they are in their nature. It was that I was looking for the body of Christ (which was not there, but perhaps in all the parish not one converted person); and collaterally, *because I believed in a divinely appointed ministry.* If Paul had come, he could not have preached (he had never been ordained); if a wicked ordained man, he had his title and must be recognized as a minister; the truest minister of Christ unordained could not. *It was a system contrary to what I found in Scripture.*[55]

Such a destabilization of Darby's view of the English (and the established Irish) church led inevitably to the search for a new and better ecclesiology. As early as 1827, in a letter to William Magee, he described what he now meant by *church.* It is, he argued,

> a congregation of souls redeemed out of "this naughty world" by God manifest in the flesh, a people purified to Himself by Christ, purified in the heart by faith, knit together, by the common bond of this faith in Him, to Him their Head sitting at the right hand of the Father, having consequently their conversation *(commonwealth)* in heaven, from whence they look for the Saviour.[56]

---

[55]Turner, *John Nelson Darby*, 18.
[56]Darby, *Considerations*, 5.

As Clarke has said, key themes emerging from this ecclesial definition, by which much of Darby's later considerations around election
and predestination were informed, include (a) an emphasis on the
church as a gathering or assembly, (b) that this assembly is of redeemed
and purified people, and (c) that members of the church are oriented
toward heaven and thus set in contrast to the "naughty world" from
which they have been plucked.[57] An important nuance to this last
point, however, is that Darby's ecclesiology does not divorce the church
from its existence in the world. For example, the church is not an assembly that finds its unity in heaven alone. Rather, each local expression
of the church is a manifestation of the *one* church that exists in singularity on earth. This has important ramifications for Darby's understanding of ecclesial catholicity. In his scheme, no local denominational
assembly could rightly be considered a church, because it would be a
gathering *only* of those Christians within that locality who identified
themselves with *that* denomination and not another. Darby contrasts
this ecclesiological ontology with the being and purpose of pre-
Christian Israel:

> The Jewish dispensation which preceded His coming into the world had
> for its object, not to gather the church upon earth, but to exhibit the gov-
> ernment of God by means of an elect nation. At this time [however] the
> Lord's purpose is to *gather* as well as to *save*, to realize unity, not merely
> in the heavens, where the purposes of God shall surely be accomplished,
> but here upon earth, by one Spirit sent down from heaven.[58]

Nevertheless, there is a more fundamental idealization of the church's
this-worldly life that is a consequence of the nature of the church's
membership. Insofar as the church is an assembly of the purified and
the redeemed, the realization of its perfected fullness cannot be de-
ferred to a future manifestation but must be eschatologically realizable—
and in fact realized—in the here and now. To find his way around the

---

[57]Clarke, "Ecclesiology of John Nelson Darby," 79.
[58]J. N. Darby, "On the Formation of Churches" (1840), in *Collected Writings*, 1:139.

obvious difficulty of the Augustinian "mixed economy" of ecclesial belonging, Darby did indeed accept the presence of the unredeemed.
Among the elect sheep can be found the occasional apostate wolf.[59] They
were, however, to be understood as merely "external appendages": participants in the *house* of God but not members of God's *church*. While
the house of God may fail—and will of necessity do so because it is built
by human effort—the church as such neither will nor can.[60]

For our purposes, of course, the key aspect of Darby's ecclesiology
is his dispensationalist distinction between church and the prior people
of Israel. Much as Calvin's concept of "double predestination" has,
rightly or wrongly, come to be an index for whether one is a Calvinist,
so too this distinction has come to be definitive of authentic dispensationalism. To quote Charles Ryrie, "The most basic theological test of
whether or not a person is a dispensationalist . . . [is whether they]
distinguish between Israel and the church consistently."[61] For Darby,
this distinction was essential.

The distinction, however, is not between an elect church and a non-
elect Israel. Neither Darby himself nor dispensationalist theology more
broadly draws such a naive dichotomy. Indeed, Ben Witherington has
noted that, for all its questionable elements, dispensationalism ought
to be credited for its consistent pushback against supersessionism.[62]
Nonetheless, the election of Israel is, for Darby, of a fundamentally different nature than that of the church. Israel, he says, had a "national
election." To be sure, "the laws of the country were God's own laws, the
presence of God was there, and the abuses and corruptions did not alter
that." Nonetheless, this form of election is not to be confused with the

---

[59]R. H. Krapohl, "A Search for Purity: The Controversial Life of John Nelson Darby" (unpublished PhD diss., 1988), 453.
[60]See J. N. Darby, "Remarks on 'The Church and the World'" (1866), in *Collected Writings*, 15:348; and *Familiar Conversations on Romanism: Apostolicity and Succession* (1860), in *Collected Writings*, 22:234-36.
[61]C. C. Ryrie, *Dispensationalism* (Chicago: Moody Bible Institute, 1995), 39.
[62]B. Witherington, "Dispensationalism," in *The Cambridge Dictionary of Christian Theology*, ed. I. A. MacFarland, D. A. S. Fergusson, K. Kilby, and I. R. Torrance (Cambridge: Cambridge University Press, 2011), 142.

election of individuals to salvation. While some in Israel may participate in that, it is dependent on their having been individually chosen
by God, not as a result of their belonging to an elect nation.[63] As he
says elsewhere, "The Jews were a community, but not of saved persons;
[rather, they were] a national community of the sons of Jacob."[64]
Moreover, unlike what we have seen with Ignatius and Origen, there is
no preexistent church in and among the people of Israel in the Darbyite
ecclesiology; it does not exist even *in nuce*. On the contrary, Darby
insists that the church is not merely "hidden" but is in fact nonexistent
until the day of Pentecost.[65] Because the union of Christians with
Christ is grounded in the resurrection and ascension of Christ, it is
temporally impossible for the church to have existed prior to this.

If, then, there is a difference between the election of a nation and the
election of individuals to salvation, and if therefore the elected character of Israel is thus different from the elected character of those who,
as members of the church, are recipients of salvation, what does
election actually mean for Darby? In a letter from 1878, he explains it
in this way:

> Election supposes a large number out of whom God chooses; and if we
> take it as eternal, or no time with God, still a number are in view out of
> whom a choice is made. Predestination is the proper purpose of God as
> to these individuals: even supposing there were no others, God had them
> in His mind—surely for something, which is thus as we see connected
> with it; but it is a blessed idea that God had His mind thus set on us
> without thinking of others.[66]

---

[63]Darby, *The Claims of the Church in England Considered; being the close correspondence between the Rev. James Kelly of Stillogan, Ireland, and J.N. Darby*, (London: W.H. Broom, 1964), 34-35.

[64]Darby, *Law* (1868), in *Collected Writings*, 10:33. Cited in Clarke, "Ecclesiology of John Nelson Darby," 92.

[65]Clarke, "Ecclesiology of John Nelson Darby," 93. One curious consequence of this dispensation-alist timetable is that, insofar as the church does not come into existence until Pentecost, Darby argues that God was still engaging with the Jewish people up until that time. The "Jewish dispensation" does not, in fact, come to a close until the stoning of Stephen; it is at this point that Saul/Paul is called to be an apostle to the Gentiles, which signals the end of a nation-specific community of God and the opening up of that community to people of all nations.

[66]Darby, *The Letters of JND* (Winschoten, Netherlands: H. L. Heijkoop, 1971), 3:476.

God therefore makes an eternal choice for some and against the majority. Those few who are chosen, whose "proper purpose" is to be predestined to communion with God through Christ, are from all nations and peoples (some Gentiles, some Jews). Together they constitute, as the church, the earthly form of an essentially heavenly community. This divine choice, moreover, is to be mirrored by the church in the self-separation from the non-elect. Darby argued that such separation is not schismatic but rather an imperative for holiness based on Scripture.

> The path of the saints is most simple; their portion is heavenly; to be not of the world, as Christ is not of the world; to be clear from all their plans. . . . If the saint knows this intrinsically his path is very clear, to wit the spirit of separation from the world, through the knowledge of death, and power, and glory, and coming of the Lord Jesus Christ . . . and hence growing positive separation from them all.[67]

In one of his early writings, Darby does suggest a proper purpose for Israel itself, that it will enjoy a millennial "glory which [the Jews] will possess as a nation redeemed by Christ."[68] Importantly, though, this earthly glory is radically other than the election to salvation in the church, which is retained by God as an opportunity afforded by him only to a very few.

CONCLUSION

At the start of this chapter we remarked on the peculiarly nationalistic form that European Christianity took during the nineteenth century. We noted in particular that religious feeling intensified by nationalistic zeal led, typically and not unsurprisingly, to a sense of national (or, at times, ethnic) chosenness. While this may have been most evident in Germany, it was not without its counterpart in places such as France. Yet neither Schleiermacher nor Darby fell victim to it despite the fact that, in Schleiermacher's day, a distinctly German sense of identity was

---

[67]Darby, *The Christian Witness* (1834), 29. Cited in Carter, *Anglican Evangelicals*, 243.
[68]Darby, *The Purposes of God* (1839), in *Collected Writings*, 2:266. Cited in Clarke, "Ecclesiology of John Nelson Darby," 99.

imposing itself through various cultural media in response to Napo-leonic aggression and, in Darby's time, Ireland was flexing its anti-English muscle.

Rather, the character of election—what it might mean to be "chosen" by God—took on a more expansive nature for both men. For Schleier-macher, the indivisibility of God's creative, redemptive, and sanctifying works, and their collective enactment under the covering of God's eternal good pleasure, requires that the idea of an ultimately fixed di-chotomy between the elect and the non-elect must be eschewed. In Darby's case, while a particular national election is affirmed for Israel, this elect status is decidedly earthbound and is not to be identified with election for salvation. Those who enjoy the latter are, for Darby, an eternally predestined few. They, the church, are to be distinguished from the "hangers-on"—those who inhabit the *house* of God but not his kingdom—yet they include both Jews and Gentiles, from every local expression of church in every land. Given the spread of increas-ingly toxic xenophobia during Darby's day that, as we have seen, took on a deliberately religious hue, even his exclusivist doctrine of election was, in its ethnic blindness, expansive in its own way. In the first half of the twentieth century, however, the doctrine of election was overlaid with precisely that sort of toxic racism that was missing from Darby's theology. Nowhere was this more clearly exemplified than in National Socialist Germany.

KARL BARTH'S RECONSIDERATION OF THE DOCTRINE OF ELECTION

DURING THE WINTER OF 1941–1942, and with another period
of military service with the Swiss Army auxiliary troops imminent,[1]
Karl Barth completed the second part-volume of *Church Dogmatics II.*
He had started work on it in the summer semester of 1939 as Europe
was on the cusp of yet another devastating conflict. Without a doubt,
the outbreak of war in September of that year and the ramping-up of
various resistance activities over the subsequent months influenced
Barth's material considerations while he wrote. As Barth put it in a letter
to Otto Weber ten years later, everything that was taught in the Basel
lecture theater during this period "had a wartime background."[2] In
stark contrast to the caricaturized "other-worldly Barth," whose theology was, so it is claimed, so devoted to the transcendent God to be
of no earthly (and certainly no political) use, the Barth who wrote *CD*

This chapter first appeared, in a slightly different form, in S. Hattrell, ed., *Election, Barth, and the French Connection: How Pierre Maury Gave a "Decisive Impetus" to Karl Barth's Doctrine of Election* (Eugene, OR: Pickwick Publications, 2016), 107-28.

[1]Barth's duties were to guard bridges and public buildings against sabotage. See M. Barth, "Current Discussions on the Political Character of Karl Barth's Theology," in *Footnotes to a Theology: The Karl Barth Colloquium of 1972*, ed. H. M. Rumscheidt (Waterloo, Ontario: Corporation for the Publication of Academic Studies in Religion in Canada, 1974), 77. He was not, by his own admission, very good at it. On one occasion he allowed an entire squad he was leading to desert their posts to a hut where there was a warm fire and hot coffee! See "Witness to an Ancient Truth," interview with K. Barth, *Time*, April 20, 1962.

[2]'Der Hintergrund von dem Allem war ja die Kriegszeit...' K. Barth to O. Weber, 20 June 1949. Cited in E. Busch, *Karl Barths Lebenslauf: Nach seinen Briefen und autobiographischen Texten* (Munich: Christian Kaiser, 1975), 315.

II/2 was deeply implicated in a total and unconditional (*unbedingt*) resistance against the Hitler regime.[3] Part of that resistance included his letters of support to churches in war-torn countries, his sheltering of Jewish refugees and provision of financial aid to various underground networks in Germany, and (later in 1944) his attempts to secure rescue for Hungarian Jews facing deportation to Auschwitz.[4]

Despite his hatred of Nazism and unqualified opposition to it, in this second volume of his *Doctrine of God*, Barth exemplifies the principle he articulated in 1933—doing theology "as if nothing had happened" (*als wäre nichts geschehen*).[5] The overtures of global war and the fight against fascism did not intrude directly into his dogmatic work. On the contrary, he continued with his determination to refuse Hitler and Nazism any constitutive theological significance at all. Barth had built this principle into his theological methodology when, in the second volume of his *Prolegomena* he had insisted that the critical function of dogmatic theology must be the summoning again of the teaching church to the voice of Jesus Christ alone.[6] Through her dogmatic task, the church is called to return ever anew to the Word and revelation of God that has been spoken in Jesus Christ and to which the Old and New Testaments attest. That is, it is vital that the church is called by her dogmatic work to return to a Word *already spoken*, not to try to find a new word for a new day:

> The requisite modernity and actuality of dogmatics cannot consist in the fact that it speaks to any time, to any political, intellectual, social or ecclesiastical structures of the present, as though this can be the standard of Church proclamation. . . . In the present, and for the sake of the present,

[3]Busch, *Lebenslauf*, 316.
[4]See especially chapter 7 of my *Covenanted Solidarity: The Theological Basis of Karl Barth's Opposition to Nazi Antisemitism and the Holocaust* (New York: Peter Lang, 2001); and D. Kranzler, *The Man Who Stopped the Trains to Auschwitz: George Mantello, El Salvador and Switzerland's Finest Hour* (New York: Syracuse University Press, 2000).
[5]K. Barth, *Theologische Existenz heute!* (1933), in *Karl Barth Gesamtausgabe III: Vorträge und kleinere Arbeiten, 1930–1933*, ed. M. Beintker, M. Hüttenhoff, and P. Zocher (Zurich: TVZ, 2013), 280.
[6]*CD* I/2, 812.

dogmatics will not inquire about the voices *of* the day, but about the voice of God *for* the day.[7]

Consequently, in the lectures that formed the basis of the *Doctrine of God* and indeed all volumes of the *Church Dogmatics*, Barth felt himself to be constrained by Scripture and not by political events, no matter how tumultuous those events became. In this light, the particular emphasis of *CD* II/2 was neither the war raging throughout Europe nor the ideological heresies underpinning Nazi Germany's aggression but rather a locus of dogmatic enquiry that gave Barth "much pleasure, but even greater anxiety"—specifically, the doctrine of election.[8]

But this is not the whole story. Barth's theology was never as contextually vacant as his methodology might suggest or as his many critics have complained.[9] Notwithstanding his consistency in dogmatically inquiring after the voice of *God* rather than the voice of the *day*, an undercurrent of political rhetoric becomes evident in Barth's treatment of election if one is prepared to see it. Perhaps Barth's anxiety about this locus was not only because of the evangelical weightiness of the subject, and not only because of how sharply he departs from his Reformed predecessors, but also because of his awareness that in his manner of treating it he *does* say something of specific political intent that stood in opposition to and accusation against the prevailing Nazi racism.

In this chapter, I will seek to assess Barth's doctrine of election in three steps. First, I will outline the major aspects of his articulation of election. Second, I will describe the political-rhetorical context in which Barth reflected on this locus. And third, I will show how the particularities of his doctrine of election stand in self-conscious resistance to the National Socialist war against the Jews.

---

[7]*CD* I/2, 843.

[8]*CD* II/2, x.

[9]See, for example, W. G. Jeanrond, "From Resistance to Liberation Theology: German Theologians and the Non-Resistance to the National Socialist Regime," *Journal of Modern History* 64, suppl. (1992): 188-90; R. Gutteridge, *Open Thy Mouth for the Dumb! The German Evangelical Church and the Jews, 1879–1950* (Oxford: Basil Blackwell, 1976), 124-25; R. Niebuhr, "Barth's East German Letter," *Christian Century* 76, no. 6 (February 1959): 167-68.

THE OUTLINES OF DOCTRINAL REVISION

Volume two of the *Church Dogmatics* was not the first time Barth had attempted to articulate the doctrine of election. In his first cycle of dogmatics in Göttingen (1924–1925), Barth introduced the idea of God's gracious election as the counterpoint and correspondent to the dialectical veiling/unveiling of God in his revelation.[10] Election, and its "parent" locus of predestination, most properly exists dogmatically in the closest possible relationship to the doctrine of God and not, as Lutheran theology typically has it, subsumed within the doctrine of creation as a corollary to justification.[11] We will soon return to why Barth thinks this must be the case. In truth, however, his treatment of the doctrine in these early years of his academic life betrays what he knew at that time to be true of himself—that his knowledge of theological texts was limited and that "he had much catching up to do."[12] As he put it in 1927, "I can now admit that at the time I did not even have a copy of Reformed confessions, and I certainly hadn't read them."[13] His way of catching up was to read incessantly: "All day long I am reading pell-mell hundreds and hundreds of pages: Heim, Thomas Aquinas, Fr. Strauss, Alex. Schweizer, Hermann."[14] What he relied on most, though, was a turgid volume of Heinrich Heppe's *Reformed Dogmatics*. His later reflections on this are now well known:

> It was out-of-date, dusty, unattractive, almost like a logarithm table, dreary to read . . . [But] fortunately I did not dismiss it too lightly. I read, I studied, I pondered and found myself rewarded by the discovery . . . of a dogmatics which had both form and substance (*Gestalt und Substanz*).[15]

---

[10]*GD*, 440-75.

[11]*GD*, 444. Bruce McCormack argues that this placement of the locus of election exemplifies the classically Reformed stance that Barth takes here. B. L. McCormack, *Karl Barth's Critically Realistic Dialectical Theology: Its Genesis and Development, 1909–1936* (Oxford: Clarendon, 1997), 371.

[12]D. L. Migliore, preface, *GD*, xvii-xviii.

[13]K. Barth, autobiographical sketch, *Fakultätsalbum der Evangelisch-theologischen Fakultät Münster*, (1927). Cited in E. Busch, *Karl Barth: His Life from Letters and Autobiographical Texts*, trans. J. Bowden (Grand Rapids: Eerdmans, 1994), 129.

[14]K. Barth to E. Thurneysen, 20 March 1924. Cited in J. Smart, trans., *Revolutionary Theology in the Making: Barth-Thurneysen, 1914–1925* (London: Epworth Press, 1964), 176.

[15]K. Barth, introduction to H. Heppe, *Reformed Dogmatics: Set Out and Illustrated from the Sources*, trans. G. T. Thomson (London: George Allen & Unwin, 1950). See also Busch, *Lebenslauf*, 167.

With this as his primary educative text, and then with two lecture series on John Calvin (1922) and the Reformed confessions (1923) under his belt,[16] it is hardly surprising that his first attempt at an explication of the doctrine of election was thoroughly Reformed in nature.

What it means to say that Barth's early understanding of election was Reformed can be gleaned from the way John Calvin himself approached the matter. "The covenant of life," says Calvin in his *Institutes*, "is not preached equally to all, and among those to whom it is preached, does not always meet with the same reception."[17] In other words Calvin, who (like Barth) was a preacher at heart, was exercised by his pastoral observation that some people respond to the gospel whereas others do not. The "primary function" of his doctrine of election is thus to explain this curiosity. As McGrath says, "Calvin's predestinarianism is to be regarded as reflection upon the data of human experience."[18]

This is fundamentally the same point that Barth wishes to stress in his Göttingen lectures. Predestination is, "in its strict form," nothing other than the truth that there is a "twofold possibility" according to which there exists "the simultaneous presence and succession of faith and unbelief in different individuals or even in the same individual." One might know or not know, believe or not believe—and whatever the situation may be, it is *God's* work through his eternal election of grace.[19] For Barth, of course, this twofold possibility is inextricably connected to his dialectics of revelation, in which God's self-revealing is always *hidden*. Christ is always revealed only in the incognito, "in the

---

[16]K. Barth, *The Theology of John Calvin*, trans. G. W. Bromiley (Grand Rapids: Eerdmans, 1995); K. Barth, *The Theology of the Reformed Confessions*, trans. D. J. Guder and J. J. Guder (Louisville: Westminster John Knox Press, 2000).

[17]*Inst*, 3.21.1.

[18]A. E. McGrath, *Christian Theology: An Introduction*, 2nd ed. (Oxford: Blackwell, 1997), 452. See also McGrath's very similar comment in his *Reformation Thought*, where he states: "Calvin's predestinarianism is to be regarded as *a posteriori* reflection upon the data of human experience, interpreted in the light of Scripture, rather than something which is deduced *a priori* on the basis of preconceived ideas concerning divine omnipotence. Belief in predestination is not an article of faith in its own right, but is the final outcome of scripturally informed reflection on the effects of grace upon individuals in the light of the enigmas of experience." See McGrath, *Reformation Thought: An Introduction*, 2nd ed. (Oxford: Blackwell, 1993), 127.

[19]*GD*, 443-44.

likeness of sinful flesh" (ἐν ὁμοιώματι σαρκὸς ἁμαρτίας) (Rom 8:3)—
that is, only where it could be explained away as something *other than*
the revelation of God.[20] One should also note that unbelief—seeing
only the incognito and *not* the revelation—is, in Barth's view, the far
more reasonable path. It is only *belief* that needs any explanation.

But for the Barth of the Göttingen years, the key point to note is that
this twofold possibility is, as it was for Calvin, an utterly real possibility.
Rejection, or reprobation, may be accorded an unequal weighting
relative to election—God's yes speaks even out of the no, and his no
tends always toward his yes. Nonetheless, anyone who wishes to hold
a Reformed view of predestination must, says Barth, be willing to say
both A and B. God's yes and no are both real possibilities for him to
declare over different individuals, or even over the same individual at
different times.[21]

And to whom is this twofold possibility spoken? Or, to put it otherwise, who does Barth consider to be the objects of divine election and
reprobation? At this place, Barth does part company with Calvin, Jo-
hannes Heidegger, and others of his Reformed predecessors. Against
their view that there are two separate and fixed groups of "certain
people" who are eternally predestined by God to be either blessed believers or damned unbelievers, Barth insists rather that "both are
both."[22] Exemplifying the actualism[23] with which Barth's entire theological method is pervaded, predestination becomes, under this scheme,

> exclusively a basic description of God's dealings with us, of his free and
> actual use at every moment of the possibility of saying Yes or No to us, of
> electing or rejecting us, of awakening us to faith or hardening us, of giving
> us a share in the hope of eternal salvation or leaving us in the general
> human situation whose end is perdition.[24]

---

[20]*GD*, 446.
[21]*GD*, 452, 455, 461.
[22]*GD*, 454.
[23]See G. Hunsinger, *How to Read Karl Barth: The Shape of His Theology* (New York: Oxford University Press, 1991), 30-32.
[24]*GD*, 455-56.

As McCormack notes, Barth's understanding of election in his Göttingen years is thus actualistic and theocentric.[25] The focus is on the *freedom* of *God's* actions and decisions. Insofar as it is God's determination for any individual that is in play, the doctrine is theocentric. Insofar as those determinations are freely made moment by moment for individuals, and not eternally mandated for fixed groups of people, it is actualistic and consequently at odds with Barth's Reformed tradition.

What is strikingly missing from Barth's doctrine of election at this time is any substantive reference to Jesus. Indeed, in the whole section there are only half a dozen references to him. One also might well complain that Barth's early view of actualistic election provides no ground for salvific certainty—that according to this view one could find oneself to be in one moment elect and in the next moment rejected. Barth came to recognize that these two problems are not different but are in fact the two sides of the *same* problem. Thus, it was precisely by taking more seriously the person of Jesus Christ, by reorienting his doctrine Christologically, that this double-sided deficit was overcome. Indeed, this is what Barth does in *CD* II/2, to which we now turn.[26]

By the time Barth began work on volume two of the *Dogmatics*, nearly fifteen years after his first cycle of dogmatics in Göttingen, two things of determinative significance had happened. First, Barth had radically reconstructed his theological method on the basis of his (re) discovery of the ancient doctrine of the anhypostasia/enhypostasia.[27] True, Barth had begun to orient his theology according to this formula from as early as 1924. When compared with his *Romans* period, for

---

[25]McCormack, *Karl Barth's Critically Realistic Dialectical Theology*, 373.

[26]It should be noted that Barth did not address the problem of election at all in his Münster dogmatics of 1927, so it is possible only to compare what he said in Göttingen with his more developed articulation of this doctrine in the *Church Dogmatics*.

[27]The anhypostatic/enhypostatic distinction refers to the insistence of much post-Chalcedonian Christology that the humanity of Jesus has no independent existence of its own as a hypostasis—that is, a self-subsistent reality in abstraction from the hypostatic union. That is to say, the human nature of Jesus "acquires" hypostatic identity only in and with its union with the Logos. As Barth puts it, "The human nature of Christ has no personhood of its own. It is *anhypostatos* . . . or, more positively, it is *enhypostatos*. It has personhood, subsistence, reality, only in its union with the *Logos* of God." *GD*, 157.

example, Barth's Göttingen theology gave the incarnation as such much greater significance; it was not relegated simply to a mathematical point, as it had been in 1922. Yet curiously, and as we have seen above, this incarnational reorientation did not at the time decisively impact Barth's understanding of election, which remained fundamentally oriented toward the free activity of God. But second, in 1936 Barth traveled to Geneva, where he heard French pastor Pierre Maury deliver his lecture "Election and Faith" at the International Calvin Congress.[28] In that lecture, in which Barth heard of a very different type of twofold election to that which he had taught previously—one that located both election and reprobation in Christ himself—Barth was provided with the resources he needed to bring his Christology to its logical conclusion. Bruce McCormack and Matthias Gockel have shown that the full articulation of this logic was not presented until the early 1940s.[29] Nonetheless, the foundations of Barth's theological reorientation—in which election was grounded Christologically or, to put it another way, in which Christology became the fountainhead of the knowledge of the electing God—can be traced back to 1936.

In *CD* II/2, Barth adopts, and takes significantly further, Maury's conception of election. It is not simply that Jesus Christ is the locus of both election and rejection, although he is indeed that. Maury crystallized for Barth the "particularist" nature of the knowledge of election; that is, "Outside of Christ, we know neither of the electing God, nor of His elect, nor of the act of election."[30] But Barth went somewhat further,

---

[28]The lecture was later translated by Charlotte von Kirschbaum and published under the title *Erwhählung und Glaube*, Theologische Studien 8 (Zurich: Evangelischer Verlag, 1940). Note that Barth in all likelihood missed the delivery of the lecture itself and had to read the text afterward. See B. Reymond, *Karl Barth-Pierre Maury Nous qui pouvons encore parler Correspondance, 1928-1956: Introduction, Notes et Traductions de Bernard Reymond* (Paris: Symbolon, L'Age d'Homme, 1985), 94.

[29]B. L. McCormack, "Seek God Where He May Be Found: A Response to Edwin Chr. Van Driel," in *Orthodox and Modern: Studies in the Theology of Karl Barth*, ed. B. L. McCormack (Grand Rapids: Baker Academic, 2008), 263; Gockel, *Barth and Schleiermacher on the Doctrine of Election*, 162n14.

[30]Maury, *Erwählung und Glaube*, 7. "Particularism" is, of course, one of the four motifs that George Hunsinger uses to construct a hermeneutical framework for interpreting Barth's theology. See Hunsinger, *How to Read Karl Barth*, 32-25.

with his Christologically circumscribed doctrine of election speaking directly, and controversially, to the eternal being of God himself. In order fully to grasp the revolutionary significance of Barth's doctrine, as well as its utility as a piece of theological resistance, we need to consider both of these aspects.

Consistent with his dialecticism, as well as with what he had gleaned from Maury, Karl Barth's most obvious dogmatic move was to orient both the yes and no of God's electing will toward the person of Jesus Christ. Jesus is identified as the (only) one in whom both our election to mercy and our rejection to judgment cohere. He is the one truly elected man and also the only one who is truly rejected. Of no one else can either be said, without this Christological caveat.

Thus, Barth is led to claim that the particular partner "over against God which cannot be thought away . . . , which is so now adjoined to the reality of God that we cannot and should not say the word 'God' without at once thinking of it" is none other than the man Jesus of Nazareth.[31] In particularist terms, Jesus of Nazareth is "not merely *one* of the elect, but *the* elect of God" (*nicht nur* ein Erwählter, sondern der Erwählte Gottes).[32]

> Of course, the election has to do with the whole of humanity . . . although materially it has to do first and exclusively with the one man. . . . Thus the doctrine of election is rightly grounded when in respect of elected men as well as the electing God it does not deal with a generality or abstraction in God or man, but with the particularity and concretion of the true God and true man.[33]

In order to properly ground our understanding of election, we are therefore to look solely, and at least in the first instance, to Jesus Christ, who is himself the "particularity and concretion of the true God and true man" and therefore as such the true elect man.[34]

---

[31]*CD* II/2, 8.
[32]*KD* II/2, 125; *CD* II/2, 116.
[33]*CD* II/2, 51.
[34]*CD* II/2, 58-59.

But by the same token, this Jesus is also the (only) one who is truly rejected. Living by the grace of God, Jesus is also "branded by the wrath of God" (*von Gottes Zorn Gezeichnete*). He is at one and the same time, and the one because of the other, both the elected and the rejected one, (zugleich *der von Gott Erwählte* und *der von Gott Verworfene ist*).[35] Both Cain and Abel, Isaac and Ishmael are to be found paradigmatically in him.

Importantly, while this has infinite soteriological benefit for humankind, it also has profoundly devastating consequences for God's own being. For Barth, God's freely willed condescension into humanity's own state means that God "has declared Himself guilty of the contradiction against Himself in which man was involved," that God has taken on Godself the "wrath and judgment to which man had brought himself; that he took upon Himself the rejection which man had deserved; that He tasted Himself the damnation, death and hell which ought to have been the portion of fallen man."[36] This is not merely a suffering of these things *alongside* humankind but a bearing of them *in humanity's place*. No wonder that Barth calls this a "severe self-commitment" (*schwerste Kompromittierung*)![37] Of course, all this accrues most properly to the one Jesus of Nazareth. As the electing God and elected man, he is also the elected *and rejected* man, on behalf of all. To be genuinely and actually lost and abandoned is in fact the concern *only* of Christ. There is, says Barth, "only one Rejected, the Bearer of all man's sin and guilt . . . and this One is Jesus Christ."[38]

In the first instance, by locating the traditional polarities of predestination—election and reprobation—*in Christ* rather than in individuals or in distinct groupings of people, this move undercut the existential uncertainty that has typically infused this doctrinal locus. Instead of making the determination of election or rejection subsidiaries of, on

---

[35]*KD* II/2, 403-4; *CD* II/2, 366.
[36]*CD* II/2, 164.
[37]*KD* II/2, 179.
[38]*CD* II/2, 346, 352.

the one hand, an unknowable *decretum absolutum* (Calvin) or, on the other hand, an unstable actualism (Barth's Göttingen iteration of the doctrine), Barth was able to honor the real seriousness (or the serious reality) of God's righteous judgment and yet at the same time affirm the unqualified scope of God's grace.

In a very real sense, this Christological revision of the old theory of "double predestination" was a thoroughgoing refutation of Reformed orthodoxy. What is more germane to our purposes here, however, is the fact that Barth's doctrine of election underwent a foundational and (therefore) material change between its first articulation in Göttingen and its final statement in *CD* II/2. Moreover, it is crucial to recognize that this change was not initiated by Barth's own theological creativity, as though he were reflecting *in abstracto*. On the contrary, it was precipitated, among other things but perhaps preeminently, by Maury's lecture in 1936, then refined in its articulation by the peculiar historical circumstances in which the doctrine was developed. After the following short excursus, we will turn to this more contextual matter of authorship.

EXCURSUS: IMPLICATIONS OF BARTH'S DOCTRINE OF ELECTION FOR THE DOCTRINE OF GOD

Until the mid-1990s it was routinely assumed that this Christological revision of earlier Reformed teaching was the most striking aspect of Barth's reconsideration of the doctrine of election. Yet since the publication of Bruce McCormack's groundbreaking 1995 book, and his equally provocative follow-up contribution to the *Cambridge Companion to Karl Barth*,[39] it has been a quite different aspect of Barth's understanding of election that has generated heated (if not hostile) controversy. As suggested earlier, Barth's truly revolutionary contribution within this particular locus concerns the eternal being of the triune God. Orienting this doctrine with reference to Jesus Christ

---

[39]B. L. McCormack, "Grace and Being: The Role of God's Gracious Election in Karl Barth's Theological Ontology," in *The Cambridge Companion to Karl Barth*, ed. J. Webster (Cambridge: Cambridge University Press, 2000), 92-110.

leads him to posit a fundamentally new way of thinking about God's very nature.[40]

According to Bruce McCormack, who has taken the lead in identifying what he regards as the inescapable logic of Barth's doctrine, Barth's identification of Jesus Christ as the subject of election means that election is not simply the sum of the gospel but part of the very doctrine of God itself. Election is not simply something that God does but rather is intrinsic to God's very being. Indeed, it is the decision by which God constitutes God's own being as triune.[41] In McCormack's words, "God is what he is in the eternal decision of election and not in a state or mode of existence that is above or prior to that decision."[42] That is, the works of God *ad intra* (the trinitarian processions) find their ground in the first of the works of God *ad extra* (election). This entails a dissolution of the distinction between the *Logos asarkos* and the *Logos ensarkos*, between the *incarnatus* and the *incarnandus*.[43] The *Logos asarkos* never exists—not even within the immanent Trinity—in abstraction but only ever in the most complete identification with the *Logos incarnandus*. In

---

[40]Robert Jenson concurs: "The doctrine of election, of God's choice 'before all time,' is for Barth the center of the doctrine of God's being." R. W. Jenson, *Systematic Theology I: The Triune God* (New York: Oxford University Press, 1997), 140.

[41]See also Eberhard Jüngel: "As the beginning of all the ways and works of God, God's election of grace is not only an *opus Dei ad extra* (external work of God) or, more precisely, an *opus Dei ad extra externum* (external work of God directed outwards); it is at the same time an *opus Dei ad extra internum* (external work of God directed inwards). For election as such is not only a decision made by God and in so far an election which also certainly concerns him; it is equally a decision which affects God himself. . . . If, then, the decision of the election of grace not only affects elect humanity but also at the same time affects God in a fundamental way, then it is dogmatically consistent to treat the doctrine of predestination as a part of *the doctrine of God*. E. Jüngel, *God's Being Is in Becoming: The Trinitarian Being of God in the Theology of Karl Barth*, trans J. Webster (Edinburgh: T&T Clark, 2001), 83-84. See also B. Myers, "Election, Trinity and the History of Jesus: Reading Barth with Rowan Williams," in *Trinitarian Theology After Barth*, ed. M. Habets and P. Tolliday (Eugene, OR: Pickwick Publications, 2011), 121-37.

[42]B. L. McCormack, "Election and the Trinity: Theses in Response to George Hunsinger," *Scottish Journal of Theology* 63, no. 2 (2010): 223.

[43]See, for example, McCormack, "Grace and Being," 92-110; and McCormack "Seek God Where He May Be Found." Note, however, that McCormack vehemently insists that he does not thereby collapse the economic Trinity into the immanent Trinity, as Paul Molnar suggests. "Talk of a 'collapse' makes it sound as though there is only an economy of God, that there is no immanent Trinity 'before the foundations of the world.' On the contrary, to say that God constitutes Himself as the triune God in an *eternal* act is to say that God is already triune before He creates a world." B. L. McCormack, "Let's Speak Plainly: A Response to Paul Molnar," *Theology Today* 67 (2010): 63-64.

the incarnation of the Son, therefore, what happens economically has ontological bearing on what is and has been true for God *immanently*.[44] Importantly, McCormack does not claim this as his own idea but as the necessary consequence of Barth's own logic.

As is well known among Barth scholars, Paul Molnar and George Hunsinger have been in the vanguard of those who reject McCormack's thesis. They do so both from the perspective of their own exegesis of Barth's theology and also on account of the dogmatic implications of such thinking. Paul Molnar has taken issue with McCormack's view that, for Barth, the immanent Trinity is a product of God's will to be *pro nobis* in the economic Trinity.[45] Rather, Molnar contends that the immanent Trinity is vital to any theological endeavor to retain God's being in freedom. Indeed, if McCormack is correct that (in Barth's theology) God's work *ad extra* determines his being *ad intra*, then his being as triune is dependent on the world that needs saving. Moreover, if God's being *a se* is predicated on God's decision and action *pro nobis*, then God is thus constituted anthropomorphically and not in terms of his own free perfection.[46]

Similarly, George Hunsinger has rebutted McCormack's interpretation of Barth by questioning the dissolution of the *Logos incarnatus* and the *Logos incarnandus*. Hunsinger argues that to say Jesus Christ is the subject of election does not mean that the eternal Son had no existence apart from election. On the contrary, a perichoretic Christology would enable one to maintain a distinction between the eternal Son and the Son *incarnatus*, "who mutually coinhere with one another without losing their real distinctiveness."[47] The decision for election *emerges from* God's perfect triunity but does not constitute it.

---

[44]P. D. Jones, "Obedience, Trinity and Election: Thinking with and Beyond the *Church Dogmatics*," in *Trinity and Election in Contemporary Theology*, ed. M. T. Dempsey (Grand Rapids: Eerdmans, 2013), 149-50.

[45]Dempsey, *Trinity and Election*, 7.

[46]See P. Molnar, *Divine Freedom and the Doctrine of the Immanent Trinity: In Dialogue with Karl Barth and Contemporary Theology* (London: T&T Clark, 2002). Much debate centers on how one defines, respectively, God's self-*determination* and his self-*constitution*.

[47]Dempsey, *Trinity and Election*, 10. See also G. Hunsinger, "Election and the Trinity: Twenty Five Theses on the Theology of Karl Barth," *Modern Theology* 24, no. 2 (2008): 179-98.

An abundance of articles, books, and PhD theses have been written on this debate, and to rehearse their several conclusions here would be neither constructive nor relevant to the present project. Regardless of which side one takes in this particular debate, the simple fact remains: Karl Barth's articulation of the doctrine of election has generated renewed interest not simply in the doctrine itself but in the God who lies behind it, as its sole Subject. And for Barth, of course, the character of this electing Subject was—and is—one who must eternally be known as he who loves, overabundantly, in his own self-determined freedom.

THE DEVELOPMENT OF THE DOCTRINE IN ITS POLITICAL CONTEXT

As we have already seen in an earlier section of this chapter, volume two of the *Church Dogmatics* was not the first time Barth had attempted an articulation of the doctrine of election. However, the circumstances in which Barth developed the doctrine the second time around were markedly different from what they had been in 1924–1925. Barth's Göttingen years coincided, of course, with the disastrous Weimar Republic, about which Barth had initially been enthusiastic. As McCormack has put it, "However 'watered down' the socialism represented by the Weimar government . . . Barth regarded it as the best hope for Germany in the present."[48] Yet in spite of his keen observations, his theology was not greatly impacted by the German politics of the day. In part, his initiation into teaching left him little time for anything other than lecture preparation. As Barth himself said, "I had to work in my study." He "simply had no time at this point for entangling [him]self in political activity."[49] What did exercise him somewhat more were the toxic politics of his own university, not least within the Faculty of Theology. Relations were constantly strained, particularly with Carl Stange and Emanuel Hirsch. In early 1924 Barth wrote to Eduard Thurneysen, "My relation to the faculty is now worse than ever. . . . All of them are now

---

[48]McCormack, *Karl Barth's Critically Realistic Dialectical Theology*, 200.
[49]K. Barth, *Letzte Zeugnisse* (Zurich: EVZ-Verlag, 1969), 42-43; Busch, *Karl Barth*, 148.

outspokenly unfriendly to me. But that is mutual."[50] In other words, during his first attempt to write about election, Barth was more occupied with securing his own place in the university than thinking through the doctrine with any great novelty.

Yet during the writing of *CD* II/2, Barth could not fail to be affected by wider issues. There was, indeed, a global seriousness to the context from which Barth could not, and did not want to, escape. The production of this volume, and the lectures of which it consists, was bookended by, on the one side, *Kristallnacht* (November 9–10, 1938) and, on the other, by the start of Operation Barbarossa (June 22, 1941), the beginnings of the mass deportation of Jews, and the construction of the Bełżec and Chełmno *Totenlargeren* (December 1941–March 1942). Far more than internal faculty backbiting, Barth's writing and thinking about the doctrine of election were thus contextualized by the early horror of the Shoah. Critically, Barth's theological work was affected by this context.

In 1938, Hitler had removed the last voices of moderation from his government. Initially, Economics Minister Hjalmar Schacht, Foreign Minister Konstantin von Neurath, and Generals Fritsch and Blomberg had acted as brakes on some of the regime's more extreme policies. But within five years of seizing power, Hitler had had enough. With their removal, the way was open for the more radical elements of the party to enact their ideas. As a result, the Jews

> were attacked simultaneously on all fronts with a fervor unknown since the heady . . . days of 1933. Boycotts were organized, Aryanisation was accelerated, legislation was promulgated, deportation was attempted, and for the first time large numbers of Jews were herded into concentration camps.[51]

Then, coinciding with the annexation of Austria, Adolf Eichmann was given chief responsibility for solving the "Jewish problem."

---

[50]K. Barth to E. Thurneysen, 4 March 1924. Cited in Smart, *Revolutionary Theology in the Making*, 175.

[51]K. A. Schleunes, *The Twisted Road to Auschwitz: Nazi Policy Toward German Jews, 1933–1939* (Urbana: University of Illinois Press, 1970), 216.

In the midst of all this, Barth was not silent. In March 1938, during his Gifford Lectures, he noted (in agreement with article 14 of the Scottish Confession), "Under certain conditions there may be resistance to the political power, which is not merely allowed but enjoined by God . . . a resistance which can in certain circumstances be a matter of opposing force by force."[52] He continued this tone later in the year in his *Rechtfertigung und Recht*, in which he made plain that when faced with the specter of an unjust state, the church's fulfillment of its political duty takes shape in "responsible decision about the validity of laws, responsible care for their maintenance, in a word, political action, which may and must also mean political struggle [*politischen Kampf*]."[53]

In the aftermath of *Kristallnacht*, Barth put into practice precisely this action on behalf of the persecuted Jews of Germany. In stark contrast to the rest of the Confessing Church, which stood by wordlessly, Barth perceived the destruction of the synagogues as the tipping point, after which it was only ever possible for the church to say an uncompromising no to Nazism. "The really decisive, biblical-theological" reason for the church's necessary rejection of National Socialism was its inherent anti-Semitism: "Were this to stand by itself it would in itself justify the sentence: National Socialism is the anti-Church fundamentally hostile to Christianity."[54] But Barth went further. Recognizing that anti-Semitism was an attack not only on the Jews but on the Jew Jesus, he condemned it roundly as the sin against the Holy Spirit and, as such, the most damnable blasphemy.[55]

Of course, once the war itself had begun, Barth was back in Switzerland. But this did nothing to stop his efforts on behalf of both Christians and Jews in the Nazi-occupied territories. He sheltered Jewish

---

[52]K. Barth, *The Knowledge of God and the Service of God* (London: Hodder & Stoughton, 1938), 229.

[53]K. Barth, *Rechtfertigung und Recht*, Theologische Studien 104 (Zurich: Theologischer Verlag, 1989), 44.

[54]K. Barth, "Die Kirche und die politische Frage von heute," in *Eine Schweizer Stimme, 1938–1945* (Zurich: TVZ, 1985), 89-90.

[55]Barth, "Die Kirche und die politische Frage von heute," 90.

refugees in his own home in Basel, gave financial support to Gertrud
Staewen's underground resistance movement, and coordinated an attempt in 1944 to help rescue Hungary's Jews from deportation.[56]

These, then, were the contextual bookends within which Barth was
busy writing his revised doctrine of election between 1939 and 1942.
Unlike the surrounding circumstances within which the Göttingen
doctrine had been prepared, these events did not fail to make their
mark on Barth, both personally and theologically. As we shall see in the
final part of this chapter, Barth's articulation of election during the war
years, far from being doctrinal abstraction, was in fact itself a piece of
theological *Widerstand*.

ELECTION AS RESISTANCE

To say that Karl Barth's doctrine of election resonates politically as resistance against Nazism is, admittedly, a statement that needs some
nuancing. First, it does not mean that Barth was seeking to write this
volume as a self-conscious manifesto against Hitler. His intent here, as
in all his writings, was to serve the church by expounding as best he
could the biblical witness to Christ and, in so doing, subjecting dogmatic tradition to the scrutiny of Scripture. Neither Barth's doctrine of
election nor any other part of the *Church Dogmatics* is what we could
properly call "political theology."

Nonetheless, that does not thereby render it apolitical. I have argued
elsewhere that Barth seems to have been dogmatically unmoved by the
Holocaust. At least, it does not rate a mention in any of the places one
might expect it to appear, such as *CD* III/3, where Barth speaks of
radical evil in the form of *das Nichtige*.[57] I remain convinced that this
constitutes a serious lacuna in Barth's theology. However, I do not
therefore claim that Barth was either unaware of or unaffected by the
horrors of Nazism. That Barth did not foreground the geopolitical

---

[56]See, for example, my *Covenanted Solidarity*, 241-70; and *Barth, Israel and Jesus: Karl Barth's Theology of Israel* (Aldershot, UK: Ashgate, 2007), 31-35.

[57]See, for example, my *Reading Auschwitz with Barth: The Holocaust as Problem and Promise for Barthian Theology* (Eugene, OR: Wipf & Stock, 2014), chap. 4.

context of World War II and the Shoah in his dogmatic work does not mean it was of no material consequence to him.

Moreover, the historiography of the Nazi period provides ample evidence that there was not just one type of resistance to Nazism, but many. To put it another way, the grammar of resistance can be parsed in multiple ways. The syntax of that grammar includes Hans and Sophie Scholl's "White Rose" movement and the von Stauffenberg bomb plot of July 1944. But it also includes nonviolent resistance, such as the innumerable acts of *Kiddush Hashem* (sanctification of the Name) performed by Jewish prisoners in the concentration camps, as well as intellectual dissent like that of Helmut von Moltke's Kreisau Circle. As von Moltke wrote to his wife, Freya, on the eve of his execution, he and his fellow conspirators were condemned not for what they had done but for what they had *thought*.[58] It is in this context of what we might call "discursive resistance"—resistance that deliberately *en*counters, and then *counters*, the prevailing ideology—that Barth's revisioning of election in the context of Nazi anti-Semitism can be located. And so we must ask, in what way(s) was *CD* II/2 discursively resistant against the Nazis' war on the Jews?

To answer that question adequately, it is necessary first to recognize the extent to which the Nazis deliberately appropriated the Christian language of election. As far back as *Mein Kampf*, Hitler had indicated the need for a reversal of revelatory potential. The Jew, he said, was "an incarnate denial of the beauty of God's image," whereas Aryans were "that highest image of God amongst His creatures."[59] Consistent with a long Romantic tradition of seeing *Gottestum* in *Deutschtum*—a trend at which we looked briefly in the previous chapter—this divinization of the German *Volk* stood in dialectical necessity alongside the demonization of the Jews. Thus, Reinhold Krause could say, in his infamous

---

[58]H. J. von Moltke, *Letters to Freya: A Witness Against Hitler* (London: Collins Harvill, 1991), 404. Cited in S. J. Plant, *Taking Stock of Bonhoeffer: Studies in Biblical Interpretation and Ethics* (Aldershot, UK: Ashgate, 2014), 13.

[59]A. Hitler, *Mein Kampf*, trans J. Murphy (London: Hurst & Blackett, 1939), 157, 322.

Sports Palace speech of November 1933, that on the one hand the "essence of Jesus' teaching . . . is completely identical with the demands of National Socialism" and on the other "the Jews are not the people of God."[60] Both statements stood side by side in necessary and logical harmony—indeed, the one entailing the other.

But the Jews were not, of course, simply sidelined by the Nazis into covenantal ambiguity—they were determined for destruction, with their final moments resembling a macabre parody of the last judgment. In Matthew 25, Jesus places the "sheep" (those who enter the kingdom) on the right hand of the Son of Man, while the "goats" (those destined for punishment) are turned to the left. So it was also at the Nazi death camps. Raul Hilberg notes that, when trains arrived at the Auschwitz platform, the SS sent to the left those who were to be taken immediately to the gas chambers. Those who were to be, at least temporarily, spared from execution were sent to the right.[61] Nazi selection procedures thus intentionally reflected biblical imagery and iconography of divine judgment. The difference, though, was that the Jews *as a people* were by definition determined for the "left" (that is, death) because National Socialist ideology had already decreed them to be *Lebensunwertes Leben* (life unworthy of life).

Barth's rhetoric speaks directly to this situation. We are forbidden, he insists, to conceive of election as "bifurcating into a rightward and leftward election." Left and right, insofar as they denote one's determination for life or death, are meaningless in Barth's system except in relation to Jesus himself. There is a leftward election, but its object is God and not humankind, neither as a whole nor in any of its individuated parts.[62]

---

[60]See C. Mosely, *Nations and Nationalism in the Theology of Karl Barth* (Oxford: Oxford University Press, 2013), 112-13.

[61]R. Hilberg, *The Destruction of the European Jews* (London: W. H. Allen, 1961), 626. See also Martin Weiss, "Selection at Auschwitz," at www.ushmm.org/remember/holocaust-survivors/first-person-conversations-with-survivors/first-person/martin-weiss-selection-at-auschwitz. Those who were sent to the right were given only a temporary stay of execution. They were put to hard physical labor—during which many died anyway—and then, once they had become too ill or weak for that, were sent to the gas chambers.

[62]*CD* II/2, 172.

Barth's doctrine also repudiated the arrogation of divinity that Nazism, and SS officers in particular, had taken to themselves. Elie Wiesel writes that,

> substituting himself for God, the SS man sought to recreate the universe in his own image. His endeavor was ontological . . . One was not allowed to look into the eyes of an SS man, for the SS man was God, and you cannot look into the face of God, just as you cannot look into the face of the Angel of Death.[63]

This image of *potentia absoluta* was precisely what was reflected on the ramp at Auschwitz, and indeed anywhere that guards and soldiers could decide with arbitrary justification whether a particular Jew would in that moment live or die. But Eberhard Busch reminds us that Barth's doctrine of election was predicated not on the idea of God as *potentia absoluta* but on the decision of God that is in its entirety and very foundation utterly *gracious*.[64]

In other words, in his rejection of both bifurcated election and of a subject of electing will who could be correlated to "power in itself," Barth confounded the rhetoric and reality of Nazi ideology. But Barth's counterpoint to the National Socialist dogma of election went further, in particular, in its elevation of the Jews' covenantal status.

Precisely what place postbiblical Israel has in Barth's schema has been a matter of intense debate. Katherine Sonderegger is the most articulate exponent of those who view Barth's theology to be ultimately, if unwillingly, infected by anti-Semitic prejudice.[65] Eberhard Busch and I, on the other hand, represent a smaller number of interpreters who read Barth far more positively than that, with his doctrine of election providing abundant evidence of his theological solidarity with

---

[63]E. Wiesel, "Some Questions That Remain Open," in *Comprehending the Holocaust*, ed. A. Cohen, J. Gelber, and C. Wardi (New York: Peter Lang, 1988), 11.

[64]E. Busch, *Unter dem Bogen des Einen Bundes: Karl Barth und die Juden, 1933–1945* (Neukirchen-Vluyn: Neukirchener Verlag, 1996), 451. Barth also states, "It is not 'the Almighty' who is God . . . For the 'Almighty' is bad, as 'power in itself' [*potentia*] is bad. The 'Almighty' means Chaos, Evil, the Devil." K. Barth, *Dogmatics in Outline*, trans. G. T. Thomson (London: SCM Press, 1955), 48.

[65]K. Sonderegger, *That Jesus Christ Was Born a Jew: Karl Barth's "Doctrine of Israel"* (University Park: Pennsylvania University Press, 1992).

the Jews. While space precludes a thorough treatment of this topic here,[66] the key aspects are readily identified.

First, Barth insists there is a community that is elected in Christ, identifiable with "the reality of both Israel and the Church."[67] While this community offers a twofold witness, yet nonetheless it is manifestly a *single* community, the unity of which is inviolable:

> Just as the electing God is one and the elected man Jesus Christ is one, so too the community as the primary object of the election which has taken place in Jesus Christ is one (*Eine*). Everything that is to be said of it in the light of the divine predestination will necessarily result in an emphasizing of this unity.[68]

In other words, the strict dichotomy drawn by Nazis and the *Deutsche Christen* between Jews and Christians—and even the dichotomy often drawn by the Confessing Church during the *Kirchenkampf* between Christians and Jewish Christians—becomes meaningless in Barth's work. The one indivisible God elects one indivisible community. There are not two covenants but one—"the bow of the one covenant"[69] (of grace) arches over both Israel and the church. The reason for this is inherently Christological, for Jesus—who is the very personification of the covenant within which both exist—

> is the promised son of Abraham and David, the Messiah of Israel. And he is simultaneously the head and Lord of the Church . . . In both these characters he is indissolubly one. And as the One he is ineffaceably both. As Lord of the Church he is the Messiah of Israel, and as the Messiah of Israel he is Lord of the Church.[70]

Second, and in consequence, it becomes impossible to identify the church or Israel as, independently of the other, objects of election or reprobation. On the contrary, "the object of election is neither Israel for

---

[66]Interested readers can consider the arguments put forward by Busch in his *Unter dem Bogen des Einen Bundes*; and in my *Covenanted Solidarity*, esp. chap. 6.

[67]*CD* II/2, 196.

[68]*CD* II/2, 197.

[69]*CD* II/2, 199.

[70]*CD* II/2, 197-98.

itself nor the Church for itself, but both together in their unity."[71] Even in the so-called Judas Passage in which Judas is portrayed as the archetypical figure of rejection and who prima facie represents Israel, Barth insists on a radical continuity between the "elect" and the "rejected." Judas, says Barth, is "undoubtedly a disciple and apostle," standing in the closest proximity to the church. Indeed, Jesus was betrayed to death not by Judas acting alone but *"from within the Church."* At this most decisive juncture, "the Church stands and acts in identity with the Israel which rejected its Messiah, together with the heathen world which allied itself with this Israel." At this point, therefore, "the apostles have to share the guilt of Israel and the Gentile world."[72] If election accrues to both Israel and the church in indissoluble unity, then so too does the burden of rejection. It is not, and cannot be, borne by just one covenantal partner alone.

Third, Barth grounds his doctrine in the freedom of God to act independently of humanity's actions. God is, in this sense, radically *apathetic* —insofar as that means that his eternal determination *pro nobis* is not altered or undercut by human resistance and disobedience. Whereas traditional supersessionism has relegated Israel to judgment and reprobation on account of the Jews' rejection of the gospel, Barth steadfastly contends for God's faithfulness. Not by any action of its own can Israel "annul the covenant of mercy . . . [or] alter the fact that the promise is given and applies to itself, that in and with the election of Jesus Christ *it and no other* is God's elected people."[73] Neither biblical nor postbiblical Israel, says Barth, can "create any fact that finally turns the scale against their own election."[74] The uncaused freedom of God to act in this way, for this people, is why, irrespective of their faith or

---

[71] *CD* II/2, 199.

[72] *CD* II/2, 459-61. As David Demson has rightly said, whenever Barth uses the term *lost and defecting Israel*, he "uses it as the middle term between the first term 'lost and defecting apostolate' and the last term 'lost and defecting mankind.'" D. E. Demson, *Hans Frei and Karl Barth: Different Ways of Reading Scripture* (Grand Rapids: Eerdmans, 1997), viii. That is, neither Barth's hermeneutic nor his discourse make it possible to conceive of the idea of a "rejected Israel" in isolation.

[73] *CD* II/2, 237.

[74] *CD* II/2, 209.

unbelief, "the fundamental blessing, the election, is still confirmed. . . . [The] final word is one of testimony to the divine Yes to Israel."[75]

CONCLUSION

It would, of course, be disingenuous to suggest that Barth's theology of Israel was a model of philo-Semitic sympathy. There are places within his doctrine of election in which both his phraseology and his logic are susceptible to profound critique. Indeed, Barth has not escaped censure from some for betraying a latent supersessionary intent. Nonetheless, it is equally evident that his articulation of election—conceived and taught during the first murderous phase of the Holocaust—represented a singularly powerful counterpoint to Nazi ideology. His contending for the continuing election of the Jews, their inviolable solidarity with the church, and their determination by God for *life* and not death, both within the pages of his *Dogmatics* and the lecture theaters of his university, was in remarkable contrast to the anti-Jewish propaganda that had infected European Christianity for centuries.

As we have seen, the theological bases on which Barth was able to affirm this were grounded in (a) God's eternally free decision to be for and not against us—a decision that is not vulnerable to human vicissitudes but, on the contrary, is secured by God's sovereignty—and (b) the unifying bond of the One who is both subject and object of election, Jesus Christ the *Yahweh-Kyrios*, Messiah and Lord.

Yet we have also seen that Barth's doctrine of election evolved over time. The form of its articulation in Göttingen was far more actualistic and far less Christological. One of the consequences of this was a prioritization of the status at any given moment of the *individual*, which meant that the *community* of the elect, and Israel in particular, was removed almost entirely from consideration. All this changed when Barth read Pierre Maury's 1936 Geneva paper. From that point on, Barth was no longer able to conceive of election apart from its locus in Jesus Christ and the community that is thus elected in him.

---

[75]*CD* II/2, 15.

The Göttingen view of election would have been acutely ill-equipped to oppose Nazi ideology. In contrast, the revised form of that doctrine, as Barth taught it between 1939 and 1942, was so thoroughly reconstituted around the eternal yes of God in Christ Jesus that it was able, as we have seen, to offer "discursive resistance" to both National Socialist anti-Semitism and the Holocaust to which it gave birth. Maury's influence on Barth must therefore rightly be seen to have had not only theological but also political ramifications. If, in a post-Holocaust world, some of the language and logic of *CD* II/2 needs further revision, we should nevertheless not lose sight of how sharply it countered the prevailing prejudices. And for that we have not only Barth but also Pierre Maury to thank.

RECONSTITUTING ELECTION IN THE AFTERMATH OF THE HOLOCAUST

THE HEBREW-CHRISTIAN TRADITIONS HAVE, in a variety of both affirmative and pejorative ways, frequently referenced the Jews as God's "chosen people." We saw this in particularly clear form in chapter one through the various texts from Genesis, Deuteronomy, Romans, and Ephesians. Throughout the rest of the book, we have seen that theme of chosenness recurring in a variety of contexts and with both hopeful and hateful connotations. In some (mostly Christian, economically supersessionist) paradigms, Jewish chosenness is an attribute that once described a particular people—namely, the ethnic Hebrew worshipers of YHWH—but that has, since the execution of Jesus Christ, been transferred instead to the church. In other renditions—such as dispensationalist Christian Zionism that has an intellectual lineage which can be traced to figures like John Darby—the Jews continue as the chosen people of God, with their returning to the land of Israel in 1948 proving that identity and, further, proleptically vindicating a certain form of world-oriented apocalyptic. In such readings, Israel as both nation and geography is the central stage of world history.[1] In yet another variant, Christian

---

[1]It should be remembered that the idea of a final earthly victory of Israel over its enemies is not the same as an affirmation of the ultimate salvation of the Jews and their reception into God's heavenly kingdom. As we have seen with Darby, "Israel" can be glorified on earth, as the proper *telos* of its election, yet still not participate in the community of the redeemed.

punitive supersessionism regards the Jews as still the chosen of God— but now chosen for collective damnation instead of for redeemed life. In his lectures of 1976–1977, Markus Barth posed these alternatives in this way: "Is the people of God in its New Testament form the competitor, successor, or partner of the elect people, the Jews?"[2] Of course, Barth's sympathies—at least the theological ones, if not the political— lay with the Jewish people.[3] Nonetheless, what unifies all three readings—as well as Barth's own summary of them—is that each, in varying ways, objectifies Jewish people and imposes on them a definition of chosenness that is alien from every and all Jewish understandings of what it means to be elect. To be frank, these three alternatives consider the relationship of the Jewish people to God only through a prior commitment to Christian primacy. Insofar as this is their common starting point, any consequent definition of Jewish election is predetermined to be foreign to any and every Jewish definition. In this final chapter, then, we will seek to subvert that privileging of the Christian voice by exploring what Jews themselves have said about their election and how those views have changed over time. Having seen earlier what some of the texts of the *Torah* say on this matter, we will turn now in this final chapter to consider some later understandings, with an emphasis on post-Holocaust readings.

---

[2]M. Barth, *The People of God*, JSNT Supplement Series 5 (Sheffield, UK: JSOT Press, 1983), 12.

[3]There is no doubt in Barth's mind that to speak of "the people of God" must mean to speak of the church. But he is equally clear that the church's identity as the people of God is only ever conditional, secondary, and fragmentary. The church as a community of people made alive to God in Christ must be considered in light of the fact that "a house and temple . . . already existed *before* there was a church. . . . God *had* a household and a people for the revelation of his grace and glory, *even Israel.*" This is not in itself, of course, a novel insight, nor even a particularly philo-Semitic one. Even the strongest advocates of supersessionism accept that the church's place in God's covenant was chronologically second, even if not providentially so. But Barth goes beyond simply stating the obvious point that Israel came before the church in history. Rather, he insists that the very historical primacy of Israel secures its continuing election, and the church's subsequence renders her conditional. It is not, he argues, the Jews' place within the household of God that is in question. What is problematic, however, is the name, the claim, the existence of the church. Is this (in its majority Gentile) body really the people of God? The certain answer is: only when incorporated in the people elected forever." See M. Barth, *The Broken Wall: A Study of the Epistle to the Ephesians* (London: Collins, 1960), 53, 119.

RABBINIC READINGS

In that great work known as the Talmud, "a literature written by Jews for Jews," the people of the earth are classified dichotomously as "Israel *and the other nations.*"[4] In other words, for the six hundred years during which this collection of rabbinic teachings was compiled, it was axiomatic that, in the divine ordering of humankind, there existed only the Jews whom God had chosen, then everyone else. As Abraham Cohen once put it, "It was a cardinal dogma that Israel was the chosen people." Moreover, he says, this dogma "receive[d] its richest amplification in the treatment of the Rabbis."[5] And so in the Talmud we read rulings such as this: "The Holy One, blessed be He, said to Israel, 'I am God over all who come into the world, but I have only associated my Name with you.'"[6] Or, as the midrash on the book of Genesis says, "Israel was in the thought of God before the creation of the Universe."[7] Writing four to five centuries after the compilation of the Talmud, the incomparable Maimonides (ca. 1135–1204) likewise noted that, "[HaShem] is ever mindful of His covenant . . . that He made with Avraham, swore to Yitzchak, and confirmed in a decree for Yaakov, for Yisrael, as an eternal covenant (*Tehillim*, 105: 8-9)."[8]

These affirmations of Jewish chosenness notwithstanding, there are two critical points to make in reflection on them. First, this rather selective group of texts implies an elected exclusivity that was never really

---

[4]A. Cohen, *Everyman's Talmud: The Major Teachings of the Rabbinic Sages* (1975; repr., New York: Schocken Books, 1995), 59. My emphasis.

[5]Cohen, *Everyman's Talmud*, 59. In the twentieth century, the founder of Reconstructionist Judaism, Rabbi Mordecai Kaplan (1883–1983), advocated an entirely different view. At a conference in New York in 1945, Kaplan reportedly said that "The idea of the Chosen People was justifiable religious doctrine in ancient Judaism [but] today it is not merely untenable, but also detrimental to a normal adjustment of the Jew to his environment. . . . That idea is warranted, to be sure, in the realm of opinion as an assertion of Judaism's contribution to the religion of mankind in the past, but it is not as such an opinion that it is included in the traditional Prayer Book. There it is in the realm of dogma and is meant to affirm that the Jewish people has been chosen to occupy forever the central place in the divine scheme of salvation. As such it neither is nor can be any longer accepted by modern-minded Jews."

[6]Ex R xxix.4 (*Sh'mot Rabba* is the midrash on the book of Exodus).

[7]Gen R i.4.

[8]A. Y. Finkel, *The Essential Maimonides: Translations of the Rambam* (Northvale, NJ: Jason Aronson, 1996), 22.

intended to be such. It was, and is, an election utterly unlike the racially circumscribed notion of divine supremacy that characterized both French and especially German religiopolitical ideologies of the nineteenth and twentieth centuries, because it was, and is, an election that looks outward to the other nations as well. As the late Chief Rabbi Baron Immanuel Jakobovits put it,

> Yes, I do believe the chosen people concept as affirmed by Judaism in its holy writ, its prayers, and its millennial tradition. [But] in fact, I believe that *every people*—and indeed, in a more limited way, every individual—is "chosen" or destined for some distinct purpose in advancing the designs of Providence.[9]

Or, in the words of Martin Buber, "Israel was chosen from of old . . . to work not on others but on itself. This work, however, was to shine in the midst of the world of nations, to win souls for God and thus to become the beginnings of His kingdom."[10]

Second, just as Israel's chosenness—that is to say, its election—has never, in midrashic teaching, been thought to denote an ethnic or religious superiority, it has also, from time to time, been regarded as a burden that the Jewish people carry vicariously for "the other nations." And so we read such as this: "The Nation of Israel is likened to the olive. Just as this fruit yields its precious oil only after being much pressed and squeezed, so Israel's destiny is one of great oppression and hardship, in order that it may thereby give forth its illuminating wisdom."[11] Or as the redoubtable Tevye says to God in *The Fiddler on the Roof*, "I know, I know, we are your chosen people. But once in a while, can't you choose someone else?" And in André Schwarz-Bart's evocative novel, *Le derniers des Justes*, Mother Judith asks (only very slightly rhetorically), "When will God stop *miracling* us this way?" In each instance, there is a recognition that the blessing of election sometimes carries

[9]Cited in D. Mackenzie, T. Falcon, and J. Rahman, eds., *Religion Gone Astray: What We Found at the Heart of Interfaith* (Woodstock, VT: Skylight Paths, 2011), 21.
[10]M. Buber, *The Prophetic Faith* (New York: Macmillan, 1949), 233.
[11]Ex R xxxvi.1.

consequences that are hard to bear. Nowhere was this more evident than in the National Socialist "war against the Jews,"[12] the Shoah, in which six million of God's chosen were hunted down and industrially murdered. It is no wonder that the Jewish people's concept of election has been turned upside down since the ending of the Holocaust.

JEWISH THEOLOGIES OF ELECTION AFTER THE SHOAH

In 1982, the late Jewish philosopher Emil Fackenheim claimed that the Holocaust[13] was an event of such extraordinary and unprecedented evil that it was no less than a decisive rupture of all epistemological and cultural categories, including history, philosophy, and theology.[14] He argued that neither the world nor its organizing patterns of thought and discourse could ever be the same after Auschwitz. Not everyone has found this claim for singularity compelling or persuasive. To make and then stand by this claim means, first, to imply a judgment about other events that may, at first glance, appear to fall within a similar category of event and, second, to risk mythologizing the Holocaust itself (and therefore its participants, both victims and perpetrators) into historical inaccessibility. Illustrative of a third difficulty with Fackenheim's thesis on the singularity of Auschwitz—this time a theological rather than historiographical difficulty—is Markus Barth's furious, and at times vitriolic, debate with Fackenheim on precisely this point. Barth saw in Fackenheim's insistence on the hermeneutical centrality of the Holocaust a form of natural theology that was, for him—as the son of his father!—anathema. Was it not "perverse" of Fackenheim to go back "again and again [to] the horrors of Hitler?" Would it not be better, urged Markus, to "throw behind you the unbearable guilt and suffering of those endless years and uncounted martyrs" and refuse to "make sin the

---

[12]The phrase comes from Lucy Dawidowicz's 1975 book, *The War Against the Jews, 1933–1945* (New York: Holt, Rinehart & Winston, 1975).

[13]Note that I use the terms *Holocaust, Shoah,* and (occasionally) *Churban* interchangeably to denote the same event. It is important to appreciate, however, that while each of these terms is, for various reasons, inexact and even inappropriate, Jewish custom has tended to favor *Shoah.*

[14]E. Fackenheim, *To Mend the World: Foundations of Post-Holocaust Jewish Thought* (1982; repr., New York: Schocken Books, 1989).

basis of [y]our theology?"[15] Yet, as the Catholic ethicist John Pawlikowski has said, whether we like it or not—and the younger Barth clearly did not!—"the face of Auschwitz" has ushered in "a significantly new era."[16]

Notwithstanding his positing a deeply problematic universal singularity for the Holocaust, Fackenheim's claim is at heart an epistemological one. The Shoah has come to be recognized, in many circles at least, as *the* rupturing event of the modern era. Indicative of this rupturing character is the so-called *Historikerstreit* of the 1980–1990s, during which historians and philosophers of history debated the legacy of Nazism in the overall evaluation of German history.[17] Regardless of which side one took in this debate, there was one point on which agreement was reached, one fundamental historiographical truth that could not be escaped—the Holocaust was and is, for Germany at least, an unmasterable history. It is a *Vergangenheitsbewältigung*; it is a past that will not go away.[18]

This sort of ontological determination that arose out of the so-called Historians' Debate inevitably raised the status of the Holocaust to an event of more than mere history. Marvin Prosono, for one, has argued with some concern against such a sacralizing of the Holocaust. Instead of it being regarded and studied simply as a series of discrete events, the Holocaust has, he says, become "a metaphysical conceptualization . . . which [has come] to stand for something more." Prosono cautions that we must be wary of interpreting the Holocaust as a "sacred text."[19] Yet for

---

[15]M. Barth to E. Fackenheim, 18 December 1966, Markus Barth Collection, Princeton Theological Seminary, Series II, Box 13, file 375. See my "Jewish-Christian Dialogue from the Underside: Markus Barth's Correspondence with Michael Wyschogrod (1962–84) and Emil Fackenheim (1965–80)," *Journal of Ecumenical Studies* 53 (Summer 2018): 334.

[16]J. Pawlikowski, "Christian Ethics and the Holocaust: A Dialogue with Post-Auschwitz Judaism," in *Theological Studies* 49 (1988): 650.

[17]For an excellent overview and analysis of this debate, see especially P. Baldwin, *Hitler, the Holocaust and the Historians Dispute* (Boston: Beacon Press, 1990); R. Kühnl, ed., *Vergangenheit, die nicht vergeht: Die "Historikerdebatte"; Darstellung, Dokumentation, Kritik* (Cologne: Pahl-Rugenstein, 1987); and C. Maier, *The Unmasterable Past: History, Holocaust and German National Identity* (Cambridge, MA: Harvard University Press, 1988).

[18]See E. Nolte, "Die Vergangenheit, die nicht vergehen will," *Frankfurter Allgemeine Zeitung* (June 6, 1986).

[19]M. Prosono, "The Holocaust as a Sacred Text: Can the Memory of the Holocaust Be Tamed?,"

all his insistence that the Holocaust *not* be universalized and thus vacated of *particular* meaning, Yehuda Bauer has nonetheless, and perhaps reluctantly, recognized that the Shoah has indeed "become a cultural code."[20] It is a paradigmatic event, a symbol, that stands for more than itself. By its very nature, the Holocaust stands apart from the normative sweep of history and disrupts the routine categories of explanation.

To return to Fackenheim's diagnosis, the Holocaust renders the assumption of historical continuity between past and present fragile, at best, if not in fact untenable: "Historical continuity is shattered because at Auschwitz not only man [*sic*] died, but also the idea of man." In Fackenheim's opinion, the Holocaust represents not merely a temporary "relapse into barbarism" out of which humanity will escape (if it has not already done so) but rather "a total rupture" in the very understanding of what humanity is.[21] Chief among all categories of thought and being that are torn asunder by the Holocaust is the notion of the intrinsic dignity of human life. In National Socialist ontology, not all life was equally worthy; Jews, indeed, were *Lebensunwertes Leben*— life unworthy of life—and were, by definition, expendable. Even more pointedly, to snuff out Jewish life was a moral good. Martin Rumscheidt has correctly pointed out that there was a very specific "ethic that functioned in the planning and execution of the Holocaust," but it was "an ethic that did not define the arrest, brutalization, deportation, selection and gassing of Jews as wrong, but, in fact, as ethically tolerable and even as good."[22] With this insight, we are thrust back into the question of election and how—if this ultimate expendability of the Jews was what

in *Remembering for the Future: The Holocaust in an Age of Genocide*, vol. 3, ed. J. K. Roth and E. Maxwell (Houndmills, UK: Palgrave, 2001), 384-87.

[20]Y. Bauer, "A Past That Will Not Go Away," in *The Holocaust and History: The Known, the Unknown, the Disputed and the Reexamined*, ed. M. Berenbaum and A. J. Peck (1998; repr., Bloomington: Indiana University Press, 2002), 22.

[21]Fackenheim, *To Mend the World*, 250-51, 253, 261. As Neil Levi and Michael Rothberg remind us, a deep engagement with the events of the Shoah necessitates "an imperative to rework conventional categories of understanding in the face of their limits." Levi and Rothberg, eds., *The Holocaust: Theoretical Readings* (Edinburgh: Edinburgh University Press, 2003), 1-2.

[22]H. M. Rumscheidt, "Professional Ethics After Auschwitz," in 30th Annual Scholars' Conference on the German Churches and the Holocaust, March 4–7, 2000, 251-52.

they experienced under Nazism—modern Judaism has had to redefine what it means to be chosen.[23]

THE HOLOCAUST IN CONTEMPORARY JEWISH THEOLOGY

In the decades since the ending of the Holocaust, there has been an unsurprisingly robust engagement within the sphere of modern Jewish theology with the legacies and lessons of the Shoah. This is not, as some might have it, because the Holocaust was purely and simply a *Jewish* event. It was not.[24] Such a naive categorization of the Holocaust fails utterly to comprehend both its enormity and the reach of its moral and cultural consequences. Moreover, it is a categorization that recapitulates the marginalization of Jews that has been so much a part of their collective history. Nor is it to suggest that there is a broad consensus within contemporary Judaism about the impact and importance of the Holocaust. The response of the Haredi Jews, for example, is radically different from that of Reform Jewish scholars such as Richard Rubenstein and Ignaz Maybaum and from that of the liberal Jewish theologian Marc Ellis. As Zev Garber has correctly noted, Jewish responses to the Shoah "cover the gamut of Jewish thought."[25] Indeed, this is precisely how it should be. This is partly generational. Eliezer Berkovits reminds us that those who were not there *must* respond but *cannot* respond in the way that is possible for those who were: "We are not Job and we dare not speak and respond as if we were."[26] The late Catholic scholar Harry J. Cargas put it bluntly when he said that the Shoah

---

[23]The material in this sub-section is adapted from my book *Reading Auschwitz with Barth*, 15-17.

[24]However, I do not mean by this what Markus Barth once meant: "Would you consider it blasphemous if I said that we Christians have not also been criminals who committed [*sic*] Auschwitz but at the same time also victims of their deeds . . . Auschwitz also happened to me." Letter, M. Barth to E. Borowitz, March 2, 1967, Markus Barth Collection, Princeton Theological Seminary, Series II, Box 13, file 381. See my "Jewish-Christian Dialogue from the Underside," 336. By this Barth wished to affirm the solidarity of Christians with the Jewish people on account of their joint election. Nonetheless, this way of expressing solidarity caused quite understandable offense.

[25]Z. Garber, *Shoah: The Paradigmatic Genocide; Essays in Exegesis and Eisegesis*. Studies in the Shoah 8 (Lanham, MD: University Press of America, 1994), 2.

[26]E. Berkovits, *Faith After the Holocaust* (New York: Ktav Publishing House, 1973), 3-5.

"requires an extraordinary response. That should be plural. It requires extraordinary responses."[27]

This (quite proper) spectrum of Jewish reflections on the Holocaust notwithstanding, there is an overall agreement that at the very least the Holocaust says *something* to Jews and to Judaism, not least in terms of their election. Insofar as this something is a thing to be heard, by Christians as well as by Jews, it is to that (or those) to which we now turn.

RICHARD RUBENSTEIN

One of the more courageous and creative theological respondents to the Holocaust is Richard Rubenstein (b. 1924), whose brilliant but controversial 1966 book *After Auschwitz* remains arguably the most penetrating insight into post-Holocaust Judaism that has so far been written. To the dismay of many of his colleagues, Rubenstein argued that the near-success of Hitler's genocidal intentions for European Jewry must render belief in covenant theology and in the (ultimately benevolent) Fatherhood of God impossible and obscene.[28] The Holocaust, he said, makes it simply impossible these days to retain the notion of a God in covenantal partnership with the Jewish people. As a "basic minimum . . . the Jews [must] give up the notion that they are the Chosen People of a personal deity."[29] This, in Rubenstein's view, is the inevitable and inescapable either-or for contemporary Jews:

> We can either affirm the innocence of Israel or the justice of God but not both. If the innocence of Israel at Auschwitz is affirmed, whatever God may be, He/She is not distinctively and uniquely the sovereign Lord of covenant and election. If one wishes to avoid any suggestion, however

---

[27]H. J. Cargas, preface to Garber, *Shoah*, xiii. Emphasis added.

[28]One of the many negative assessments of the book came from Jakob Petuchowski, who in a letter to Markus Barth noted, "While I share the anguish which prompted Rubenstein to write what he did, I also find myself much closer to the spirit of your critique than to the 'solution' offered by Rubenstein. What is missing in Rubenstein's treatment is the traditional Jewish response of faith, *we-aph 'al pi khen*, 'and yet!'" J. Petuchowski to M. Barth, 20 April 1967, Markus Barth Papers (Special Collections, Princeton Theological Seminary), Series II, Correspondence, Box 13, file 389.

[29]Garber, *Shoah*, 36.

remote, that at Auschwitz Israel was with justice the object of divine punishment, one must reject any view of God to which such an idea can
plausibly be ascribed.[30]

In Rubenstein's view, paganism—by which he means recovering again
the Jewish attachment to land and earth[31]—is now the only credible
alternative to covenant theology.

For Markus Barth, Rubenstein's alliance with the "death of God"
theologians Thomas Altizer and William Hamilton was the most
damning indictment of his post-Holocaust experiment.

> Rubenstein . . . scorns all hope, especially resurrection. He would face and
> accept blackest darkness and accept no silver linings. . . . [For Rubenstein]
> after Auschwitz man must recognize that the God from whom we come,
> in whom all history runs its course, and to whom we go, is identified with
> Nothingness. . . . *All talk of election*, mission, justification *is sheer myth
> and must be forgotten*. Thus, despair is declared holy.[32]

Arguably, however, even more disturbing than Rubenstein's no to the
God of Israel is the seriousness with which he takes the biblical witness.
He denies the God whom Israel worships, not in spite of what the Scriptures say, but because of it. The testimony of the Hebrew Bible, he
argues, is littered with accusations from Israel's prophets against Jewish
disobedience. Divine retribution cannot but fall, as the rightful response from the hand and will of the electing God. Consequently, when
theological interpretation of the Holocaust frames it in similar terms,
as God's righteous anger against a disobedient people, there is a disturbing synchronicity with the scriptural witness that makes an easy
rejection of the analysis problematic on biblical grounds. That is, such

---

[30]R. L. Rubenstein, *After Auschwitz: History, Theology, and Contemporary Judaism*, (1966; repr.,
Baltimore: Johns Hopkins University Press, 1992), 172.

[31]R. L. Rubenstein, "Some Perspectives on Religious Faith after Auschwitz," in *The German Church
Struggle and the Holocaust*, ed. F.H. Littell and H.G. Locke (Detroit: Wayne State University
Press, 1974), 267.

[32]M. Barth, review of *After Auschwitz*, in *The Pittsburgh Point*, April 6, 1967. Copy in the Markus
Barth Papers (Special Collections, Princeton Theological Seminary), Series III, Publications,
Box P11, file 6. Emphasis added.

an interpretation is "essentially in harmony with Scripture."[33] There is a logical potency about Rubenstein's thesis that is hard to dismiss. Steven Katz has observed that Rubenstein's argument, which is in all likelihood the most radical of all Jewish responses to the Shoah, takes such an extremist position that, "if his thesis is correct, then all other less radical responses . . . , which are predicated on some continued affirmation of . . . [God], are not viable."[34]

I have written elsewhere about the inconsistencies and (in my view, fatal) flaws in Rubenstein's thesis, and I will not rehearse those criticisms again here.[35] Suffice it to say that, notwithstanding the rupturing effect of the Holocaust to which reference has already been made, Jewish history cannot be telescoped into the single interpretive lens of the Shoah. As Steven Katz affirms, Jewish history does not begin with Auschwitz—nor does it end with Auschwitz. There is a Jewish survival after and separate from Auschwitz, and to deny that historical reality is to grant Hitler the posthumous victory, of which Fackenheim spoke and then forbade.[36] The late Conservative Orthodox rabbi David Hartman has put it this way: "Auschwitz, like all Jewish suffering of the past, must be absorbed and understood within the normative framework of Sinai. We will mourn forever because of the memory of Auschwitz. [But] we will build a healthy new society because of the memory of Sinai."[37]

This, however, is what Rubenstein is unable either to comprehend or to permit. On the one hand, he insists on a certain uniqueness for Auschwitz and for all that that place signifies. It is only because the Holocaust is sui generis that it can convey the determinative impact

---

[33]Rubenstein, *After Auschwitz*, 170. As we have seen, the strict either-or of Rubenstein's argument means that, if one wishes to keep God "in the picture," as it were, then the Shoah must be seen as an act of divine justice.

[34]S. Katz, *Post-Holocaust Dialogues: Critical Studies in Modern Jewish Thought* (New York: New York University Press, 1983), 174.

[35]See my *Reading Auschwitz with Barth*, chap. 1.

[36]Katz, *Post-Holocaust Dialogues*, 176-77. See also Fackenheim on the 614th commandment in Fackenheim, *To Mend the World*, xix-xx. The idea of a 614th *mitzvah* was first aired by Fackenheim at a symposium in March 1967 in New York titled "Jewish Values in the Post-Holocaust Future."

[37]D. Hartman, "New Jewish Religious Voices II: Auschwitz or Sinai?," *Ecumenist* 21, no. 1 (1982): 8.

for him and (he claims) for Judaism as a whole. On the other hand, Rubenstein's phenomenology of history requires that he disconnect it from all the other key events in Jewish memory—the Exodus and Sinai traditions, the First and Second Temples, and the various exilic-and-return experiences—apart from which its uniqueness is indemonstrable and through which Israel's election, its chosenness, is itself made manifest. In other words, because Rubenstein parses election only through the dark prism of the Holocaust, and without reference to these other determinative events of Jewish history, election itself is understood by him as nothing less, and nothing other, than an inescapable path toward "elected fatality" and not (as we have named it earlier in the book) "elected sociality." To be an elect Jew is, for Rubenstein, to be elected by God unto only death. This is undoubtedly the logical consequence of his interpretive method, and it makes perfect sense why he would repudiate both the consequence and the type of electing God whom he sees as originator of the consequence. Yet, as people such as Steven Katz and Markus Barth have observed, there are other ways of parsing both Jewish history and the understanding of Jewish election to which that history points that are less narrowly defined and that thus lead to less pessimistic conclusions.

IGNAZ MAYBAUM

If Richard Rubenstein provokes consternation because of his "death of God" theology, with its peculiar phenomenological underpinning, Ignaz Maybaum (1897–1976) is equally controversial, but for entirely different reasons. His most articulate writing on the subject appears in his seminal 1965 book, *The Face of God After Auschwitz*.[38] Like Rubenstein, Maybaum writes from a Reform Jewish perspective. Again, like Rubenstein, Maybaum's thesis is posited on the basis of a particular historiography. But there the similarities end. In stark contrast to Rubenstein, who seeks to evacuate the Holocaust from its historical connectedness, Maybaum

---

[38]I. Maybaum, *The Face of God After Auschwitz* (Amsterdam: Polak & Van Gennep, 1965).

insists on seeing the Shoah in close continuity with Israel's past. Curiously, this leads him to his second major departure from Rubenstein. Whereas Rubenstein reads the Shoah as incontrovertible evidence of the death of God and the illegitimacy of any continuing talk of Israel's election, Maybaum argues instead that the death of the Jewish victims of Nazism should be interpreted through the lens of Christological hermeneutics. The murdered Jews are reflective of a new crucifixion, through which God raises humanity to a greater level of maturity and leads the world into a new era of progress. As remarkable as it sounds, "In Auschwitz Jews suffered vicarious atonement for the sins of humankind." Therefore, "The Golgotha of modern mankind is Auschwitz. The cross, the Roman gallows, was replaced by the gas chamber."[39]

In Maybaum's paradigm, there is an inner connectedness between Israel's biblical-prophetic history, Auschwitz, and Christianity's own redemption story:

> Jews have a history to which the Servant-of-God texts in the Book of Isaiah provide the pattern. In Auschwitz . . . Jews suffered vicarious death for the sins of mankind. It says in the liturgy of the Synagogue in reference to the first and second *churban*, albeit centuries after the event: "because of our sins." After Auschwitz Jews need not say so. Can any martyr be a more innocent sin-offering than those murdered in Auschwitz! The millions who died in Auschwitz died "because of the sins of others." Jews and non-Jews died in Auschwitz, but the Jew hatred which Hitler inherited from the medieval Church made Auschwitz the twentieth-century Calvary of the Jewish people.[40]

Maybaum's extraordinary conclusion is predicated on what he sees as two fundamental aspects of the divine-human relationship within history. On the one hand, he affirms the very thing that Rubenstein feels compelled to deny—that is, the uniqueness, the chosenness, of Israel within divine providence. To the anti-Semite, the Jews' existence is an ontological offense:

---

[39]Maybaum, *Face of God After Auschwitz*, 21.
[40]Maybaum, *Face of God After Auschwitz*, 35.

> After millennia of a varied history the election of the Jewish people still existed as a living and strong factor . . . Hitler also knew that the Jew, historically and existentially, even without any personal choice, stands for justice, mercy and truth . . . But they [Jews] proved to be what others, what millions were not: they were chosen. In the apocalyptic hour of modern mankind the Jews did not bow before the Moloch. *God did not let them. They were his people. Their election was still valid.* Again it was demonstrated that to be chosen means to have no choice. God chooses. The Jewish people were again chosen to be not like the gentiles.[41]

Maybaum points to the very essence of the Jewish scandal, and the thing to which Karl Barth himself points. As Barth says, in the context of his doctrine of providence, "Jews as Jews were not meant to have any continued existence . . . *But they always have had, and they still have today; and today genuinely so.*"[42] Or again,

> Therefore the Jews can be despised and hated and oppressed and persecuted and even assimilated, but they cannot really be touched; they cannot be exterminated; they cannot be destroyed. They are the only people which necessarily continues to exist, with the same certainty that God is God, and that what He has willed and said and done according to the message of the Bible is not a whim or a jest, but eternally in earnest.[43]

Barth thus affirms what Maybaum also says: the reason why the Nazi war against the Jews was ultimately unsuccessful is because the Jews were and are chosen.

On the other hand, Maybaum refutes the uniqueness of the Shoah event and interprets it, on the contrary, as yet another occurrence in Israel's history that mediates atonement. "It is," says Maybaum, "our prophetic task to interpret Auschwitz as awful portent (*mophet*) in the exodus from our past into the future. None of us needs to blush when expected to do what the biblical prophets did."[44] Therefore, not only is the Holocaust on a continuum with other decisive events in Israel's

---

[41]Maybaum, *Face of God After Auschwitz*, 25-26. Emphasis added.
[42]*CD* III/3, 212. Emphasis added.
[43]*CD* III/3, 218-19.
[44]Maybaum, *Face of God After Auschwitz*, 200.

history but so too are post-Holocaust Jewish theologians on a continuum with the biblical prophets. The continuities within history are striking. Like the destruction of the First and Second Temples, Auschwitz is *Churban*—destruction not for its own sake but for the sake of the sociocultural evolution, first of the Jews and then, through them, of all humanity.

Self-evidently, these two predicates belong inseparably to one another. The only reason that a Jewish Churban can be at all evolutionary and progressive is because the Jews as such are God's elect and thus chosen as the mediators of the divine providential overruling in world history. However, serious ramifications of Maybaum's metaphysic of history render his position theologically untenable.

Maybaum's thesis depends on his understanding of Churban, which in turn is informed by his belief in the eternal providence of God. Churban is not simply a catastrophic event, although it is at least that. More to the point, though, it is an event that "make[s] an end to an old era and creates a new era. The *Churban* is a day of awe, of awe beyond human understanding."[45] There is, in other words, a creative aspect to Churban. It has a peculiarly dialectical structure, being at once an event of total destruction and yet simultaneously the herald of a new dawn. It carries this significance because, in essence, the Churban is a distinctly providential event; it happens in, through, and at the will of God, with the express purpose of drawing the Gentile nations to Godself. It is a historical expression of the function of Israel's election: to be a light to the nations. Transcending "the parameters of Israel's own existence, [it] affects world history and informs the life of the nations." As Steven Katz observes, in precisely this way, Churban is a "revelatory moment that brings the gentiles to God by addressing them in a language they find intelligible."[46]

The imperative inherent in the Maybaumian thesis to retain faith in both Israel's election and in the electing God of Israel is no doubt a

---

[45]Maybaum, *Face of God After Auschwitz*, 32.
[46]Katz, *Post-Holocaust Dialogues*, 158.

more palatable response to Auschwitz than Rubenstein's paganistic alternative. Nevertheless, the way in, and the purpose for, which Maybaum ascribes revelatory status to the Shoah—that it functions as a redemptive vehicle for the nations' return to God—makes for uncomfortable, indeed impossible, reading.

For the Christian reader, of course, Maybaum's contention that the Holocaust somehow stands as a modern-day equivalent to the cross of Christ, and carries with it a similar redemptive effect, is an intolerable concession to make. But it is equally impossible to the Jewish reader, perhaps for a similar reason. It is not primarily that Maybaum's thesis devalues the atoning singularity of Jesus' death. It certainly does so, but one can hardly criticize a Jewish theologian for that. In any case, there are enough arguments within Christian discourse about the way in which the cross is redemptively effectual for Maybaum's argument not to be decisively repudiated on those grounds alone.[47] That is, we should not reject Maybaum's Auschwitz-atonement theory out of hand simply because it does not conform to a particular Christian model of atonement, of which there are several. Rather, the problem with Maybaum's argument is of a different nature entirely, one that should resonate equally with Christians and Jews—and indeed with people of all faith traditions and none. The overriding difficulty with it is the moral repugnance of the atonement that is here suggested, by which Jews are, again as throughout their history, sacrificed for some hypothetical *summum bonum.*

If we are to take Maybaum seriously, then the Jewish victims of the Nazi death camps were sacrificial victims—truly, "lambs to the slaughter"—on behalf of others. Their deaths secured the liberation of those who did not die. There are two insuperable difficulties with this claim, one ontological and one theological. Maybaum misconstrues the

---

[47]As Robert Jenson has put it, "If you deny that Christ is 'of one being with the Father,' or that the Son and Jesus are but one hypostasis, you are formally a heretic. But you can deny any explanation of how the atonement works . . . or even deny that any explanation is possible, and be a perfectly orthodox believer." Jenson, "On the Doctrine of the Atonement," *Princeton Seminary Bulletin* 27, no. 2 (2006): 100.

nature of Jesus' crucifixion by seeking to interpret Auschwitz as an
event of similar type. They are patently different. The Christian confession of the cross is that there, at that historical moment, God took
on Godself the sin of humanity. Irrespective of one's view of the (im)
possibility of God, Christian doctrine and dogma across the ages and
the ecumenical spectrum agree at least that on the cross, the incarnate
second person of the Trinity went to his death, willingly and for others.
And because such a sacrifice overflows from the abundance of divine
selfhood and is indeed a sacrifice of God by God, this is no demonstration of caprice or malevolence but rather of God's beneficent self-
giving. In Steven Katz's words, "There is thus no terrible cruelty or
unspeakable 'crime' but only Divine Love, the presence of unlimited
Divine Grace."[48]

It is not hard to see, however, that the Shoah is an utterly different
sort of event. Notwithstanding the possibility of acts of *Kiddush
Hashem*[49] (קִדּוּשׁ הַשֵּׁם) (of which there were many), the victims of the
Nazi *Einsatzgruppen* and the gas chambers did not go to their deaths
willingly. In their case, God chose not himself to die, but them. Indeed,
that Maybaum argues that the Holocaust exists in history as a moment
of God's providence necessarily means that God willed and caused (at
least as a first cause) the deaths of the Nazis' victims. Here, then, must
be an instance not of overwhelming and unlimited grace but of overwhelming and inexpressible cruelty. Moreover, Katz begs the vital
question: If these deaths at Auschwitz were in the service of vicarious
atonement, "is it not the case that the nature of the atonement is far
more criminal and infinitely more depraved than the sins for which it
atones?"[50] Clearly, there is a dis-analogy between the Holocaust and
the crucifixion. To claim they are of the same type is to make a fundamental category error.

---

[48]Katz, *Post-Holocaust Dialogues*, 252.
[49]קִדּוּשׁ הַשֵּׁם —the *mitzvah* (commandment) for the "sanctification of the Name," to bring glory to
   God by being holy, as God is holy.
[50]Katz, *Post-Holocaust Dialogues*, 253.

There remains the overarching theological difficulty of Maybaum's thesis—theological, because it relates primarily to the nature of the God to whom Maybaum ascribes the providential causality of the Shoah. Maybaum wants to insist that God was present in Auschwitz. Of course, if the psalmist is right, and God is present even in the grave (Ps 139:8), then Maybaum must also be right. There is, it is true, a degree of comfort in the idea that not even the hellish conditions of the death camps could entirely separate God from his people.[51] But Maybaum does not wish to limit God's presence in the Holocaust simply to that of suffering solidarity. As we have seen, God is far more culpable than that. He is causally present: "Hitler was an instrument. . . . God used this instrument to cleanse, to purify, to punish a sinful world; the six million Jews, they died an innocent death; they died because of the sins of others."[52]

No one could reasonably refute Maybaum's claim that the world is utterly sinful; if the Holocaust proves anything, it proves that. Nor could anyone these days seriously argue against the innocence of those Jews who died at the Nazis' hands (although tragically and nonsensically, there are still some ultra-conservative Christian groups for whom Jesus' blood is on the Jews' and their descendants, [Mt 27:25] hands, and to whom the accusation of deicide remains as potent a cause of anti-Semitic hatred as ever). But the contention that God himself caused and used the Holocaust as a vehicle of redemptive cleansing is deeply problematic and poses afresh the theodicy problem. If God was not involved, if divine providence played no part, then one must question the omnipotence of a God who did not (could not?) step in. In John Pawlikowski's confronting phrase, "The paradigm of an all-powerful God who will intervene to halt human and creational destruction is simply dead after the Holocaust."[53] If God was involved, then one must question

---

[51]Elie Wiesel's *Night* presents perhaps the most poignant of all expressions of the divine presence in Auschwitz, in the story of the young boy hanged on the gallows. There is, however, no lingering comfort in Wiesel's account—only despair. See E. Wiesel, *Night*, trans. S. Rodway (London: Penguin, 1981), 75-76.

[52]Maybaum, *Face of God After Auschwitz*, 67.

[53]J. Pawlikowski, "Human Responsibility: Contemporary Reflections in Light of Nazi Ideology,"

whether in fact perfect love and moral rectitude are at the essence of the divine being. To again quote Katz,

> Once one attributes [the Shoah] directly—causally—to God, it becomes impossible to understand or to justify, for an omnipotent, omniscient Being must be able to instruct His creation and to lead it where He will in ways other than Auschwitz. If he cannot then he is not the all-encompassing Absolute of Maybaum's metaphysics. If he does not then he is not the moral deliverer of Judaism.[54]

Maybaum is to be applauded for his courageous efforts to protect the redemptive possibility of God's action, even in the midst and in spite of the most horrendous tragedy of the Jews' history. Moreover, he does so by defiantly insisting that the redemptive nature of the Holocaust depends on the continuing status of the Jewish people as God's chosen, as the apple of his eye (Zech 2:8). Nonetheless, his framework poses more problems than it resolves, and it condemns Hitler's victims to being mere playthings of a malfeasant God whose providential plan is depicted as being more important than even his own elected people.

ELIEZER BERKOVITS

Eliezer Berkovits (1908–1992) is representative of a third strand of contemporary Jewish responses to the Shoah to which we also need to give some consideration. As we shall see, however, his contribution does not lie in the radicality of his argument but in its very orthodoxy. Unlike Rubenstein, who insists on taking Scripture so seriously that in a post-Shoah world he cannot accept the image of the God who is therein described, and unlike Maybaum, who interprets the Jewish sufferings through the redemptive lens of reconfigured Christology, Berkovits approaches the problem of the Holocaust from an Orthodox rabbinic perspective. Vitally, this includes, like Maybaum, his insistence on the continuing election of the Jewish people. Indeed, it is his cleaving to,

---

in *Remembering for the Future: The Holocaust in an Age of Genocide*, ed. J. K. Roth and E. Maxwell (Houndmills, UK: Palgrave, 2001), 2:149.

[54]Katz, *Post-Holocaust Dialogues*, 263.

and deep familiarity with, halachic tradition that sets him apart from most other Jewish thinkers and theologians who have wrestled with the impact and import of the Holocaust.[55] That this is his standpoint also renders his understanding of the Shoah fundamentally flawed.

As far as Berkovits is concerned, the Holocaust poses no new challenge to God or theology. In this he stands in direct conflict with Rubenstein but in agreement with David Hartman and Michael Wyschogrod, for both of whom Auschwitz is not and cannot be ultimately decisive in any serious sense. This is not to say that he regards it as insignificant. On the contrary, his deep reverence for the integrity of humanity requires him to say that the horror of suffering, and the dilemma that the reality of suffering poses to our concept of God, is the same whether one Jew dies or six million. The basic question remains: How could God allow it? Thus, Berkovits does not underestimate the worth of the six million, as some have claimed, but instead places the highest of premiums on *each* individual. On this basis he is compelled to affirm that, "From the point of view of the problem, we have had innumerable Auschwitzes."[56] The sufferings of one, or the suffering of many, equally challenge the vision of God's beneficence and mercy. The problem, says Berkovits, is as old as creation itself—or at least as old as creation's estrangement from God.

> While in absolute terms the horrors of the German death camps by far surpassed anything that preceded it, in terms of subjective experience the impact of the catastrophe on the major tragic occasions of Jewish history was no less intense than the impact of the horrors of our own experience. The problem of God's providential presence is always raised in relationship to man's [*sic*] subjective experience of his presence. The objective quantitative magnitude of the tragedy has little to do with it. It is for this reason that while the Holocaust is unique in the objective magnitude of its inhumanity, it is not unique as a problem of faith.[57]

---

[55]Katz, *Post-Holocaust Dialogues*, 268.
[56]Berkovits, *Faith After the Holocaust*, 90.
[57]Berkovits, *Faith After the Holocaust*, 90.

It is evident from this that Berkovits is in no way trying to minimize the enormity of the Holocaust horror. It is indeed "unique in the objective magnitude of its inhumanity." Theologically, however, there is nothing that the Holocaust presents that has not been presented before. The Holocaust simply reifies in the modern world the problem of how to affirm both the love of God and the reality of evil.

How, then, does Berkovits respond to this age-old dilemma? True to his commitment to Jewish tradition and orthodoxy, he reverts to the defensive position of free will theodicy, which is predicated in turn on the divine "hiddenness"—the *hester panim* (hidden face) of God. That is, God must be absent in order for humanity to have authentic moral agency. "That man may be," says Berkovits, "God must absent Himself."[58] Or, in Simone Weil's words, "God can only be present in creation under the form of absence."[59] "Man can only exist because God renounces the use of power on him. This, of course, means that God cannot be present in history through manifest material power. Such presence would destroy history [which is] the arena for human responsibility."[60] If God intervenes with material power in the world of human historical occurrence, then humankind itself is robbed of the opportunity to choose the good over the evil and is thus cheated of the essential element of its humanity. The corresponding problem, though, is that for as long as God "shows forbearance with the wicked, He must turn a deaf ear to the anguished cries of the violated."[61]

Inasmuch as this is a restatement of free will theodicy, it is as coherent as any other theodical response to massive evil. But the converse is also true; inasmuch as it a restatement of free will theodicy, the same objections retain their rebuttive force. That is, could not an omnipotent, omniscient, and eternally beneficent God have created a world that was both free of evil and retentive of human freedom? Alternatively, would

---

[58]Berkovits, *Faith After the Holocaust*, 124.
[59]S. Weil, *Gravity and Grace*, trans. E. Craufurd (London: Routledge and Kegan Paul, 1963), 99.
[60]Berkovits, *Faith After the Holocaust*, 109.
[61]Berkovits, *Faith After the Holocaust*, 106.

it not have been possible for such a God to facilitate a place for human moral responsibility without so much evil? Steven Katz goes even further: "It increasingly seems to me that it would have been . . . morally preferable, to have a world in which 'evil' did not exist, at least not in the magnitude witnessed during the *Sho'ah*, even if this meant doing without certain heroic moral attributes or accomplishments."[62] For Katz, moral freedom is simply not worth the ever-threatening menace of evil. Far better to be morally deficient and safe than morally free and at risk of malevolent destruction.

While Eliezer Berkovits's response to the Holocaust thus falls victim to the same philosophical deficiencies as any other theodicy, his thesis insists on a thoroughgoing affirmation of God's care for Israel, precisely because they are and continue to be bound together under his covenant. Notwithstanding all that the Jewish people have suffered through the absence of God, this very absence is paradoxically the proof of his merciful presence. "Evil will not ultimately triumph."[63] On the contrary, and in a manner reminiscent of Karl Barth, the survival of the Jews despite all they have endured proves God's miraculous, mysterious intrusion into Israel's historical story. In their wondrous endurance, against all the odds, we are compelled to affirm none other than "the presence of a hiding God in history."[64] God, in order to safeguard human moral responsibility, had to remain hidden. But in his hiddenness, God was nevertheless present in order to safeguard the future of his beloved people. This is Berkovits's claim. It cannot be proven. It can only be believed (or not).

Berkovits thus advances a thoroughly orthodox response to the Shoah. Awful in magnitude, the Holocaust nonetheless poses no greater threat to our vision of God than any other tragic occurrence, precisely because God himself cannot ultimately be challenged. Even

---

[62] Katz, *Post-Holocaust Dialogues*, 274.

[63] Berkovits, *Faith After the Holocaust*, 107.

[64] E. Berkovits, *With God in Hell, with God in Hell: Judaism in the Ghettoes and Deathcamps* (New York: Hebrew Publishing, 1979), 83. See also R. Harries, *After the Evil: Christianity and Judaism in the Shadow of the Holocaust* (Oxford: Oxford University Press, 2003), 30-31.

in his absence, he is present. Even in his supposed indifference, he is completely engaged for and on behalf of his elected people. Such a response to the Holocaust is, in this author's view, a critical parameter to keep in mind. One can only marvel at the faith in his God to which Berkovits remains, in spite of everything, committed. Nonetheless, his response is, by itself, theologically untenable. It simply does not adequately address the issues that the Shoah raises, mainly because it does not believe that there are any particular issues to be addressed. As Katz puts it, Berkovits "lacks the sense of uncertainty and ambiguity that has been a cornerstone of . . . the Jewish . . . experience"[65] and of which someone like Elie Wiesel has been such a vocal proponent. Or, in Pawlikowski's words, Berkovits has "seriously underestimated the degree to which the Holocaust forces us to readjust some of our understanding of our biblical heritage."[66]

The Holocaust does nothing if not shake our entire theological, philosophical, and epistemological foundations—yet Berkovits cannot bring himself to accept that view. Yes, he acknowledges the profundity of its impact on Israel and the West. The West can no longer claim to be or to represent a global ethic: "Auschwitz ushered in the final phase of the moral disintegration of Western civilization."[67] Yet Berkovits ultimately has faith and retains his hope. The survival of Israel—specifically, the people, on the land—represents both riddle and response. The Jews should not be, yet they are. They have survived against all odds, and in so doing have shown not only that they are the chosen people of God but that there is indeed a God who has chosen them. In this hope for Israel, says Berkovits, there is hope for humanity.[68]

In considering the works of Rubenstein, Maybaum, and Berkovits, we have encountered three very different Jewish theological responses to the Holocaust, each of which addresses the question of Jewish

[65]Katz, *Post-Holocaust Dialogues*, 96.
[66]Pawlikowski, "Christian Ethics and the Holocaust," 655.
[67]Berkovits, *Faith After the Holocaust*, 36.
[68]Berkovits, *Faith After the Holocaust*, 167.

election in a different way. Richard Rubenstein—posing a dichotomous either-or between, on the one hand, the Jews' innocence in the face of Nazi exterminationism and, on the other, the concept of covenant—sides (rightly) with the Jewish people. The casualties of this decision, however, are any talk of election and the covenantal care of God for his people as well as that electing God himself. In stark contrast, Ignaz Maybaum defends—indeed, insists on—the continuing chosenness of Israel as God's beloved people. But he does so because he exegetes the Holocaust as a cross-like redemptive event that, precisely because it happened to the elect people of Israel, has salvific ramifications for all of humanity. The Shoah is, in Maybaum's thesis, the event by which Israel at last lives into its mission as a light to the nations. Finally, Eliezer Berkovits takes yet another approach. Unlike Rubenstein and Maybaum, Berkovits refuses to grant the Holocaust any particular historiographical significance. It is not unique; it is not sui generis. What it does show, however, is that the people of Israel survive. They continue to live, even after the most monstrous attempt to get rid of them. And this, argues Berkovits, surely demonstrates both their election as God's covenant people and the ultimate victory of God's providential care.

Not surprisingly, none of these interpretations has garnered a consensus of support. They each pose creative possibilities as well as untenable challenges. But they each also demonstrate a renewed engagement by Jewish theologians with the vexed matter of what it means to be divinely chosen. They are not the only ones to do so. Perhaps more remarkably, even the Roman Catholic Church has, in the aftermath of the Holocaust, been forced into its own reconsideration. It is to that instance to which we now turn in the final substantive section of this book.

VATICAN II: NOSTRA AETATE

In 1967, the Canadian-Israeli historian Pinchas Lapide responded to Rolf Hochhuth's controversial 1963 play *The Deputy* (*Der Stellvertreter*) by defending the wartime actions of Pope Pius XII and arguing that, under his papacy, the Roman Church had been responsible for the rescue of more than eight hundred thousand Jews. Lapide's defense of such a divisive pope was remarkable, not only because it came from a Jewish scholar but because it was so obviously at odds with what had become a near-unanimous castigation of Pius's pontificate.[69] However, his admiration for Pope Pius XII notwithstanding, Lapide was far more qualified in his assessment of the Catholic tradition as a whole. He was quick to recognize that whatever good Pius XII might have done was in stark contrast to the majority of Roman Catholic history. "How [Catholic] leaders for eighteen centuries succeeded in reconciling the basic Christian doctrine of love with a persistent policy of anti-Judaism is perhaps the most baffling problem of modern theology."[70]

Lapide, however, was not only writing in the wake of Hochhuth's controversial play. In the nearer background was the just-concluded Second Vatican Council (1962–1965), out of which had emerged, among a remarkable set of other significant changes, a radically new articulation of the relationship between Roman Christianity and non-Christian religions. The special connection of the church with Israel was particularly in view, and the resulting document, *Nostra Aetate*,[71] was an intentional repudiation of precisely that 1,800-year-old "persistent anti-Judaism" of which Lapide was to speak two years later. With remarkable candor, Cardinal Walter Kasper said, toward the end of

---

[69]Hochhuth's play is a searing critique of Pope Pius XII, presenting him as a callous yet cowardly figure who refused to use his considerable influence to take action against the Nazi regime or to speak out against the Holocaust. Hochhuth's characterization of Pius XII was routinely accepted for years, culminating in John Cornwell's extraordinarily ill-titled *Hitler's Pope: The Secret History of Pius XII* (London: Penguin Books, 1999). More recent scholarship, however—including by renowned historians Martin Gilbert and Owen Chadwick—has not only helped restore Pius's reputation but has also cast suspicion on Hochhuth himself, who has been named as a (possibly unwitting) pawn of the Cold War–era Soviet disinformation bureau, Seat 12.

[70]P. Lapide, *The Last Three Popes and the Jews* (London: Souvenir Press, 1967), 25. Lapide's claims have not been without controversy themselves. Susan Zucotti, Carol Ritner, and John K. Roth are among influential Holocaust historians who have criticized Lapide's factual accuracy as well as his use of "problematic sources." See S. Zuccotti, *Under His Very Windows: The Vatican and the Holocaust in Italy* (New Haven, CT: Yale University Press, 2000); and C. Ritner and J. K. Roth, eds., *Pope Pius II and the Holocaust* (New York: Leicester University Press, 2002).

[71]Second Vatican Council, "Declaration on the Relation of the Church to Non-Christian Religions, *Nostra Aetate*, Proclaimed by His Holiness Pope Paul VI on October 28, 1965," www.vatican.va/archive/hist_councils/ii_vatican_council/documents/vat-ii_decl_19651028_nostra-aetate_en.html.

2001, that *Nostra Aetate* "was and is an historical breakthrough"—but that it was so only "after a long and sad history of indifference, misunderstanding, discrimination, denunciation, oppression and persecution."[72] Unfortunately, however, and despite the best of intentions of "the Good Pope" John XXIII,[73] *Nostra Aetate* was not as complete a success as it might have been.[74]

The declaration, which commences (oddly, it must be said[75]) with the observation that international and cross-cultural relations between people groups are becoming stronger, turns its attention in that very particular light to the relationship between the world religions. Acknowledging the innate quest for meaning as the most primal bond shared by all people, the declaration exhorts "the sons" of the church to honor and appreciate whatever forms such a quest might take in and across the various religions of the world.[76] A short paragraph then mentions "the Moslems," noting that the church "regards [them] with esteem."[77]

---

[72]W. Kasper, "Some Reflections on *Nostra Aetate*," November 23, 2001, www.vatican.va/roman_curia /pontifical_councils/chrstuni/card-kasper-docs/rc_pc_chrstuni_doc_20011123_kasper-nostra -aetate_en.html.

[73]Pope John XXIII had a long history of aiding Jewish people. As Apostolic Delegate to Istanbul during the 1940s, then Angelo Giuseppe Roncalli issued thousands of false baptismal certificates to Jews, who were thus able to escape Nazi occupation under the pretense of being Catholic. In 1959, he ordered the removal of the term *perfidious Jew* from the Good Friday liturgy. Then, in 1961, he commissioned the drafting of *Decretum de Judaeis*—the precursor to *Nostra Aetate*, which, due to his untimely death in 1963, John XXIII never saw promulgated. For a brief textual history of both documents, see J. D. Small, "The Legacy of *Nostra Aetate* in Mainline Protestant Churches," in *A Jubilee for All Time: The Copernican Revolution in Jewish-Christian Relations*, ed. G. S. Rosenthal (Cambridge: Lutterworth Press, 2017), 79-81.

[74]W. A. Visser't Hooft, first secretary-general of the World Council of Churches, described *Nostra Aetate* as a disappointing document that was bereft of substance, apart from a few polite comments about non-Christian religions. Karl Barth similarly thought the entire council to be something of a lost opportunity for the Roman Catholic Church to fully and prophetically engage with modernity. With particular respect to *Nostra Aetate*, Barth queried why Judaism was treated as though it were on the same plane "as Hinduism, Buddhism, and Islam, as a 'non-Christian' religion" when in fact it is "the sole natural . . . proof of God." K. Barth, *Ad Limina Apostolorum: An Appraisal of Vatican II*, trans. C. R. Kim (Eugene, OR: Wipf & Stock, 2016), 35-36.

[75]It is odd because the catastrophe of World War II was only twenty years in the past, the Cuban Missile Crisis (which had threatened the world with nuclear annihilation) had occurred only three years previously, President Lyndon Johnson was escalating the US effort in the Vietnam War, the American civil rights movement was in full swing, and the Indo-Pakistani War, which, although short, had witnessed the largest tank battle since World War II, had ended just over one month before the promulgation of the declaration.

[76]*Nostra Aetate*, §§1-2.

[77]*Nostra Aetate*, §3.

Given where Roman Catholic teaching had been in relation to other Christian traditions—even in the year 2000, the Vatican was still referring to non-episcopal Christian traditions as "defective communities"[78]—the note of respect and even honor that characterized *Nostra Aetate*'s references to other religions is extraordinary. None of this, however, was an affirmation of their redemptive nature. As Piet van der Merwe has correctly observed, "The declaration [did not] address issues which, according to the Church, are of essential meaning to the relationship between the church and non-Christian religions; [in particular] it did not address the salvific position of non-Christian religions."[79] Although the bulk of the declaration tackled the question of Catholic-Jewish relations head-on, it did so necessarily hampered by this dogmatic blind spot.

In turning to what *Nostra Aetate* has to say specifically about the people of Israel—or, as the declaration words it, "Abraham's stock"— one of the most necessary tasks it achieved was, at long last, a formal repudiation of deicide: the accusation that all Jews are, and always will be, collectively responsible for the crucifixion. True, the language used to speak about Jewish culpability for the death of Jesus is somewhat equivocal. "Jerusalem," it is insisted, "did not recognize the time of her visitation, nor did the Jews in large number, accept the Gospel; indeed not a few opposed its spreading." Moreover, "the Jewish authorities and those who followed their lead pressed for the death of Christ." Yet one significant concession upturned Catholic teaching since at least the time of John Chrysostom: "What happened in His passion *cannot be charged against all the Jews*, without distinction, *then alive, nor* against the Jews of *today*."[80]

---

[78]Congregation for the Doctrine of the Faith, "Declaration *Dominus Iesus*, On the Unicity and Salvific Universality of Jesus Christ and the Church," August 6, 2000, §4.17, www.vatican.va /roman_curia/congregations/cfaith/documents/rc_con_cfaith_doc_20000806_dominus-iesus _en.html.

[79]P. van der Merwe, "Commentary on the Documents *Nostra Aetate* and *Lumen Gentium*," *HTS Theological Studies/Teologiese Studies*, supplement 12, 73, no. 6 (2017): 20.

[80]*Nostra Aetate*, §4. Emphasis added. See Harries, *After the Evil*, 159-60. It should be noted that Karl Barth wondered why there was no specific confession of guilt for the centuries of Christian anti-Semitism. Such a confession, he said, would have been appropriate. Barth, *Ad Limina Apostolorum*, 36.

Even more significantly from the perspective of this present project is that the matter of Jewish election was reopened. For example, the declaration identifies the Jews as the genesis of the mystery that is the church and indeed the "beginnings of her faith and her election."[81] Joshua Furnal clearly overstates the case when he says that *Nostra Aetate* depicts the Jewish people as "uniquely . . . God's chosen people."[82] This is simply not the language that the text employs. Indeed, the declaration is emphatic that it is the church that is "the new people of God."[83] While it is the case that divine election finds its first expression in the "Patriarchs, Moses and the prophets," participation in that election is shared only by those who, as members of Christ's church, "believe in Christ." Following the well-worn route of Paulinism, the document expresses unequivocal hope only for those Jews who are "Abraham's sons according to faith."[84]

Nevertheless, this is not the only word to be said, because "the Jews should not be presented as rejected or accursed by God, as if this followed from the Holy Scriptures." Quite the contrary: "God holds the Jews most dear for the sake of their Fathers [and] does not repent of the gifts He makes or of the calls He issues."[85] Whether such a concession anticipates a future salvation of all Israel apart from their evangelization and conversion is not clear from the text. Kevin Hart, for example, has argued that, while *Nostra Aetate* is "rich in theological possibilities," it is still "silent as regards the salvation of those who

---

[81]*Nostra Aetate*, §4.

[82]J. Furnal, "Abraham Joshua Heschel and *Nostra Aetate*: Shaping the Catholic Reconsideration of Judaism During Vatican II," *Religions* 7, no. 6 (2016). It would be true to say that the declaration describes Israel's election as unique, in the sense of being the original election into which the church is now included and which is therefore somehow different from the church's election. But it is patently false to argue that Israel's election is unique if by that it is being suggested that Israel *alone* is the elect people of God.

[83]In *Lumen Gentium*, published almost a full year before *Nostra Aetate*, the church is identified in multiple places as "the new Israel." Second Vatican Council, "Dogmatic Constitution on the Church *Lumen Gentium* Solemnly Promulgated by His Holiness Pope Paul VI on November 21, 1964." See especially §2.9, www.vatican.va/archive/hist_councils/ii_vatican_council/documents/vat-ii_const_19641121_lumen-gentium_en.html.

[84]*Nostra Aetate*, §4.

[85]*Nostra Aetate*, §4.

practice other religions," including Judaism.[86] But at the very least, even if the council was not completely giving up the legitimacy of Jewish missions, it was emphatically repudiating "hatred, persecutions, [and] displays of anti-Semitism, directed against Jews at any time and by anyone."[87] That is to say, just because *Nostra Aetate* did not say all that it could have does not mean it said nothing at all.

CONCLUSION

Evidently the decades since the Holocaust have witnessed not only substantial rethinking from the Jewish side as to the nature of divine election but also a somber reassessment of the Jews' place in God's salvific plan from the Christian perspective. If *Nostra Aetate* pioneered official ecclesial *metanoia* from centuries of anti-Semitic hostility, other non-Catholic traditions were soon to follow. In 1980, the EKiR (Deutsche Evangelische Kirche im Rheinland) issued the groundbreaking *Towards a Renewal of the Relationship of Christians and Jews*, in which the synod affirmed "the permanent election of the Jewish people as the people of God."[88] Across the Atlantic, and seven years later, the United Church of Christ followed suit when, at its Sixteenth General Synod, the delegates voted in favor of a resolution affirming that "God's covenant with the Jewish people has not been abrogated."[89]

None of this has been without difficulty. As we have seen, the range of responses from Jewish theologians does nothing other than instantiate the complex and sometimes contradictory attitudes of contemporary Jewish thought to both the definition and desirability of chosenness. From the Christian aspect, there is not only little clarity (and

[86]K. Hart, "Who Shall Be Saved? The Lord's Prayer After *Nostra Aetate*," ABC Religion & Ethics, October 28, 2015, www.abc.net.au/religion/who-shall-be-saved-the-lords-prayer-after-nostra-aetate /10097714.

[87]*Nostra Aetate*, §4.

[88]"Towards Renovation of the Relationship of Christians and Jews," Synod of the Evangelical Church of the Rhineland, 1980, www.bc.edu/content/dam/files/research_sites/cjl/texts/cjrelations /resources/documents/protestant/EvChFRG1980.htm.

[89]"Relationship Between the UCC and the Jewish Community," Sixteenth General Synod of the United Church of Christ, http://d3n8a8pro7vhmx.cloudfront.net/unitedchurchofchrist/legacy_ url/1140/87-gs-jewish.pdf?1418424574.

even less consensus) about how *both* Christians and Jews could at the same time enjoy God's electing favor but also the risk that the entire question will be hijacked by the complexity of Israeli foreign policy. That is to say, retreat by Christians and churches into a traditional, supersessionary anti-Judaism is more often than not the knee-jerk response to acts of Israeli state aggression against Palestinians—no matter how categorically distinct the issues are.

There remains much work to do.

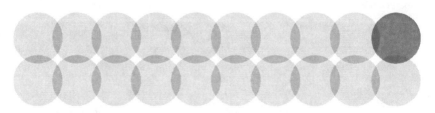

CONCLUSION

HUMANS ARE TRIBAL CREATURES. We like, and need, to know with whom we belong. There is nothing wrong with this; indeed, we could, without too much difficulty, find scriptural warrant for it.

> Then the LORD God said, "It is not good that the man should be alone; I will make him a helper as his partner." So out of the ground the LORD God formed every animal of the field and every bird of the air, and brought them to the man to see what he would call them; and whatever the man called every living creature, that was its name. The man gave names to all cattle, and to the birds of the air, and to every animal of the field; but for the man there was not found a helper as his partner. So the LORD God caused a deep sleep to fall upon the man, and he slept; then he took one of his ribs and closed up its place with flesh. And the rib that the LORD God had taken from the man he made into a woman and brought her to the man. Then the man said, "This at last is bone of my bones and flesh of my flesh; this one shall be called Woman, for out of Man this one was taken." (Gen 2:18-23)

From the moment Adam confessed that his partner was not to be found among the other creatures, simple company has never been an adequate replacement for genuine companionship. And that is as it should be.

The problem is not that we want to know, and to be with, the people who are *ours*—those whom we recognize as being our kin, "flesh of our flesh," as it were. No, the problem is that, throughout the history of humankind, belonging to one group has almost inevitably meant deciding that we do *not* belong to another. Companioning with one has entailed alienating another. Knowing and owning our own corporate identity has mutated all too easily, and all too frequently, into an "othering" of those with whom we feel we do not belong. As Jonathan Sacks so powerfully puts it,

> Groups unite and divide. They divide as they unite. Every group involves the coming together of multiple individuals to form a collective Us. But every Us is defined against a Them, the ones not like us. The one without the other is impossible. Inclusion and exclusion go hand in hand.[1]

It should come as no surprise that the idea of election (of being chosen *by* God to be *with* God) has, as we have seen, traditionally been paired with the idea of reprobation (of being chosen *by* God to *not* be with God). Moreover, the social power of religion is and has been so great that this "not belonging" has never simply been comprehensible as a mere temporary marginalization from God's good will on this side of history but has almost always been parsed as an eternal lostness.

Thus, the natural human proclivity to form groups, and the religious import of defining the eternal destinies of such groups, has tended toward the assumption of a bifurcation of humanity into the lost and the saved. Within the Christian traditions, at least, membership of either group has generally been understood to be a matter of divine pleasure and free decision—the composition of both groupings is and eternally has been ultimately located in God's choice alone. Consequently, membership within the elect has been recognized to be at best only partly conditioned by, and even less observable through, the merits that may accrue to any individual—thus the Pauline-Lutheran refrain that we are saved by *faith*, through *grace*, with both faith *and* grace being divine gifts that we do not have in and of ourselves.

Conversely, while Christian theological consensus has typically agreed that no natural human merits are intrinsically salvific, some

---

[1] J. Sacks, *Not in God's Name: Confronting Religious Violence* (New York: Schocken Books, 2015), 30-31.

attributes have nevertheless been frequently understood as inherently reprobative. A murderer, a blasphemer, or even a despotic ruler need not inevitably be destined for damnation, no matter how bad her or his deeds. But within normative Christian construals of God's electing pleasure, to be a Muslim—or even worse, a Jew—has almost always meant exclusion from the elect, simply on account of being Muslim or Jewish, no matter how righteous one might otherwise have been. In other words, the "othering" that is necessary to relegate some to perdition has, in the case of Jews and Muslims, been justified on grounds of identity, not fidelity.[2] To put it slightly differently, while Christian doctrine has made much of our human inability to know the definitive makeup of the elected community of God—that composition being a matter of gracious gift rather than human attainment—it has found it far easier to populate the community of the lost.

Yet all of this has been predicated on the a priori assumption that it is God's eternal determination—whether that be a willing or a reluctant determination—to so divide his human creation into these two camps. But what if that assumption is wrong? To return again to David Congdon's suggestion, such a bifurcation of human destiny makes sense *only if* God's justice, which (it is claimed) has to be satiated by the non-salvation of most, is made somehow more palatable by a merciful redemption of a favored few. The intolerable consequence that lurks beneath this idea is that God's just condemnation of the many is a work that is more proper to him than is his gracious salvation of the few.

This simply will not do. If, as Barth insists, God is the One who loves in freedom[3]—if, indeed, God is the One who, as perfectly revealed in Jesus Christ, is himself love—then righteous anger leading to reprobation

---

[2]It is worth noting that Stephen Haynes has argued for a dichotomous representation of Jewish identity in Dante's *Divine Comedy*. According to Haynes, Dante depicts the righteous patriarchs and matriarchs of Israel who are to be found in Limbo—Abel, Noah, Abraham, Moses, David, and Rachel—are best described as "Hebrews," whereas "Jews" per se are better identified with Judas, who is to be found in the ninth circle of hell, inside Lucifer's mouth. S. R. Haynes, *Jews and the Christian Imagination: Reluctant Witnesses* (Houndmills, UK: Macmillan, 1995), 2-3.
[3]*CD* II/1, 257-321.

can surely not be more properly characteristic of him than a mercy that leads to life. Here we must again take a determined stand against Thomas Aquinas's contention that both election and rejection—salvation and damnation—are equally illustrative of God's love. If, after the Holocaust—and like Rubenstein, Katz, and Pawlikowski—we can no longer accept the notion of a God who would sacrifice his children Israel to the gas chambers of Auschwitz, then we surely cannot accept the notion of a God who, as a viable demonstration of one of his modes of love, would allow any of his beloved children to be relegated eternally to the nothingness of reprobation.

Therefore, perhaps at least part of the solution is to refuse any such bifurcating will on the part of God. Perhaps, even if we as human beings tend always to separate ourselves into camps—the Us and the Them—that is not in fact what God chooses to do.

In 1942 Karl Barth famously, and at the time provocatively, insisted that Jews and Christians live together *unter dem Bogen des einen Bundes*—under the covering of the one covenant, in elected solidarity. Equally famously, and equally provocatively, he was later to imply that the boundaries of God's one covenant community may have to be understood in even broader terms. Commenting on the parable of the Good Samaritan, Barth insisted that the good and merciful neighbor is not (or at least not *only*) the church. Even those whom the church, in its hubristic action as priest and Levite, has excluded from its own community "can assume and exercise the function of a compassionate neighbor." Why? Because, as a consequence of God's reconciling work in Christ, those we deem to be Them are in fact already *in* Christ and therefore in fellowship with God, with Us. They *are* Us, albeit presently incognito. In Barth's words, the Samaritan—the archetypical outsider—is already "the brother of tomorrow."[4] While neither Scripture nor Christian tradition, he said, endorses an

---

[4]*CD* IV/2, 809. Hans Frei puts it this way: "Humanity at large is the neighbor given to the church, through whom Christ is present to the church." H. W. Frei, *The Identity of Jesus Christ* (Eugene, OR: Wipf & Stock, 1997), 192.

unequivocal proclamation of universal salvation, nor do they un-equivocally reject its possibility.

I would suggest that this humble recognition of our incapacity fi-nally and fully to know the mind and will of God ought to direct our thinking and our theologizing about this vexed concept of election. Whereas so many teachers and leaders of the church throughout the centuries have furnished us with definitive pronouncements (*only* a few will be saved; they will be saved *only* in *this* way; the many who are lost are sent to their perdition because either God has *willed* it or his justice *requires* it; and so on), perhaps we would do better—as theolo-gians, priests, and pastors—to admit that on this question, at least, we come to the edge of knowability. And at that incomprehensible edge, rather than speculating on the things we cannot know, perhaps it is better to rest and trust in the remembrance that the final words in Scripture, just as the beginning words in Genesis, are life-givingly cre-ative: "Let *everyone* who is thirsty come. Let *anyone* who wishes take the water of life" (Rev 22:17).

BIBLIOGRAPHY

Alighieri, Dante. *The Divine Comedy*. Translated by C. H. Sisson. London: Pan Books, 1981.

Arminius, Jakob. *Arminius and His Declaration of Sentiments: An Annotated Translation with Introduction and Theological Commentary*. Translated by W. S. Gunter. Waco, TX: Baylor University Press, 2012.

Axt-Piscalar, Christine. *Der Grund des Glaubens: Eine theologiegeschichtliche Untersuchung zum Verhältnis von Glauben und Trinität in der Theologie Isaak August Dorners*. Beiträge zur historischen Theologie 79. Tübingen: J.C. Mohr, 1990.

Baldwin, Peter. *Hitler, the Holocaust and the Historians Dispute*. Boston: Beacon Press, 1990.

Bangs, Carl. *Arminius: A Study in the Dutch Reformation*. Grand Rapids: Zondervan, 1985.

Barth, Karl. *Ad Limina Apostolorum: An Appraisal of Vatican II*. Translated by C. R. Kim. Eugene, OR: Wipf & Stock, 2016.

———. *Church Dogmatics*. Edited by Geoffrey W. Bromiley and Thomas F. Torrance. 4 vols. in 13 parts. Edinburgh: T&T Clark, 1936–1969.

———. *Der Römerbrief, Erste Fassung*. In *Gesamtausgabe* II.16. Edited by Hermann Schmidt. Zurich: TVZ, 1985.

———. *Der Römerbrief 1922*. 1940. Reprint. Zurich: Theologischer Verlag, 2015.

———. "Die Kirche und die politische Frage von heute." In *Eine Schweizer Stimme, 1938–1945*. Zurich: TVZ, 1985.

———. *Dogmatics in Outline*. Translated by G. T. Thomson. London: SCM Press, 1955.

———. *The Epistle to the Romans*. Translated by Edwin C. Hoskyns. 6th ed. Oxford: Oxford University Press, 1933.

———. *Geschichte der protestantischen Theologie seit Schleiermacher*. Zurich: Hans Walt, 1943.

———. *Gespräche, 1959–1962*. In *Gesamtausgabe* IV.25. Edited by Eberhard Busch. Zurich: TVZ, 1995.

———. *The Knowledge of God and the Service of God*. London: Hodder & Stoughton, 1938.

———. *Letzte Zeugnisse*. Zurich: EVZ-Verlag, 1969.

———. *Protestant Theology in the Nineteenth Century*. London: SCM Press, 2001.

———. *Rechtfertigung und Recht*. Theologische Studien 104. Zurich: Theologischer Verlag, 1989.

———. *Theologische Existenz heute!* (1933). In *Karl Barth Gesamtausgabe III: Vorträge und kleinere Arbeiten, 1930–1933*. Edited by Michael Beintker, M. Hüttenhoff, and P. Zocher. Zurich: TVZ, 2013.

———. *The Theology of John Calvin*. Translated by Geoffrey W. Bromiley. Grand Rapids: Eerdmans, 1995.

————. *The Theology of the Reformed Confessions*. Translated by Darrell L. Guder and Judith J. Guder. Louisville: Westminster John Knox Press, 2000.

Barth, Markus. *The Broken Wall: A Study of the Epistle to the Ephesians*. London: Collins, 1960.

————. "Current Discussions on the Political Character of Karl Barth's Theology." In *Footnotes to a Theology: The Karl Barth Colloquium of 1972*. Edited by H. Martin Rumscheidt. Waterloo, Ontario: Corporation for the Publication of Academic Studies in Religion in Canada, 1974.

————. *Ephesians 1–3*. Anchor Bible 34. New York: Doubleday, 1974.

————. *The People of God*. JSNT Supplement Series 5. Sheffield, UK: JSOT Press, 1983.

Bauer, Yehuda. "A Past That Will Not Go Away." In *The Holocaust and History: The Known, the Unknown, the Disputed and the Reexamined*. Edited by Michael Berenbaum and A. J. Peck. 1998. Reprint. Bloomington: Indiana University Press, 2002.

Baur, Ferdinand C. *Lehrbuch der christlichen Dogmengeschichte*. 1847.

Beaulac, S. "The Westphalian Model in Defining International Law: Challenging the Myth." *Australian Journal of Legal History* 8, no. 2 (2004).

Behr, John. *Formation of Christian Theology*. Vol. 1, *The Way to Nicaea*. New York: St. Vladimir's Seminary Press, 2001.

Beinert, R. A. "The Meaning and Practice of Conversion: A Comparison of Calvin's and Luther's Theologies." *Lutheran Theological Review* 22 (2009–2010).

Beker, Johan C. *Paul the Apostle*. Edinburgh: T&T Clark, 1980.

Benedict, Philip. *Christ's Churches Purely Reformed: A Social History of Calvinism*. New Haven, CT: Yale University Press, 2002.

Bennet, Gillian. *Bodies: Sex, Violence, Disease and Death in Contemporary Legend*. Jackson: University of Mississippi Press, 2005.

Berkovits, Eliezer. *Faith After the Holocaust*. New York: Ktav Publishing House, 1973.

————. *With God in Hell, with God in Hell: Judaism in the Ghettoes and Deathcamps*. New York: Hebrew Publishing, 1979.

Bethune-Baker, James F. *Early History of Christian Doctrine*. 1903. Reprint. London: Methuen, 1962.

Boguslawski, Steven C. *Thomas Aquinas on the Jews: Insights into His Commentary on Romans 9–11*. Mahwah, NJ: Paulist Press, 2008.

Bouwsma, William J. *John Calvin: A Sixteenth-Century Portrait*. Oxford: Oxford University Press, 1988.

Bowman, Donna. *The Divine Decision: A Process Doctrine of Election*. Louisville: Westminster John Knox Press, 2002.

Brecht, Martin. *Martin Luther: Shaping and Defining the Reformation, 1521–1532*. Translated by J. L. Schaaf. Minneapolis: Fortress Press, 1990.

Breiner, B. F., and C. W. Troll. "Christianity and Islam." In *The Oxford Encyclopedia of the Islamic World*. Oxford Islamic Studies Online. www.oxfordislamicstudies.com/article/opr/t236/e0149.

Brent, Allen. *Cyprian and Roman Carthage*. Cambridge: Cambridge University Press, 2010.

————. *Ignatius of Antioch*. London: T&T Clark, 2007.

Brockliss, Laurence W. B. *The University of Oxford: A History*. Oxford: Oxford University Press, 2016.

Brown, Stephen F. "Medieval Theology." In *The Blackwell Companion to Modern Theology.* Edited by Gareth Jones. Oxford: Blackwell, 2004.

Brown, Stewart J. *Providence and Empire: Religion, Politics and Society in the United Kingdom, 1815–1914.* London: Routledge, 2013.

Bruce, Frederick F. *Galatians.* New International Greek Testament Commentary. Grand Rapids: Eerdmans, 1982.

Brueggemann, Walter. *Genesis.* Atlanta: John Knox Press, 1982.

Brunner, Emil. *The Christian Doctrine of God: Dogmatics, Vol. I.* Translated by Olive Wyon. London: Lutterworth Press, 1962.

———. *The Christian Doctrine of the Church, Faith and the Consummation Dogmatics, Vol. III.* Translated by Thomas H. L. Parker and D. Cairns. Cambridge: James Clarke, 2002.

Buber, Martin. *The Prophetic Faith.* New York: Macmillan, 1949.

Burn, Andrew E. *An Introduction to the Creeds and to the Te Deum.* London: Methuen & Co., 1899.

Busch, Eberhard. *Karl Barth: His Life from Letters and Autobiographical Texts.* Translated by John Bowden. Grand Rapids: Eerdmans, 1994.

———. *Karl Barths Lebenslauf: Nach seinen Briefen und autobiographischen Texten.* Munich: Christian Kaiser, 1975.

———. *Unter dem Bogen des Einen Bundes: Karl Barth und die Juden, 1933–1945.* Neukirchen-Vluyn: Neukirchener Verlag, 1996.

Calvin, John. *Institutes of the Christian Religion.* Translated by Henry Beveridge. Grand Rapids: Eerdmans, 1995.

———. *Instruction in Faith.* Edited and translated by P. T. Furhmann. Louisville: Westminster John Knox Press, 1992.

———. *The Letters of John Calvin.* Vol. 1. Edited by Jules Bonnet. Eugene, OR: Wipf & Stock, 2007.

———. *Sermons on the Book of Micah.* Edited and translated by Benjamin W. Farley. Phillipsburg, NJ: P&R Publishing, 2003.

Carter, Grayson. *Anglican Evangelicals: Protestant Secessions from the Via Media, c. 1800–1850.* Oxford: Oxford University Press, 2001.

Catherine of Siena. *The Dialogue.* Translated by S. Noffke. New York: Paulist Press, 1980.

Chazan, Robert, ed. *Church, State and Jew in the Middle Ages.* New York: Behrman House, 1980.

Clarke, G. W., ed. *The Letters of St. Cyprian of Carthage.* Vol. 1, *Letters 1–27.* Ramsey, NJ: Paulist Press, 1984.

Clarke, Matthew A. "A Critical Examination of the Ecclesiology of John Nelson Darby." Unpublished manuscript, 2009.

Clements, Ronald E. *God's Chosen People: A Theological Interpretation of the Book of Deuteronomy.* London: SCM Press, 1968.

Coffey, David. "The Holy Spirit as the Mutual Love of the Father and the Son." *Theological Studies* 51 (1990).

Cohen, Abraham. *Everyman's Talmud: The Major Teachings of the Rabbinic Sages.* 1975. Reprint. New York: Schocken Books, 1995.

Cohn-Sherbok, Dan. *The Crucified Jew: Twenty Centuries of Christian Anti-Semitism*. London: Fount, 1993.

Congdon, David W. *The God Who Saves: A Dogmatic Sketch*. Eugene, OR: Cascade Books, 2016.

Coolman, Holly Taylor. "Romans 9–11: Rereading Aquinas on the Jews." In *Reading Romans with Aquinas*. Edited by Matthew Levering and M. Dauphinais. Washington, DC: Catholic University of America Press, 2012.

Cornwell, John. *Hitler's Pope: The Secret History of Pius XII*. London: Penguin Books, 1999.

Cross, Richard. *Duns Scotus*. In *Great Medieval Thinkers*. Edited by Brian Davies. Oxford: Oxford University Press, 1999.

———. *Duns Scotus on God*. Aldershot, UK: Ashgate, 2005.

———. *The Physics of Duns Scotus: The Scientific Context of a Theological Vision*. Oxford: Clarendon Press, 1998.

Croxton, Derek. "The Peace of Westphalia of 1648 and the Origins of Sovereignty." *The International History Review* 21, no. 3 (1999).

Cunliffe-Jones, Hubert, ed. *A History of Christian Doctrine*. Philadelphia: Fortress Press, 1984.

Darby, John Nelson. "Analysis of Dr Newman's *Apologia pro Vita Sua*: With a Glance at the History of Popes, Councils, and the Church." In *The Collected Writings of J. N. Darby*. Edited by W. Kelly. Kingston-on-Thames, UK: Snow Hill, n.d.

———. *Considerations Addressed to the Archbishop of Dublin* (1827). In *Collected Writings*. Vol. 1. Winschoten, Netherlands: H. L. Heijkoop, 1971.

———. "On the Formation of Churches" (1840). In *Collected Writings*. Vol. 1. Winschoten, Netherlands: H. L. Heijkoop, 1971.

———. *The Letters of JND*. In *Collected Writings*. Vol. 3. Winschoten, Netherlands: H. L. Heijkoop, 1971.

———. "Remarks on the Church and the World." In *Collected Writings*. Vol. 15. Winschoten, Netherlands: H. L. Heijkoop, 1971.

———. "Familiar Conversations on Romanism: Apostolicity and Succession" (1860). In *Collected Writings*. Vol. 22. Winschoten, Netherlands: H. L. Heijkoop, 1971.

———. *The Claims of the Church in England Considered; being the close correspondence between the Rev. James Kelly of Stillogan, Ireland, and J.N. Darby*. London: W. H. Broom, 1964.

Davies, Brian. *Thomas Aquinas's Summa Theologiae: A Guide and Commentary*. Oxford: Oxford University Press, 2014.

Dawidowicz, Lucy. *The War Against the Jews, 1933–1945*. New York: Holt, Rinehart & Winston, 1975.

de Greef, Wulfert. *The Writings of John Calvin: An Introductory Guide*. Expanded edition. Translated by L. D. Bierma. Louisville: Westminster John Knox Press, 2008.

Demson, David E. *Hans Frei and Karl Barth: Different Ways of Reading Scripture*. Grand Rapids: Eerdmans, 1997.

Duffy, Eamon. *Reformation Divided: Catholics, Protestants and the Conversion of England*. London: Bloomsbury, 2017.

Dumont, Stephen. "Duns Scotus, John (c.1266–1308)." In *The Routledge Encyclopedia of Philosophy*. London: Taylor and Francis, 1988.

Erickson, Millard. *Christian Theology*. Grand Rapids: Baker Academic, 1985.

Esposito, John. *Islam: The Straight Path*. Oxford: Oxford University Press, 1988.

Fackenheim, Emil. *To Mend the World: Foundations of Post-Holocaust Jewish Thought*. 1982. Reprint. New York: Schocken Books, 1989.

Fasolt, Constantin. *The Limits of History*. Chicago: University of Chicago Press, 2013.

Fiala, Andrew. "Fichte and the *Ursprache*." In *After Jena: New Essays on Fichte's Later Philosophy*. Edited by D. Breazeale and T. Rockmore. Evanston, IL: Northwestern University Press, 2008.

Fichte, Johann Gottlieb. *Addresses to the German Nation*. Translated by I. Nahkimovsky, B. Kapossy, and K. Tribe. Indianapolis: Hackett Publishing, 2013.

Finkel, Avraham Y. *The Essential Maimonides: Translations of the Rambam*. Northvale, NJ: Jason Aronson, 1996.

Frei, Hans F. *The Identity of Jesus Christ*. Eugene, OR: Wipf & Stock, 1997.

Furnal, Joseph. "Abraham Joshua Heschel and *Nostra Aetate*: Shaping the Catholic Reconsideration of Judaism During Vatican II." *Religions* 7, no. 6 (2016).

Ganoczy, Alexandre. "Calvin's Life." In *The Cambridge Companion to John Calvin*. Edited by Donald L. McKim. Cambridge: Cambridge University Press, 2004.

Garber, Zev. *Shoah: The Paradigmatic Genocide; Essays in Exegesis and Eisegesis*. Studies in the Shoah 8. Lanham, MD: University Press of America, 1994.

Gerrish, Brian. "The Place of Calvin in Christian Theology." In *The Cambridge Companion to John Calvin*. Edited by Donald L. McKim. Cambridge: Cambridge University Press, 2004.

Gifford, Edwin Hamilton. *The Epistle of St. Paul to the Romans*. London: John Murray, 1886.

Gockel, Matthias. *Karl Barth and Schleiermacher on the Doctrine of Election: A Systematic-Theological Comparison*. Oxford: Oxford University Press, 2007.

Gordon, Bruce. *John Calvin's Institutes of the Christian Religion: A Biography*. Princeton, NJ: Princeton University Press, 2016.

Green, Garrett. "Modernity." In *The Blackwell Companion to Modern Theology*. Edited by Gareth Jones. Oxford: Blackwell, 2004.

Gunton, Colin. *The Christian Faith: An Introduction to Christian Doctrine*. Oxford: Blackwell, 2002.

Gutteridge, Richard. *Open Thy Mouth for the Dumb! The German Evangelical Church and the Jews, 1879–1950*. Oxford: Basil Blackwell, 1976.

Haas, Gunther. *The Concept of Equity in Calvin's Ethics*. Carlisle, UK: Paternoster, 1997.

Hamilton, Victor P. *The Book of Genesis: Chapters 1–17*. Grand Rapids: Eerdmans, 1990.

Harries, Richard. *After the Evil: Christianity and Judaism in the Shadow of the Holocaust*. Oxford: Oxford University Press, 2003.

Hartman, David. "New Jewish Religious Voices II: Auschwitz or Sinai?" *Ecumenist* 21, no. 1 (1982).

Hattrell, Simon, ed. *Election, Barth, and the French Connection: How Pierre Maury Gave a "Decisive Impetus" to Karl Barth's Doctrine of Election*. Eugene, OR: Pickwick Publications, 2016.

Haynes, Stephen R. *Jews and the Christian Imagination: Reluctant Witnesses*. Houndmills, UK: Macmillan, 1995.

Hegel, Georg F. W. *Lectures on the Philosophy of History*. Translated by James Sibree. London: G. Bell & Sons, 1914.

———. *The Philosophy of Right*. Translated by H. B. Nisbet. Cambridge: Cambridge University Press, 1991.

Heppe, Heinrich. *Reformed Dogmatics: Set Out and Illustrated from the Sources*. Translated by G. T. Thomson. London: George Allen & Unwin, 1950.

Hesselink, I. John. "Calvin on the Relation of the Church and Israel Based Largely on His Interpretation of Romans 9–11." In *Calvin as Exegete*. Edited by P. de Klerk. Grand Rapids: Calvin Studies Society, 1995.

———. "Calvin's Theology." In *The Cambridge Companion to John Calvin*. Edited by Donald K. McKim. Cambridge: Cambridge University Press, 2004.

Hilberg, Raul. *The Destruction of the European Jews*. London: W. H. Allen, 1961.

Hitler, Adolf. *Mein Kampf*. Translated by J. Murphy. London: Hurst & Blackett, 1939.

Hodge, Charles. *Commentary on the Epistle to the Ephesians*. New York: Robert Carter & Brothers, 1866.

Hood, John Y. B. *Aquinas and the Jews*. Philadelphia: University of Pennsylvania Press, 1995.

Hunsinger, George. "Election and the Trinity: Twenty-Five Theses on the Theology of Karl Barth." *Modern Theology* 24, no. 2 (2008).

———. *How to Read Karl Barth: The Shape of His Theology*. New York: Oxford University Press, 1991.

Ingham, Mary Beth, and Mechtild Dreyer. *The Philosophical Vision of John Duns Scotus: An Introduction*. Washington, DC: Catholic University of America Press, 2004.

James, Frank A. *Peter Martyr Vermigli and Predestination: The Augustinian Inheritance of an Italian Reformer*. Oxford: Clarendon Press, 1998.

Jeanrond, Werner G. "From Resistance to Liberation Theology: German Theologians and the Non-Resistance to the National Socialist Regime." Supplement, *Journal of Modern History* 64 (1992).

Jenson, Robert W. "On the Doctrine of the Atonement." *Princeton Seminary Bulletin* 27, no. 2 (2006): 100-108.

———. *Systematic Theology I: The Triune God*. New York: Oxford University Press, 1997.

Johnson, Elizabeth A. *Abounding in Kindness: Writings for the People of God*. Maryknoll, NY: Orbis, 2015.

Johnston, Samuel Lewis. "Paul and 'Israel of God': An Exegetical and Eschatological Case-Study." In *Essays in Honor of J. Dwight Pentecost*. Edited by Stanley D. Toussaint and Charles H. Dyer. Chicago: Moody, 1986.

Jones, Paul Daffyd. "Obedience, Trinity and Election: Thinking with and Beyond the *Church Dogmatics*." In *Trinity and Election in Contemporary Theology*. Edited by Michael T. Dempsey. Grand Rapids: Eerdmans, 2013.

Jüngel, Eberhard. *God's Being Is in Becoming: The Trinitarian Being of God in the Theology of Karl Barth*. Translated by John Webster. Edinburgh: T&T Clark, 2001.

Katz, Steven. *Post-Holocaust Dialogues: Critical Studies in Modern Jewish Thought*. New York: New York University Press, 1983.

Kee, Howard Clark. *Who Are the People of God? Early Christian Models of Community*. New Haven, CT: Yale University Press, 1995.

Kelly, W., ed. *The Collected Writings of J. N. Darby*. Kingston-on-Thames, UK: Snow Hill, n.d.

Kim, Sung-Sup. *Deus providebit: Calvin, Schleiermacher, and Barth on the Doctrine of Providence*. Minneapolis: Augsburg Fortress, 2014.

Knowles, David. "The Middle Ages." In *A History of Christian Doctrine*. Edited by Hubert Cunliffe-Jones. Philadelphia: Fortress Press, 1980.

Kolnai, Aurel. *The War Against the West*. New York: Viking Press, 1938.

Kranzler, David. *The Man Who Stopped the Trains to Auschwitz: George Mantello, El Salvador and Switzerland's Finest Hour*. New York: Syracuse University Press, 2000.

Krapohl, Robert H. "A Search for Purity: The Controversial Life of John Nelson Darby." Unpublished manuscript, 1988.

Kugel, James L. *How to Read the Bible: A Guide to Scripture Then and Now*. New York: Free Press, 2008.

Kühnl, Reinhard, ed. *Vergangenheit, die nicht vergeht: Die "Historikerdebatte"; Darstellung, Dokumentation, Kritik*. Cologne: Pahl-Rugenstein, 1987.

Küng, Hans. *The Church*. New York: Image Books, 1976.

Lampe, Geoffrey W. H. "Christian Theology in the Patristic Period." In *A History of Christian Doctrine*. Edited by Hubert Cunliffe-Jones. Philadelphia: Fortress Press, 1980.

Lapide, Pinchas. *The Last Three Popes and the Jews*. London: Souvenir Press, 1967.

Lehmann, Hartmut. "'God Our Old Ally': The Chosen People Theme in Late Nineteenth- and Early Twentieth-Century German Nationalism." In *Many Are Chosen: Divine Election and Western Nationalism*. Edited by William R. Hutchison and Hartmut Lehmann. Minneapolis: Fortress Press, 1994.

Leith, J. H. "Foreword to the 1992 Edition." In J. Calvin, *Instruction in Faith*. Translated and edited by P. T. Furhmann. Louisville: Westminster John Knox Press, 1992.

Lenehan, Kevin. "*Etsi deus non daretur*: Bonhoeffer's Useful Misuse of Grotius' Maxim and Its Implications for Evangelisation in the World Come of Age." *Australasian Journal of Bonhoeffer Studies* 1, no. 1 (2013).

Levering, Matthew. *Predestination: Biblical and Theological Paths*. Oxford: Oxford University Press, 2011.

Levi, Neil, and Michael Rothberg, eds. *The Holocaust: Theoretical Readings*. Edinburgh: Edinburgh University Press, 2003.

Lincoln, Andrew T. *Ephesians*. Word Biblical Commentary 42. Edited by D. A. Hubbard and G. W. Barker. Dallas: Word Books, 1990.

Lindsay, Mark R. *Barth, Israel and Jesus: Karl Barth's Theology of Israel*. Aldershot, UK: Ashgate, 2007.

———. *Covenanted Solidarity: The Theological Basis of Karl Barth's Opposition to Nazi Antisemitism and the Holocaust*. New York: Peter Lang, 2001.

———. "Jewish-Christian Dialogue from the Underside: Markus Barth's Correspondence with Michael Wyschogrod (1962–84) and Emil Fackenheim (1965–80)." *Journal of Ecumenical Studies* 53 (Summer 2018).

———. *Reading Auschwitz with Barth: The Holocaust as Problem and Promise for Barthian Theology*. Eugene, OR: Wipf & Stock, 2014.

Link, Christian. "Election and Predestination." In *John Calvin's Impact on Church and Society, 1509–2009*. Edited by Martin E. Hirzel and Martin Sallmann. Grand Rapids: Eerdmans, 2009.

Lloyd-Jones, David Martyn. *Romans: An Exposition of 8:17-39; The Final Perseverance of the Saints*. London: Banner of Truth, 1975.

Luther, Martin. *The Bondage of the Will*. Translated by H. Cole. Grand Rapids: Eerdmans, 1931.

MacCulloch, Diarmaid. *Reformation: Europe's House Divided, 1490–1700*. London: The Folio Society, 2003.

Mackenzie, D., T. Falcon, and J. Rahman, eds., *Religion Gone Astray: What We Found at the Heart of Interfaith*. Woodstock, VT: Skylight Paths, 2011.

Macleod, D. "Dr T. F. Torrance and Scottish Theology: A Review Article." *The Evangelical Quarterly* 72, no. 1 (2000).

Maier, Charles. *The Unmasterable Past: History, Holocaust and German National Identity*. Cambridge, MA: Harvard University Press, 1988.

Mathews, E. G, trans. *The Armenian Commentary on Genesis Attributed to Ephrem the Syrian*. Louvain: Peeters, 1998.

Maury, Pierre. *Erwhählung und Glaube*. Theologische Studien 8. Zurich: Evangelischer Verlag, 1940.

Maybaum, Ignaz. *The Face of God After Auschwitz*. Amsterdam: Polak & Van Gennep, 1965.

McCormack, Bruce L. "Election and the Trinity: Theses in Response to George Hunsinger." *Scottish Journal of Theology* 63, no. 2 (2010).

———. "Grace and Being: The Role of God's Gracious Election in Karl Barth's Theological Ontology." In *The Cambridge Companion to Karl Barth*. Edited by John Webster. Cambridge: Cambridge University Press, 2000.

———. *Karl Barth's Critically Realistic Dialectical Theology: Its Genesis and Development, 1909–1936*. Oxford: Clarendon, 1997.

———. "Let's Speak Plainly: A Response to Paul Molnar." *Theology Today* 67 (2010).

———. "Seek God Where He May Be Found: A Response to Edwin Chr. Van Driel." In *Orthodox and Modern: Studies in the Theology of Karl Barth*. Edited by Bruce L. McCormack. Grand Rapids: Baker Academic, 2008.

———. "The Sum of the Gospel: The Doctrine of Election in the Theologies of Alexander Schweizer and Karl Barth." In *Orthodox and Modern: Studies in the Theology of Karl Barth*. Edited by Bruce L. McCormack. Grand Rapids: Baker Academic, 2008.

———. "Trinity and Election: Theses in Response to George Hunsinger." In *Trinity and Election in Contemporary Theology*. Edited by M. T. Dempsey. Grand Rapids: Eerdmans, 2011.

McDonald, Suzanne. *Re-imaging Election: Divine Election as Representing God to Others and Others to God*. Grand Rapids: Eerdmans, 2010.

McGoldrick, James E. "Luther's Doctrine of Predestination." *Reformation and Revival* 8, no. 1 (1999).

McGowan, Andrew B. *Ancient Christian Worship*. Grand Rapids: Baker Academic, 2014.

McGrath, Alister E. *Christian Theology: An Introduction*. 2nd ed. Oxford: Blackwell, 1997.

———. *Reformation Thought: An Introduction*. 2nd ed. Oxford: Blackwell, 1993.

McLeod, Hugh. "Christianity and Nationalism in Nineteenth-Century Europe." *International Journal for the Study of the Christian Church* 15, no. 1 (2015).

Meeks, M. Douglas. "Trinitarian Theology: A Review Article." *Theology Today* 38 (1982).

Migliore, Dan. *Faith Seeking Understanding: An Introduction to Christian Theology*. 2nd ed. Grand Rapids: Eerdmans, 2004.

Molnar, Paul. *Divine Freedom and the Doctrine of the Immanent Trinity*. 2nd ed. London: Bloomsbury T&T Clark, 2017.

Moo, Douglas. *The Epistle to the Romans*. Grand Rapids: Eerdmans, 1996.

Morgenthau, Hans Joachim. "The Problem of Sovereignty Reconsidered." *Columbia Law Review* 48, no. 3 (1948).

Morris, Leon. *The Epistle to the Romans.* 1988. Reprint. Grand Rapids: Eerdmans, 1992.

Mosely, Carys. *Nations and Nationalism in the Theology of Karl Barth.* Oxford: Oxford University Press, 2013.

Moss, Candida. *The Myth of Persecution: How Early Christians Invented a Story of Martyrdom.* New York: HarperCollins, 2013.

Muddiman, John. *The Epistle to the Ephesians.* Peabody, MA: Hendrickson, 2004.

Muller, Richard A. *Calvin and the Reformed Tradition: On the Work of Christ and the Order of Salvation.* Grand Rapids: Baker Academic, 2012.

———. *Christ and the Decree: Christology and Predestination in Reformed Theology from Calvin to Perkins.* 1986. Reprint. Grand Rapids: Baker Academic, 2008.

Myers, Benjamin. "Election, Trinity and the History of Jesus: Reading Barth with Rowan Williams." In *Trinitarian Theology After Barth.* Edited by Myk Habets and P. Tolliday. Eugene, OR: Pickwick Publications, 2011.

Nichols, J., ed. *The Works of James Arminius, DD.* London: Longman, Rees, Orme, Brown & Green, 1828.

Niebuhr, Reinhold. "Barth's East German Letter." *Christian Century* 76, no. 6 (February 1959).

Nolte, Ernst. "Die Vergangenheit, die nicht vergehen will." *Frankfurter Allgemeine Zeitung* (June 6, 1986).

Norden, Eduard. *Agnostos Theos: Untersuchungen zur Formengeschichte Religiöser Rede.* Berlin: Verlag B. G. Teubner, 1913.

Oergel, Maike. *Culture and Identity: Historicity in German Literature and Thought, 1770–1815.* Berlin: Walter de Gruyter, 2006.

Oord, T. J. Review of *The Divine Decision*, by D. Bowman. *The Journal of Religion* 84, no. 4 (2004).

Origen. *On First Principles.* Edited by J. Behr. Oxford: Oxford University Press, 2017.

Papandrea, James L. *Reading the Early Church Fathers: From the Didache to Nicaea.* Mahwah, NJ: Paulist Press, 2012.

Parker, Thomas H. L. *John Calvin: A Biography.* Louisville: Westminster John Knox Press, 2007.

Pawlikowski, John. "Christian Ethics and the Holocaust: A Dialogue with Post-Auschwitz Judaism." *Theological Studies* 49 (1988).

———. "Human Responsibility: Contemporary Reflections in Light of Nazi Ideology." In *Remembering for the Future: The Holocaust in an Age of Genocide.* Volume 2. Edited by John K. Roth and Elizabeth Maxwell. Houndmills, UK: Palgrave, 2001.

Picirilli, Robert E. *Grace, Faith, Free Will: Contrasting Views of Salvation—Calvinism and Arminianism.* Nashville: Randall House, 2002.

Pieper, Franz. *Conversion and Election: A Plea for a United Lutheranism in America.* St. Louis, MO: Concordia Publishing House, 1913.

Pink, Arthur W. *The Doctrine of Election.* Venice, FL: Chapel Library, n.d.

Pinson, J. Marthew. "Jacobus Arminius: Reformed and Always Reforming." In *Grace for All: The Arminian Dynamics of Salvation.* Edited by John D. Wagner and Clark H. Pinnock. Eugene, OR: Resource Publications, 2015.

Plant, Stephen J. *Taking Stock of Bonhoeffer: Studies in Biblical Interpretation and Ethics.* Aldershot, UK: Ashgate, 2014.

Poe, Shelli M. *Essential Trinitarianism: Schleiermacher as Trinitarian Theologian.* London: Bloomsbury T&T Clark, 2017.

Poggi, G. *The Development of the Modern State: A Sociological Introduction.* Stanford, CA: Stanford University Press, 1978.

Porro, Pasquale. "Henry of Ghent." In *Stanford Encyclopedia of Philosophy.* Edited by Edward N. Zalta (Fall 2014).

Pratscher, Wilhelm, ed. *The Apostolic Fathers: An Introduction.* Waco, TX: Baylor University Press, 2010.

Prosono, Marvin. "The Holocaust as a Sacred Text: Can the Memory of the Holocaust Be Tamed?" In *Remembering for the Future: The Holocaust in an Age of Genocide.* Volume 3. Edited by John K. Roth and Elizabeth Maxwell. Houndmills, UK: Palgrave, 2001.

Ramsey, Boniface. *Beginning to Read the Fathers.* Rev. ed. Mahwah, NJ: Paulist Press, 2012.

Redding, Graham. *Prayer and the Priesthood of Christ in the Reformed Tradition.* London: T&T Clark, 2003.

Rendtorff, Rolf. *Das überlieferungsgeschichtliche Problem des Pentateuch.* Berlin: De Gruyter, 1977.

Reymond, Bernard. *Karl Barth-Pierre Maury Nous qui pouvons encore parler Correspondance, 1928-1956: Introduction, Notes et Traductions de Bernard Reymond.* Paris: Symbolon, L'Age d'Homme, 1985.

Richardson, Paul. *Israel in the Apostolic Church.* Cambridge: Cambridge University Press, 1969.

Ritner, Carol, and John K. Roth, eds. *Pope Pius II and the Holocaust.* New York: Leicester University Press, 2002.

Ritschl, Albrecht. "Geschichtliche Studien zur christlichen Lehre von Gott." *Jahrbuch für deutsche Theologie* Bd.13 (1868).

Ritschl, Dietrich. *The Logic of Theology.* Translated by J. Bowden. London: SCM Press, 1986.

Ritschl, Otto. *Dogmengeschichte des Protestantismus.* Vol. 3. Göttingen, 1926.

Rowan, Frederica, ed. *The Life of Schleiermacher, as Unfolded in His Autobiography and Letters.* 2 vols. London: Smith, Elder & Co., 1860.

Rubenstein, Richard L. *After Auschwitz: History, Theology, and Contemporary Judaism.* 1966. Reprint. Baltimore: Johns Hopkins University Press, 1992.

———. "Some Perspectives on Religious Faith after Auschwitz." In *The German Church Struggle and the Holocaust.* Edited by F.H. Littell and H.G. Locke. Detroit: Wayne State University Press, 1974.

Rumscheidt, H. Martin. "Professional Ethics After Auschwitz." In *Thirtieth Annual Scholars' Conference on the German Churches and the Holocaust,* March 4–7, 2000.

Ryrie, Alec. *Protestants: The Faith That Made the Modern World.* New York: Penguin, 2017.

Ryrie, Charles C. *Dispensationalism.* Chicago: Moody Bible Institute, 1995.

Sacks, Jonathan. *Not in God's Name: Confronting Religious Violence.* New York: Schocken Books, 2015.

Scheck, Thomas. *Origen and the History of Justification: The Legacy of Origen's Commentary on Romans.* Notre Dame, IN: University of Notre Dame Press, 2008.

Schleunes, Karl A. *The Twisted Road to Auschwitz: Nazi Policy Toward German Jews, 1933–1939*. Urbana: University of Illinois Press, 1970.

Schramm, Brooks, and Kirsi Stjerna, eds. *Martin Luther, the Bible, and the Jewish People: A Reader*. Minneapolis: Fortress Press, 2012.

Schüssler Fiorenza, Francis. "Schleiermacher's Understanding of God as Triune." In *The Cambridge Companion to Friedrich Schleiermacher*. Edited by J. Mariña. Cambridge: Cambridge University Press, 2005.

Schwarz-Bart, André. *The Last of the Just*. Translated by S. Becker. New York: MJF Books, 1960.

Schweizer, Alexander. *Die Glaubenslehre der evangelish-reformierten Kirche*. Zurich: Oreil, Füssli, 1844.

Second Vatican Council. "Declaration on the Relation of the Church to Non-Christian Religions *Nostra Aetate* Proclaimed by His Holiness Pope Paul VI on October 28, 1965."

———. "Dogmatic Constitution on the Church *Lumen Gentium* Solemnly Promulgated by His Holiness Pope Paul VI on November 21, 1964."

Sinnema, Donald. "God's Eternal Decree and Its Temporal Execution: The Role of This Distinction in Theodore Beza's Theology." In *Adaptations of Calvinism in Reformation Europe: Essays in Honor of Brian G. Armstrong*. Edited by Mack P. Holt. Aldershot, UK: Ashgate, 2007.

Skinner, John. *Genesis*. Edinburgh: T&T Clark, 1910.

Slotemaker, John T., and Üli Zahnd. "Thomas and Scholasticism to 1870." In *The Oxford Handbook of Catholic Theology*. Edited by Lewis Ayres and M-A. Volpe. Oxford: Oxford University Press, 2015.

Small, Joseph D. "The Legacy of *Nostra Aetate* in Mainline Protestant Churches." In *A Jubilee for All Time: The Copernican Revolution in Jewish-Christian Relations*. Edited by Gilbert S. Rosenthal. Cambridge: Lutterworth Press, 2017.

Smart, James, trans. *Revolutionary Theology in the Making: Barth-Thurneysen, 1914–1925*. London: Epworth Press, 1964.

Sonderegger, Katherine. *Systematic Theology: Volume 1, The Doctrine of God*. Minneapolis: Fortress Press, 2015.

———. *That Jesus Christ Was Born a Jew: Karl Barth's "Doctrine of Israel."* University Park: Pennsylvania University Press, 1992.

Southern, Richard W. *Western Society and the Church in the Middle Ages*. Penguin History of the Church 2. 1970. Reprint. London: Penguin, 1990.

Stanglin, Keith D., and Thomas H. McCall. *Jacob Arminius: Theologian of Grace*. Oxford: Oxford University Press, 2012.

Steed, W. Preface to *The War Against the West*, by A. Kolnai. New York: Viking Press, 1938.

Steinmetz, David C. *Reformers in the Wings: From Geiler von Kaysersberg to Theodore Beza*. 2nd ed. Oxford: Oxford University Press, 2001.

Storms, Sam. *Chosen for Life: The Case for Divine Election*. Wheaton, IL: Crossway, 2007.

Stunt, Timothy. "John Nelson Darby: Contexts and Perceptions." In *Protestant Millennialism, Evangelicalism and Irish Society, 1790–2005*. Edited by Crawford Gribben and Andrew R. Holmes. Basingstoke, UK: Palgrave Macmillan, 2006.

Thandeka. *The Embodied Self: Friedrich Schleiermacher's Solution to Kant's Problem of the Empirical Self*. Albany: State University of New York Press, 1995.

Thompson, Mark D, ed. *Engaging with Calvin: Aspects of the Reformer's Legacy for Today*. Nottingham, UK: Apollos, 2009.

Torrance, Thomas F. "The Divine Vocation and Destiny of Israel in World History." In *The Witness of the Jews to God*. Edited by David W. Torrance. Edinburgh: Handsel Press, 1982.

———. *Scottish Theology from John Knox to John MacLeod Campbell*. Edinburgh: T&T Clark, 1996.

Towner, Wayne Sibley. *Genesis*. Louisville: Westminster John Knox Press, 2001.

Trebilco, Paul. *The Early Christians in Ephesus: From Paul to Ignatius*. Grand Rapids: Eerdmans, 2007.

Trinterud, L. J. "The Origins of Puritanism." *Church History* 20, no. 1 (1951).

Turner, Nancy L. "Jewish Witness, Forced Conversion and Island Living: John Duns Scotus on Jews and Judaism." In *Christian Attitudes Towards the Jews in the Middle Ages: A Casebook*. Edited by Michael Frassetto. New York: Routledge, 2007.

Turner, W. G. *John Nelson Darby*. London, 1990.

van der Merwe, Piet. "Commentary on the Documents *Nostra Aetate* and *Lumen Gentium*." *HTS Theological Studies/Teologiese Studies* supplement 12, 73, no. 6 (2017).

van Geest, Paul, Harm Goris, and Carlo Leget, eds. *Aquinas as Authority: A Collection of Essays; A Collection of Studies Presented at the Second Conference of the Thomas Instituut te Utrecht, December 14–16, 2000*. Leuven: Peeters, 2002.

Vander Schel, Kevin. *Embedded Grace: Christ, History, and Reign of God in Schleiermacher's Dogmatics*. Minneapolis: Fortress Press, 2013.

Vidler, Alec. *The Church in an Age of Revolution*. Penguin History of the Church 5. 1961. Reprint. London: Penguin, 1990.

Viereck, Peter. *Meta-Politics: The Roots of the Nazi Mind*. New York: Capricorn Books, 1965.

von Moltke, Helmut J. *Letters to Freya: A Witness Against Hitler*. London: Collins Harvill, 1991.

von Rad, Gerhard. *Deuteronomy: A Commentary*. London: SCM Press, 1966.

Vos, Antonie. *The Theology of John Duns Scotus*. In Studies in Reformed Theology 34. Leiden: Brill, 2018.

Vos, Antonie, Henri Veldhuis, Eef Dekker, Nico den Bok, and Andreas Beck, eds. *Duns Scotus on Divine Love: Texts and Commentary on Goodness and Freedom, God and Humans*. Aldershot, UK: Ashgate, 2003.

Wallace, David R. *The Election of the Lesser Son: Paul's Lament-Midrash in Romans 9–11*. Minneapolis: Augsburg Fortress, 2014.

Watkin, Thomas G. *The Legal History of Wales*. Cardiff: University of Wales Press, 2007.

Weil, Simone. *Gravity and Grace*. Translated by E. Craufurd. London: Routledge and Kegan Paul, 1963.

Weinfeld, Moshe. *Deuteronomy 1–11*. Anchor Bible 5. New York: Doubleday, 1991.

Weinrich, William. "Cyprian, Donatism, Augustine, and Augustana VIII: Remarks on the Church and the Validity of Sacraments." *Concordia Theological Quarterly* 55, no. 4 (October 1991).

Weithman, Paul. "Augustine's Political Philosophy." In *The Cambridge Companion to Augustine*. Edited by David Vincent Meconi and Eleanore Stumpe. 2nd ed. Cambridge: Cambridge University Press, 2014.

Welch, Claude. *Protestant Thought in the Nineteenth Century*. Volume 1, *1799–1870*. New Haven, CT: Yale University Press, 1972.

Wendel, François. *Calvin: The Origins and Development of His Religious Thought.* Translated by P. Mairet. London: Collins, 1980.

Weremchuk, Maxwell. *John Nelson Darby.* Neptune, NJ: Loiseaux, 1992.

Westermann, Claus. *Genesis 12–36: A Commentary.* Translated by J. J. Scullion. Minneapolis: Augsburg, 1985.

Wiesel, Elie. *Night.* Translated by S. Rodway. London: Penguin, 1981.

———. "Some Questions That Remain Open." In *Comprehending the Holocaust.* Edited by Asher Cohen, Joav Gelber, and Charlotte Wardi. New York: Peter Lang, 1988.

Williams, Rowan. *Arius: Heresy and Tradition.* Rev. ed. Grand Rapids: Eerdmans, 2002.

Williams, Thomas, ed. *The Cambridge Companion to Duns Scotus.* Cambridge: Cambridge University Press, 2003.

Windsor, Lionel J. *Paul and the Vocation of Israel: How Paul's Jewish Identity Informs His Apostolic Ministry, with Special Reference to Romans.* Berlin: De Gruyter, 2014.

Witherington III, Ben. "Dispensationalism." In *The Cambridge Dictionary of Christian Theology.* Edited by Ian A. MacFarland, D. A. S. Fergusson, K. Kilby, and I. R. Torrance. Cambridge: Cambridge University Press, 2011.

Zuccotti, Susan. *Under His Very Windows: The Vatican and the Holocaust in Italy.* New Haven, CT: Yale University Press, 2000.

NAME INDEX

SUBJECT INDEX

SCRIPTURE INDEX